MW00582167

Community Participation Methods
in Design and Planning

Community Participation Methods in Design and Planning

Henry Sanoff

John Wiley & Sons, Inc.
New York · Chichester · Weinheim · Brisbane
Singapore · Toronto

This book is printed on acid-free paper. ∞

Copyright © 2000 by John Wiley & Sons, Inc. All rights reserved.

Published simultaneously in Canada.

No part of this publication may be reproduced, stored in a retrieval system or transmitted in any form or by any means, electronic, mechanical, photocopying, recording, scanning or otherwise, except as permitted under Sections 107 or 108 of the 1976 United States Copyright Act, without either the prior written permission of the Publisher, or authorization through payment of the appropriate per-copy fee to the Copyright Clearance Center, 222 Rosewood Drive, Danvers, MA 01923, (978) 750-8400, fax (978) 750-4744. Requests to the Publisher for permission should be addressed to the Permissions Department, John Wiley & Sons, Inc., 605 Third Avenue, New York, NY 10158-0012, (212) 850-6011, fax (212) 850-6008, E-Mail: PERMREQ @ WILEY.COM.

This publication is designed to provide accurate and authoritative information in regard to the subject matter covered. It is sold with the understanding that the publisher is not engaged in rendering professional services. If professional advice or other expert assistance is required, the services of a competent professional person should be sought.

Library of Congress Cataloging-in-Publication Data
Sanoff, Henry.
    Community participation methods in design and planning / Henry
Sanoff.
        p.   cm.
    Includes bibliographical references (p.   ) and index.
    ISBN 0-471-35545-3 (cloth : alk. paper)
    1. City planning—Citizen participation. 2. Community
development. 3. Community organization. 4. Architecture and
society. 5. Architecture—Human factors. I. Title.
HT166.S2195   2000
307.1′2—dc21   99-25158

10 9 8 7

Dedicated
to
Joan, Ari, and Zoe

Contents

Participation Techniques 67
Participation Games 76
Workshops 80
Postoccupancy Evaluation 85
Visual Preference and Appraisal 88
Glossary of Participation Processes and Techniques 102

CHAPTER 3
Participation in Educational Facilities **105**

Self-Assessment 110
Community College Child Development Center 112
Davidson Elementary School 122
A University-School District Partnership 133
Minnesota Center for Arts Education 141
Minnesota Academies for the Blind and the Deaf 151
Montagnard Cultural Center 155
School Participatory Games 162

CHAPTER 4
Participation in Housing **181**

Farm Worker Housing 197
Assisted Living Housing 208
Housing Games 212

CHAPTER 5
Participation in Urban and Rural Environments **221**

SWOT Analysis 223
Richmond Neighborhood Charrette 224
Town of Bangalow, Australia 231
Town of Murfreesboro, North Carolina 239
Monroe Downtown Revitalization 246
Neighborhoods and Towns in Japan 250
Urban Participatory Games 274

Bibliography **281**
Additional Readings **291**
Index **299**

Preface

ommunity design is an umbrella term that also embraces *community planning,*
community architecture, social architecture, community development, and *com-*
munity participation. Community design, as a movement, emerged from a growing realization that mismanagement of the physical environment is a major factor
contributing to the social and economic ills of the world and that there are better
ways of going about design and planning. Advocates for this viewpoint come from
the professions of architecture, landscape architecture, and planning. A parallel
movement in organizational development, referred to as facility management,
includes a number of similarly minded design professionals.

Almost three decades ago, Robert Goodman (1971) attacked architecture
and planning and pointed to the ugliness, squalor, congestion, pollution, vandal-
ism, stress, and the destruction of communities that characterize the modern
urban movement in America, as well as many other parts of the world. Conventional architecture and planning approaches, rooted in the paternalistic creation
and management of the environment by experts, have not been successful in
achieving their ideals and visions. A particularly notable vision responding to the
urban crisis of the time was that of setting densely packed large buildings in park
areas to overcome the congestion of cities. Yet the resulting large public housing
and redevelopment projects representing this concept acted as barriers between
neighborhoods, and their large open spaces tended to isolate people from one
another.

Within the past two decades, however, pioneering development projects in
America and abroad have demonstrated that it is possible to build housing that

people want to live in, to give people a sense of pride and reinforce their identity with their local community, to build needed social facilities, and to develop neighborhoods and small towns that enrich people's lives by being responsive to their needs and aspirations. The core principle of community design applies to housing, workplaces, parks, social facilities, neighborhoods, and towns.

How to make it possible for people to be involved in shaping and managing their environment is what the community design movement has been exploring over the past few decades. Starting with designers and planners working with, instead of against, community groups, it has grown rapidly to include a new breed of professional in a variety of partnership programs involving the public sector with developers and financial institutions and working closely with the volunteer sector.

In *The Scope of Social Architecture* (1984), Hatch describes an international movement based on the conviction that participation is crucial to the redirection of architecture and the city it creates. Social architecture is viewed as an instrument for transforming both the environment and the people who live in it.

Community design, or social architecture, is an attitude about a force for change in the creation and management of environments for people. Its strength lies in being a movement that cuts across traditional professional boundaries. The activity of community design is based on the principle that the environment works better if the people affected by its changes are actively involved in its creation and management instead of being treated as passive consumers. Community participation, however, is neither a panacea nor a total solution for social change. It must be studied through theory and practice in order for it to become an integral aspect of democracy. Recently, many public figures have made references to democratic participation with words like *community* and *citizenship* and endorsed concepts like *community building*. New organizations such as the International Association for Public Participation and the Civic Practices Network have identified representative communities and examples of cutting-edge practices in community participation.

Yet at times participation has been distorted to mean that everything has to be checked with everyone before any decision is made. Juan Diaz Bordenave (1994) describes this as a disease called *participationitis*. Participation has also come to mean attendance at ongoing public hearings and constant meetings or donating money to a popular campaign. In my view, participation means the collaboration of people pursuing objectives that they themselves have defined.

This book, then, is intended to assist the development of community participation in design and planning by identifying the most salient principles and techniques for those professionally involved. Individuals who may find this book useful include practitioners and educators in architecture, landscape architecture, urban planning, community design, and community psychology, as well as policy planners, city managers, and community volunteers. Because community design is a worldwide movement, this book is written in such a way as to be useful to readers everywhere. Although the examples are mainly from the United States, with some from Australia and Japan, the processes and techniques are relevant to people living in other parts of the developed or developing world. The technique often referred to as "design games" is a universal language, embracing different cultures and evoking similar responses. In addition to their use in the case studies reported in this book, a number of these techniques have been applied to projects in many countries, including Brazil, Denmark, Egypt, England, France, Germany, Greece, Hong Kong, Israel, Korea, Mexico, Poland, Slovenia, South Africa, and Turkey.

The book is organized into several chapters, beginning with the purpose of participation and the underlying supportive theories. Chapter 1 examines community participation from a historical perspective and discusses different and changing viewpoints. It describes the stages of participation, who should participate, and the consequences of participation. "Participation Methods," Chapter 2, examines processes and techniques drawn from the experiences of a variety of professional designers, planners, and researchers. It explains different models applied in the United States and abroad. The remaining Chapters, 3, 4, and 5, consist of building, neighborhood, and small town projects that incorporate participatory processes and techniques. The purpose of these chapters is to emphasize the participatory process and the specific techniques applied to each project. The intent of this book is not to be unduly instructive in the description of processes, inasmuch as most professionals will have to shape approaches appropriate to various situations. However, particular techniques, proven from experience to be effective, are fully described and suggested as a format for adaptation.

The projects described in Chapters 3 through 5 represent my experiences as an architectural design consultant to The Adams Group Architects, as a consultant to public agencies and volunteer groups in Japan and Australia, and for three decades as Director of the Community Development Group (CDG) at the School of Design, North Carolina State University.

Henry Sanoff
September 1999

Acknowledgments

Although similar in purpose to a community design center, the Community Development Group (CDG) provides design and planning assistance to communities throughout the state of North Carolina. It was founded in 1969 as an outreach and extension program following the model of institutions formed under the national Land-Grant Act. CDG's mission, however, is aimed at serving low-income communities as well as organizations unable to afford or lacking access to professional design and planning assistance.

Since its formation, the CDG has responded to more than 150 requests for design and planning assistance in collaboration with North Carolina State academic units within the departments of Economics, Education, Engineering, Psychology, and Sociology, and the Cooperative Extension Service; with the University of North Carolina, Chapel Hill, School of Medicine, and the Department of City and Regional Planning; with local and state agencies such as the North Carolina (NC) Arts Council, NC Department of Aging, NC Department of Cultural Resources, NC Department of Child Development, NC Department of Labor, NC Department of Public Instruction, Habitat for Humanity, Lumbee Regional Development Association, Main Street Program, Coastal Plains Regional Commission, and with federal agencies such as the Department of Agriculture, Department of Housing and Urban Development, National Institute of Mental Health, Head Start, Office of Economic Opportunity, National Endowment of the Arts, and the Bureau of Indian Affairs.

This experience enabled the development and refinement of a variety of participatory techniques that have withstood the test of time. These efforts required the participation and commitment of many people, including my colleagues Graham Adams, during our many years of collaboration on participatory school projects, and Yasuyoshi Hayashi, who lent his support in bringing the concept of community participation to Japan. Other architects and planners who contributed to the development of material included in this book are Jennifer Amster, Aaron Bartels, Greg Brown, Greg Centeno, Wes Chapman, Tun Sing Chen, Matt Devine, Marilia DoVal, Frederick Ford, Arlene Humphrey, Holly Grubb, Tina Lesem, Pete Lassen, Jeff Levine, Ann McCallum, Naho Mochizuki, Nami Moriyama, Catalina Morales, Yoshie Ohno, Sergio Ortiz, David Polston, Chainarong Ratamachardensi, Jim Rice, Ashraf Salama, Ryoko Sato, Brad Smith, Robert Stipe, Mary Tippens, James Utley, and Peter Yen.

CHAPTER

1

Participation
Purposes

Although the idea of participation in building and planning can be traced to pre-literate societies, community participation is of more recent origin. It is commonly associated with the idea of involving local people in social development. The most important influences derive from the third world community development movement of the 1950s and 1960s, Western social work, and community radicalism (Midgley, 1986). The plans of many developing countries emphasized cooperative and communitarian forms of social and economic organization, stressing the values of self-help and self-sufficiency (Worsley, 1967), advocating that the poor and the oppressed should be mobilized to promote social and economic progress. Current community participation theory suggests that politicians and bureaucrats have exploited ordinary people and that such people have been excluded from the community development process. Leading proponents are found in international agencies such as the United Nations (UN), the World Health Organization (WHO), and the UN International Children's Emergency Fund (UNICEF). The emergence of community participation theory as an approach to social development is an outgrowth of the United Nations' popular participation programs that required the creation of opportunities for all people to be politically involved and share in the development process.

Although social work is primarily concerned with the problems of needy individuals and their families, it has also, since its inception in the late nineteenth century, focused on communities seeking to organize people to improve social services. Community organization has thus become an accepted method of social work, incorporating such notions as social planning. Conventional methods of community work were transformed into a more radical approach, urging people to take direct political action to demand changes and improvements.

The beginnings of a grass-roots democracy in America were linked to the community-based struggles of the 1960s that took place in the context of the civil rights movement, the rise of women's liberation, the anti-war movement, and the challenges of alternative cultures, all of which represented an upheaval of civil society (Castells, 1983). The revolts that occurred in American inner cities throughout that time rarely identified themselves as "urban movements." They tended to see themselves as expressions of black power, of welfare rights, of tenants' interests, or of the needs of the poor, triggered by the disruptive efforts of urban renewal. Legitimacy of this social movement was achieved by programs of social reform known as the "War on Poverty." The Community Action Program, funded by the federal Office of Economic Opportunity (OEO) provided institutional support and political legitimacy for the formation of urban grass-roots organizations in support of the demands of poor neighborhoods. Thousands of organizations arose in inner-city areas, laying the groundwork for a major neighborhood movement in America. The failure, however, of these social struggles to achieve substantial change was due to the diversity of issues related to the community organization movement and the lack of common goals. On the other hand, the Alinsky model of community organization tried to organize urban protest, improve the living conditions of the poor, empower the grass roots, and achieve greater democracy and social justice (Castells, 1983).

An advocate of Jeffersonian democracy, Alinsky (1972) believed in pluralism, government accountability, local autonomy, and widespread citizen participation. He held that the main problem with the system was the insensitivity of political institutions to the people, who were excluded because of bureaucratization, centralization, and manipulation of information.

As a community organizer, Alinsky believed that people could not be mobilized around models but could be rallied in defense of their immediate interests. Thus, his tactics were to organize people around a sensible issue and identify a clear opponent. He believed that when people achieve a victory, they feel the effort has been worthwhile. In a sense, the main outcome of the organization is the organization itself, its influence, its representativeness, and its internal democracy. Once this grass-roots empowerment has been achieved, the democratic institutions start working in their favor and economic interests become balanced.

Alinsky maintained that any organizer had to be called in by a community and had to leave the community as soon as an organization was established and led by its own elected leaders. The organizer must be paid by the community, through funds raised by the community, and must never become part of the movement. He believed that the organizer was a facilitator and educator in what was essentially a self-help effort. Most of Alinsky's experiences, however, were initiated by a single institution: the churches, which, because they represented the grass-roots expression of voluntary organizations, have traditionally been the natural form of popular organization throughout American history.

Alinsky believed in *participatory democracy* and utilized various methods to make it a reality rather than a trite phrase. In emphasizing the importance of citizen action, particularly at the neighborhood level, he stimulated the movement toward decentralization, local control, and consumer power. Criticisms of Alinsky focus on his antagonism and confrontational attitude toward the establishment.

Traditional community organizers operated from the premise that people and institutions with power will never surrender it voluntarily. Consequently, conflict organizers employed events such as rallies and picketing, involving large numbers of people, because they believed that numbers were the primary source of a community's strength. The measure of people participating in such events had simply to be counted.

The consensus organizing model, on the other hand, seeks to establish partnerships between private and public sector leaders and community groups by providing effective ways for individuals to use and develop their own skills and creativity on behalf of their community. This model emphasizes strategy, pragmatism, and relationship building. Consensus organizing in a community starts with the identification and involvement of a local institution to provide financial resources to support the organizing process.

The community organizing process begins with an assessment of community and downtown interests. An assessment of the culture of community involvement includes an analysis of the strengths and weaknesses of community groups, as well as the linkages already existing between social service and government agencies and local banks and foundations. The aim of the process is to build community organizations that allow for resident involvement and leadership development, in which every segment of the community has representation.

According to an extensive survey of community organizations initiated by Alinsky, Joan Lancourt (1979) concludes that in regard to issues of housing, schools, business, employment, welfare, and city services, the community organizations were not able to reverse the trend toward deterioration. Community control was not achieved in some instances because the organizations were not multiethnic. When they were, ethnic components fought each other. Often, organizations did not achieve community control but were instead co-opted and absorbed into the management of the programs they were supposed to control. Yet, other organizations were successfully formed on a territorial basis and were able to represent the diversity of the neighborhood's interests. The most successful experiences to emerge from the Alinsky ideology occurred in the 1970s when the new middle class, struck by economic crisis, was affected by the rapid decay of the quality of urban life. The organizations that developed were truly multiethnic and sometimes citywide, based on a broad array of issues of economic policy, ranging from taxes to nuclear power, from health services to electricity rates.

Citizen movements, such as those occurring in the inner cities in the 1960s, are reactions against centralized authority and intractable bureaucracies. This form of grass-roots democracy represents an important link in a representative democracy's becoming a true participatory democracy. In the mid-1960s, Paul Davidoff, a planner and lawyer, challenged planners to promote participatory democracy and positive social change, to overcome poverty and racism, and to reduce disparities between rich and poor. Davidoff challenged planners to become advocates for what they deemed proper. He viewed advocacy as a way of enabling all groups in society, particularly organizations representing low-income families. His article "Advocacy and Pluralism in Planning" (1965) presented a new model to the field of planning. Davidoff was instrumental in amending the American Institute of Planners code of ethics to state, "A planner shall seek to expand choice and opportunity for all persons, recognizing a social responsibility to plan for the needs of disadvantaged groups and persons, and shall urge the alteration of policies, institutions, and decisions which militate against such objectives" (Checkoway, 1994).

Community Design Centers

Influenced by Davidoff's advocacy model of planning, many design and planning professionals rejected traditional practice. Instead, they fought against urban redevelopment, advocated for the rights of poor citizens, and developed methods of citizen participation. Community design centers (CDCs) became the staging ground for professionals to represent the interests of disenfranchised community groups (Comerio, 1984). The social momentum of the Civil Rights Act (1957) and the innovations of the Ford Foundation's Gray Areas Program initiated in 1960 were rapidly building a framework for change throughout the nation. The experiences provided by the Economic Opportunity Act in community action agencies followed the Act's passage in 1964, and the stimulus of the Office of Neighborhood Development (part of the Department of Housing and Urban Development—HUD) strategically enhanced the economic development role of grass-roots organizations and the usefulness of professional advocacy networks such as the Association for Community Design. Organized in 1963, the Architectural Renewal Committee in Harlem (ARCH) fought a proposed freeway in Upper Manhattan. In Cleveland, Architecture-Research-Construction (ARC) remodeled hospital wards, community-based treatment centers, and group homes, working with patients, staff, and administrators in a participatory design process. In Tucson, the design center removed more than 100 pit privies from barrio homes and replaced them with prefabricated bathroom units. Founded in 1973, the Asian Neighborhood Design has a long history of work on issues in San Francisco's Chinatown. Today it is a full-service professional planning and architectural service, dedicated to housing and community development throughout the region, with an annual operating budget of about $4 million. In Salt Lake City, ASSIST, Inc. continues to provide accessibility design services, seeing more than 100 projects through construction each year. Architects, landscape architects, and planners, working as volunteers in the country's community design centers, complete hundreds of similar projects annually.

CDCs (see Sachner, 1983) are dedicated to the provision of planning, architecture, and development services unavailable to emerging civic organizations or established community-based development corporations (CBDOs). Design center organizational structures range from architect-led nonprofit corporations to university service-learning programs, to private practices and American Institute of Architects (AIA)/community-sponsored volunteer programs. Support for design centers is provided by Community Development Block Grants and other sources of funding to facilitate volunteerism. Services provided by most CDCs include the following:

- Comprehensive, participatory, and strategic planning
- Technical assistance in the selection and financing of development projects
- Advocacy and support for the acquisition and management of housing and community facilities

Over the last 30 years CDCs have been effective in providing a broad range of services in economically distressed communities (Curry, 1998). For the design and planning professions, community design centers have been the equivalent of what health clinics are to medicine and what legal aid is to law. People are served through pro bono professional assistance, but often after the injury has occurred. Long-term community-based planning and visioning processes require linkages between design centers and community organizations, with a full-time commitment to relieving distresses in urban and rural environments.

Many of the major nonprofit community development corporations in the United States began as civic groups resisting development. This community economic development movement has now moved from grass-roots activities to serving as a significant community building and development practice.

In response to the economic and political pressures of the 1980s some community design centers remained project based. Such a center is generally organized as a nonprofit corporation by an administrator through a local AIA chapter, and supported by Community Development Block Grants and other sources of funding to facilitate volunteerism. Other, more comprehensive community design practice is carried out by centers that promote community-based control of local projects with related community improvement activities. Because these centers concentrate on providing a variety of services, they help to generate projects for which architectural services will eventually be required. Community design centers look to organizers, neighborhood planning groups, individual low-income clients, community service committees, and nonprofit boards of directors for leadership in building communities.

Grass-Roots Participation

Although community design centers were the initial advocates of grass-roots participation, local citizens groups are now organizing and demonstrating their capability to acquire power to effect neighborhood change. Today in the South Bronx citizens practice a form of radical decentralized planning as they engage in a 300-acre revitalization project designated by the Bronx borough president. When city planning officials proposed the clearing of a 30-square-block area, neighborhood forums to discuss revitalization resulted in a protest staged by the residents. Long-term residents were outraged at the idea of being pushed out by an urban renewal plan after having remained in the neighborhood to keep it livable.

A neighborhood group was formed, calling itself "We Stay/Nos Quedamos." It started with block-by-block canvassing to explain the stakes and invite people to what would become 168 planning meetings in a single year. Meetings held twice a week allowed 6,000 residents of the neighborhood to take part.

The open meetings attracted citizens, urbanists, and environmentalists to debate neighborhood layout, community facilities, and the need to find environmentally friendly construction materials. Staff from local housing and transportation agencies were sensitized to neighborhood issues as a result of participating in the discussions with the residents and walking the streets of Melrose Commons.

A radically revised plan emerged that retained 60 percent of the existing buildings instead of effecting wholesale clearance. The residents asked for higher densities at several locations and a pedestrian mews with off-street buildings and small courtyards. They rejected a 4-acre park proposed by city planners and reduced it to 1 acre for better security and visibility. The residents also wanted a meeting center with open space for concerts for the community.

In the end, the city approved the plan as the residents designed it. The most difficult part of the whole process, reported Nos Quedamos, was to convince members of this heavily Central American and black community that they could fight city hall. The achievement of this grass-roots effort was not only to gain acceptance of a neighborhood plan, but to do so through a civic process that enhanced the dignity of people who had felt powerless.

Community Building

Federal programs of the 1960s, such as the Community Action Program and Model Cities, emphasized resident participation in improvement programs, in which outside professionals were making key decisions, controlling the budgets, and taking the risks. Today's community building, in contrast, sees resident groups playing a more central role in both planning and implementation. A term used to reflect this trend is *community driven* (Kingsley, McNeely, and Gibson, 1997), rather than the nondefining term *community participation* or the more inward-looking term *community controlled.*

Community building is a holistic approach that focuses its efforts on people. It is dedicated to the idea that residents must take control of their destiny and that of their communities. Community building grows from a vision of how communities function normally, where community members create community institutions that help to achieve their aspirations as well as strengthen community fabric.

Building social capital is the primary objective achieved by residents playing a central role in decision making and believing that they "own" the process as they move away from being dependent. Many case experiences suggest that resident-driven initiatives have a greater chance of success because residents are more aware of the realities of their own environments than outside professionals. They have a sense of what will work and what will not work.

The principles of community building are as follows (Naparstek, Dooley, and Smith, 1997):

- Involve residents in setting goals and strategies.
- Identify a community's assets as well as its problems.
- Work in communities of manageable size.
- Develop unique strategies for each neighborhood.
- Reinforce community values while building human and social capital.
- Develop creative partnerships with institutions in the city.

Community building integrates traditional top-down approaches with bottom-up, resident-driven initiatives to create a network of partnerships between residents, management, and community organizations. Through participation in setting goals and developing implementation strategies, residents assume ownership of the process. Residents involved in community building spend their time jointly working on productive activities that address the problems they have identified. This collaborative involvement builds social capital—developing friendships and mutual trust, sharing and strengthening common values. Building social capital is a means of building human capital, strengthening the capacities of individuals and families to overcome adversities and take advantage of opportunities. Utilizing local youth to conduct surveys or mobilizing residents to get involved in construction and cleanup projects helps to develop human capital.

It is important for community building to take place at the neighborhood level, because this allows for frequent face-to-face interaction and the ability for people to get to know each other in order to establish mutual trust. In American cities, neighborhoods of about 6,000 people are quite different from one another, which suggests the need for considerable variation in strategy. Because individual neighborhoods may be too small to address certain environmental problems, larger resident-driven organizations can facilitate collaboration between neighborhoods while allowing each to maintain its identity.

Residents need to develop a vision of what they want their neighborhood to become and how to get there. To start the process, a positive tone can be set by taking an inventory of community assets and then finding ways to take advantage of them in creating action programs. John Kretzman and John McKnight (1993) have said that a community's taking initiatives from the perspective of solving problems casts a negative tone on what should be a positive capacity-building process. They argue that community building should start by identifying neighborhood assets and finding ways to build on them, still recognizing that serious problems may exist in certain neighborhoods. The community-building orientation should be positive and constructive.

Kretzman and McKnight suggest that identifying assets in a neighborhood or community can dramatically alter the planning process inasmuch as assets occur at different levels, which can relate to their priority in developing programs. Assets within the neighborhood, such as resident's experience, neighborhood businesses, and citizens and business associations, should be acted on first, and assets controlled by outsiders, such as public institutions, can become assets, which requires the community to devise appropriate enabling strategies.

Current Views of Community Participation

A new pragmatic approach to participation has emerged, one that no longer views participation as defined by Arnstein's (1969) categorical term for "citizen power." The purposes of participation have been more modestly defined to include information exchange, resolving conflicts, and supplementing design and planning. "[Participation] reduces the feeling of anonymity and communicates to the user a greater degree of concern on the part of the management of administration. [With] it, residents are actively involved in the development process, there will be a better maintained physical environment, greater public spirit, more user satisfaction and significant financial changes" (Becker, 1977). Community participation, however, has a different meaning for different people and even a different meaning for the same people according to the situation; different users prefer to participate in different ways according to the situation too. Numerous definitions of participation can be found in the literature. Participation is contextual, so participation varies in type, level of intensity, extent, and frequency. In a review of participation literature, Deshler and Sock (1985) identified the following two levels of participation:

Pseudoparticipation was categorized as

- *Domestication*—This involves informing, therapy, and manipulation.
- *Assistencialism*—This includes placation and consultation.

Genuine participation was categorized as

- *Cooperation*—This refers to partnership and delegation of power.
- *Citizen control*—Which means empowerment.

People's participation wherein control of a project rests with administrators is pseudoparticipation. Here the level of participation is that of people being present to listen to what is being planned *for* them. This is definitely *non*participatory. Genuine participation occurs when people are empowered to control the action taken. The distinction between forms of participation is important, because it requires careful consideration of communication behaviors throughout the process to bring about knowledge sharing and learning by all participants (White, Nair, and Ascroft, 1994).

Participation is a general concept covering different forms of decision making by a number of involved groups (Wulz, 1986). Participation can be addressed effectively if the task of participation is thought of in terms of what is to be accomplished when there is an acknowledged need to involve citizens. Conceptualizing the issue means asking simple questions: Who, what, where, how, and when?

- Who are the parties to be involved in participation? Individuals or groups who will or should be involved in the participation activity being planned must be identified. Generally, people who will be affected by design and planning decisions should be involved in the process of making those decisions.
- What do we wish to have performed by the participation program? For example, is the participation intended to generate ideas, to identify attitudes, to disseminate information, to resolve some identified conflict, to review a proposal, or merely to serve as a safety valve for pent-up emotions?
- Where do we wish the participation road to lead? What are the goals?
- How should people be involved? Appropriate participation methods have to be identified to achieve desired objectives. Methods have to be matched to purposes. Methods such as community workshops and charrettes allow for diverse interests and promote human resource development. They may afford the opportunity for participants to have control over decisions. Public hearings, on the other hand, may provide information but may not promote community support.
- When in the planning process is participation needed or desired? It is necessary to decide where the participants should be involved, that is, in development, implementation, evaluation, or some combination thereof.

These are simple questions, yet rarely asked prior to the development of a community participation program.

The purposes of participation have been more modestly defined to include information exchange, conflict resolution, and supplementation of planning and design. Participation reduces the feeling of anonymity and communicates to the individual a greater degree of concern on the part of the management or administration. With participation, residents are actively involved in the development process; there will be a better-maintained physical environment, greater public spirit, more user satisfaction, and significant financial savings. The main purposes of participation are as follows:

- To involve people in design decision-making processes and, as a result, increase their trust and confidence in organizations, making it more likely that they will accept decisions and plans and work within the established systems when seeking solutions to problems.

- To provide people with a voice in design and decision making in order to improve plans, decisions, and service delivery.
- To promote a sense of community by bringing people together who share common goals.

An important point in the participatory process is individual learning through increased awareness of a problem. In order to maximize learning, the process should be clear, communicable, and open. It should encourage dialogue, debate, and collaboration. Thus, participation may be seen as direct public involvement in decision-making processes whereby people share in social decisions that determine the quality and direction of their lives. This requires the provision of effective communication media in order to provide suitable opportunities for users to participate in the design process. There are many benefits accruing from such an approach for the community, the users, and design and planning professionals.

First, from the social point of view, participation results in a greater meeting of social needs and increasingly effective utilization of resources at the disposal of a particular community.

Second, to the user group, it offers an increased sense of having influenced the design decision-making process and an increased awareness of the consequences of decisions made (Hester, 1990).

Third, to the professional, it provides more relevant and up-to-date information than was possible before. Creating a methodological framework can enable the use of rational decision-making methods without affecting the creative process.

Because participation includes a diversity of expression, a design and planning solution derived from this approach will have to be made *transparent* so that the impact of the decisions is understood by the people who make them. When public forums are convened that encourage community participation, people can openly express their opinions, make necessary compromises, and arrive at acceptable decisions. By involving as many interests as possible, not only is the product strengthened by the wealth of input, but the user group is strengthened as well by learning more about itself.

The types and degrees of participation depend on several factors and vary in accord with the circumstances. Burns (1979) classifies participation in four categories or "experiences" that can lead to agreement about what the future should bring:

> *Awareness.* This experience involves discovering or rediscovering the realities of a given environment or situation so that everyone who takes part in the process is speaking the same language, based on their experiences in the field in which change is proposed.
>
> *Perception.* This entails going from awareness of a situation to understanding it and its physical, social, cultural, and economical ramifications. It means people sharing with each other so that the understanding, objectives,

and expectations of all participants become resources for planning, rather than hidden agendas that may disrupt the project at a later date.

Decision Making. This phase concentrates on participants working from awareness and perception to a program for the situation under consideration. At this point participants create actual physical designs, based on their priorities, for professionals to use as a resource to synthesize alternative and final plans.

Implementation. Many community-based planning processes stop with awareness, perception, and decision making, often with fatal results to a project, because this ends people's responsibilities just when they could be of most value—when the how-to, where-to, when-to, and who-will-do-it must be added to what people want and how it will look. People must stay involved, throughout the process, and take responsibility with the professionals to see that there are results (Hurwitz, 1975).

Participation means different things to different people—and even to the same people—depending on the issue, its timing, and the political setting in which it takes place. Thus, in order to address participation effectively, the task should be conceptualized in terms of what is to be accomplished when the need to involve citizens is acknowledged. The planning that accompanies the development of any participation program should first include a determination of objectives, such as the following:

- Is the participation intended to generate ideas?
- Is it to identify attitudes?
- Is it to disseminate information?
- Is it to resolve some identified conflict?
- Is it to measure opinion?
- Is it to review a proposal?
- Or is it merely to serve as a safety valve for pent-up emotions?

The list of possible participation objectives will differ from time to time and from issue to issue. Once the objectives of community participation are stated, it becomes clear that participation is perceived according to the type of issue and people involved. If differences in perception and expectations are not identified at the outset and realistic objectives are not made clear, the expectations of those involved in the participation program will not have been met and they will become disenchanted. Planning for participation requires the following steps (Rosner, 1978):

- Identify the individuals or groups who should be involved in the participation activity being planned.
- Decide where in the design process the participants should be involved; that is, in the development, implementation, or evaluation.

- Articulate the participation objectives in relation to all participants who will be involved.
- Identify and match alternative participation methods to objectives in terms of the resources available.
- Select an appropriate method to be used to achieve specific objectives.
- Implement chosen participation activities.
- Evaluate the implemented methods to see to what extent they achieved the desired goals and objectives.

Taking the proposed steps will not automatically ensure success, but it can be claimed that the process will minimize failure. As a summary, four essential characteristics of participation can be identified:

1. Participation is inherently good.
2. It is a source of wisdom and information about local conditions, needs, and attitudes, and thus improves the effectiveness of decision making.
3. It is an inclusive and pluralistic approach by which fundamental human needs are fulfilled and user values reflected.
4. It is a means of defending the interests of groups of people and of individuals, and a tool for satisfying their needs that are often ignored and dominated by large organizations, institutions, and their inflated bureaucracies.

Experiences in the participation process show that the main source of user satisfaction is not the degree to which a person's needs have been met, but the feeling of having influenced the decisions.

The potential value of an organized approach to participation include logical, emotional, technological, and economical benefits. A review of the theories and practices of participation are summarized as follows:

- The professional's job is no longer to produce finished and unchangeable solutions, but to develop solutions from a continuous dialogue with those who will use his or her work. The energy and imagination of the professional are directed to raising the citizens' level of awareness in the discussion. The solution will come out of the exchanges between two; the professional states opinions, provides technical information, and discusses consequences of various alternatives, just as citizens state their opinions and contribute their expertise.
- Participation has a diversity of expression. A design or planning task resulting from this approach should be made "transparent" in order for the final decisions to be understood by the people who will be affected by them.
- Public forums should be convened, and participation by all members of the community should be encouraged. In this way people can openly express their opinions, make necessary compromises, and arrive at acceptable decisions. Not only does this method strengthen the product, but the user group is strengthened as well by learning more about itself.

- Participation in the design and planning process may involve technological issues, and as a result, specialists in various fields may be required to cooperate. Public education about technical matters, however, can make participation effective and efficient.
- Public comments and representation should be accepted into the process continuously. The final decision is not the end of the process. It must be managed, evaluated, and adapted to changing needs. Effective community change requires the increasing participation of citizens in defining the type of changes desired. Professionals will need to make their solutions less representative of themselves and more representation of citizens, even though difficulties in applying participation may arise.

Stages of Participation

Planning a participation program should first include the identification of objectives. Planning for participation takes considerable time. When sufficient time is allowed to analyze issues, participants, resources, and objectives prior to the choosing of participation methods, the chance of success is greatly enhanced.

Participation may be seen as direct public involvement in decision-making processes. In this type of participation, citizens share in decisions that determine the quality and direction of their lives. People will come together if change can and will clearly occur. Participation can function if it is active and directed and those who get involved experience a sense of achievement. At the same time, a reexamination of traditional planning procedures is required to ensure that participation becomes more than affirmation of a designer's or planner's intentions. The guidance of participation directed at environmental change requires a new skill of the professional—that of ensuring community participation in the design process. This requires the provision of effective tools.

The principles of participation can be summarized into the following five statements:

1. *There is no "best solution" to a design problem.* Each problem has a number of solutions. Solutions to design and planning problems are traditionally based on two sets of criteria:
   a. *Facts*—the empirical data concerning material strengths, economics, building codes, and so forth; and
   b. *Attitudes*—interpretation of the facts, the state of the art in any particular area, traditional and customary approaches, and value judgments. Thus, design and planning decisions are by nature biased and depend on the values of the decision maker(s).
2. *"Expert" decisions are not necessarily better than "lay" decisions.* Given the facts with which to make decisions, users can examine the available alternatives

and choose among them. The designer or planner involved in such an approach should be considered a participant who is expected to identify possible alternatives and discuss consequences of various alternatives and to state an opinion—not to decide among them—just as the users state opinions and contribute their expertise.

3. *A design or planning task can be made transparent.* Alternatives considered by professionals are frameworks in their own minds and can be brought to the surface for the users to discuss. After understanding the components of design decisions and exploring alternatives, the users in effect can generate their own plan rather than react to one provided for them. The product is more likely to succeed because it is more responsive to the needs of the people who will use it.

4. *All individuals and interest groups should come together in an open forum.* In this way people can openly express their opinions, make necessary compromises, and arrive at decisions that are acceptable to all concerned.

5. *The process is continuous and ever changing.* The product is not the end of the process. It must be managed, reevaluated, and adapted to changing needs. Those most directly involved with the product, the users, are best able to assume those tasks.

Consensus Building

Noted educational philosopher John Dewey believed that the transfer of knowledge between two people is self-corrective, allowing them to gain valid knowledge through experience, to learn from success and failure in a nonauthoritarian, nonhierarchical manner (Friedmann, 1987). Paulo Friere (1990), the Latin American philosopher also suggests an equal playing ground to exchange ideas and knowledge. All citizens are assumed to hold equally valid knowledge that they can contribute to an active discourse. Dewey and Friere have both written extensively on the value of social learning and an iterative discourse leading to consensus.

The idea of consensus is evident since ancient history, in the notion of *consensus gentium,* the Latin phrase for "agreement of people" (Gove and Merriam-Webster, 1986). Contemporary views of consensus have evolved from educational and political philosophy. On the grounds of equal participation and the development of consensus, Connolly (1969) coined the "arena theory," which involves an ultimate appeal to the notion of consensus. This theory advocates the exchange of expert and experiential knowledge. The assumption of the arena theory is that there is at least one agreeable outcome in regard to which all parties come to a consensus. However, there must be a willingness of groups to accommodate one another. Such consensus cannot be achieved in isolation. Through the iterative process of social learning and through the equality framework of the arena theory, there can develop a consensus.

Nicholas Rescher (1993) categorically discounts the value of consensus, opting instead for the *understanding* of individual needs and customs rather than the *compromise* of such needs and customs. Rescher argues that what matters to people are not shared goals but the recognition of a common interest. An understanding of one's motives and interests is more valid than conforming those interests to the ideals of the larger population. According to Rescher, what needs to be developed is a convergence of interests. Although it is imperative to understand the interests of others, it is not necessary to fully agree with such interests. Experience has revealed that individual interests can coexist without any agreement between them. In an era of pluralism, consensus may not be accepted with welcoming arms. While we may strive for understanding as a community, there remains to be seen the ideal of individual agreement. Consensus, however, is an appropriate means of assessment and reflection, although not as a means to justify a majority. There is the view that consensus is not necessarily a decision-making tool, but the foundation from which cooperation is possible. Out of this cooperation will develop ideas, decisions, and strategies, all of which rely on the development of consensus. "The more group members are involved in a decision-making process, the more likely it is that they will develop feelings of teamwork and cooperation, thereby increasing their motivation, commitment, and contribution to the group. This is why, generally, authoritarian leadership is not successful" (Brody, 1982).

The criticism that consensus either accepts or rejects individual proposals is largely unfounded. The process of consensus allows for the iterative dialogue of idea generation and debate toward decision making. The danger lies in limiting any access to the debate or considering any input more or less valid than others. "Consensus occurs after all members have had an opportunity to voice their opinions and can arrive at a decision that almost everyone can support. The process of arriving at a consensus is a free and open exchange of ideas, which continues until agreement has been reached. The process insures that each individual's concerns are heard and understood and that a sincere attempt is made to take them into consideration in searching for a resolution. This resolution may not reflect the exact wishes of each member, but since it does not violate the deep concerns of anyone, it can be agreed upon by all" (Brody, 1982, p. 67).

The "ideal speech situation" (Habermas, 1990) serves as an appropriate model for a communicative framework that identifies four components necessary to facilitate an iterative dialogue. First, there must be no constraints in the discussion process. The individual must be free to express his or her personal interests without intimidation from more powerful participants. Second, each participant must be given an equal platform from which to express his or her concerns. No one participant should have more or less opportunity to discuss personal desires and needs. Third, all participants assume equal power. All political hierarchies are abandoned, and no participant is allowed to exercise more influence than others. Finally, the ideal speech situation calls for the rational process of discussion. Persuasion by good reason is more effective than threats.

There are, however, participant attitudes that work at odds to the consensus process. Avery (1981, p. 15) sees competition between groups as a barrier to consensus. Such competition coincides with a general lack of interest among group members. Participants who see personal goals as the most critical to address may lack any commitment to resolving group conflict.

The notion of individual ownership of ideas has been shown to be a weakness. Individuals may look at their contributions as their own creative property and argue defensively for their own ideas rather than work toward a mutually acceptable reformulation (Avery, p. 15). Group ownership, however, is considered a significant strength in furthering the ideals of consensus. As Avery (p. 20) states, "Group ownership acknowledges that new concepts are developed through the process of members responding to previous contributions of other members." With group ownership of ideas, it is the idea itself, not the presenter, that is criticized. Through this process, all participants are involved in developing ideas and decisions.

In the face of complex problems and diverse interests, collaborative decision making encourages creativity, open communication, broad participation, and agreement. Designing a clear, well-managed collaborative process can lead to agreement, whereby all participants are likely to receive wide community support during implementation. Consensus building in a collaborative decision-making process occurs in several stages.

To begin, it is necessary for all participants to have a *shared sense of purpose.* Working together to share information and reach agreements requires a clear process and explicit operating procedures. Agreement should be reached on the following questions (Godschalk et al., 1994):

- Why is this process needed?
- What form of resolution is required?
- How will the group work toward a solution?
- How will decisions be made?
- What is the schedule?
- Who will receive and act on the final product?

Next, participants need to *share information* and identify additional information required. A common base of information is needed for effective problem solving. Site visits, personal narratives, interviews with experts, and a review of technical reports are means by which participants can become well informed about a problem.

Once the needed information is collected and discussed, the problem must be clearly and specifically stated. The problem, as articulated, should reflect the concerns of all participants and must be manageable within the time and resource constraints. There are several methods that can be used to *define a problem.* In addition to verbal descriptions, the use of diagrams, flowcharts, and models may help participants better understand a physical problem. Large complex problems may be subdivided into smaller manageable parts and assigned to various task groups that will report their findings to the larger group. The is/is not method helps to develop a problem statement by identifying the components that are parts of the problem with "is" and those that are not with "is not. " A variation of this method is to identify the forces that are either blocking or supporting change by listing them under "blocks" and "supports." For certain problems the advice of experts may help to formulate a mutually acceptable problem statement.

Consensus on a problem statement can be reached by having each participant restate the problem in his or her own words, thus ensuring that all participants understand all elements of the problem.

Clarification of a problem statement can be used in the development of a collective vision in which participants fantasize about an ideal state or long-range potential of a site. A *visioning process* may begin with individual statements by participants. A wish poem beginning with the phrase "I wish my . . ." can allow individual participants to write about their visions, which can be shared with the group as they work toward a common vision. For more complex problems, a design charrette can function to help participants visualize the three-dimensional implications of various proposals (see Chapter 2). Visual preferences, inventories, and assessments are useful for use in well-defined settings to convey positive or negative features of an existing or proposed situation (see Chapter 2).

The next step in the process calls for the *generation of ideas,* whereby criticism and discussion are withheld until the range of options is exhausted. Similar to brainstorming, this step in the process encourages the exploration of alternative solutions (see Chapter 2). To arrive at an appropriate solution, it is necessary for the participants to establish criteria for evaluation of the alternatives. Several methods are available to evaluate options. Participants can rank order options from the most desired to the least desired, or advantages and disadvantages can be identified for each option. More systematically, options can be compared with evaluation criteria through the use of a matrix. Once the options are evaluated, participants reach consensus either by selecting the highest-ranking option or by combining options.

Implementation of the recommendations is the final step in the process. An action plan identifying who, what, and when is an effective means for establishing responsibility.

Who Should Participate

People participate in issues in response to some perceived interest and remain involved as long as that interest persists. Clearly, different segments of the public will choose to participate on different issues. People choose to participate if they see themselves affected by an issue because of a possible threat or benefit of a proposed facility, if they have an economic interest in the outcome of a particular decision, if they need to protect or increase access to the use of a facility or service, if they perceive an environmental or health risk associated with a proposed action, or if an issue affects strongly held religious or political beliefs. Therefore, the size and composition of the participant group will be different for each decision-making process (Creighton, 1994).

People need to participate at their own levels of interest and expertise. There will always be various levels of involvement, depending on differences in technical expertise, roles in the community, and willingness to commit time and energy. Different groups may choose to be involved at different stages of the process, especially in larger projects. People may also participate more in some stages of the process than in others. In technical areas that may involve data collection and analysis, people with such expertise may be instrumental, whereas stages in which choices are made may attract a larger public. Therefore, the number and type of participants can change during the course of the planning process.

Public participation programs rarely involve the general public, but the general public should be informed about an issue so that people can decide whether to participate. However, those who are most affected by a decision should have the greatest voice in that decision. People should be informed about the consequences of not participating. They should also know how to participate if they wish to do so, and all viewpoints and interest groups within the community should be sought out.

Youth Participation

Participatory processes are also a means of enhancing the role of youths in society. Young people's involvement in community activities creates a necessary sense of belonging and an opportunity to become socially productive. Youths want to contribute to their community and believe themselves capable of doing so, but are often constrained by adult expectations. Isolation in school, for example, deprives youth of community participation, of socially productive work, and limits their chances to develop personal responsibility, tolerance, cooperation, and creativity.

Children who exist in isolated environments, such as schools, focusing on individual achievement, develop simplistic relationship skills, dependence on external validation, and antisocial behaviors (Kurth-Schai, 1988). In contrast, in nonindustrialized societies children traditionally hold a variety of household and societal responsibilities. The role of children as nurturers in developing countries is widespread and significantly influences the quality of life. In all cultures children have the capacity to renew creative activity in adults.

Community development and youth development are inextricably related because both hinge on the basic health of the functions of family and citizenship and are long-term strategies for reducing youth and community problems. In 1994, the National Network for Youth (NNY) embraced the idea of "community youth development" as a vision of working in partnership with young people to strengthen their ties to community and working with communities to value and support youth (Pittman, 1996). Investment in the human and social capital of young people through their participation in community problem solving is the best way to build skills and connections.

Through participatory processes, youths are taking on roles that make them active members of their communities. The Dudley's Young Architects and Planners Project resulted from the energy and vision of youth (Medoff and Sklar, 1994). A youth focus group for a planned community center attracted more than twice the number of participants invited. The focus group was successful as a visioning tool, and the youth requested continuation of the process. The resulting participatory process engaged youth in community ownership, taught them new skills, and produced a model for a neighborhood community center. In presenting their model to the community, the youth group conveyed clearly that they had designed the center with everyone in the neighborhood in mind.

The Du Sable/Farren Outdoor Learning Center in the South Side of Chicago, an oasis located between an elementary school and a high school, was conceived and designed by at-risk youth under the guidance of landscape architects (Dickey, 1996). Students took, and were allowed, a central role in the process and in the design of the project. Professionals in the process saw themselves as tools to assist the students who were the "heart and soul" of the project. A landscape architect on the project noted, "We learned that the process we took the kids through was as important as the product" (Dickey, p. 54). Learning resulted in a change of behavior for one professional firm involved in the project, whereby it changed its traditional approach to a public participation approach. Community work is seen as a way to fill the need for a sense of community and a sense of practical accomplishment (Boyte, 1991). Youths focus their attention on activities in which they can make a difference close to home. Today's youths are more tolerant, accepting, and open to diversity of race, ethnicity, and gender than those of previous generations.

The environmental and perceptual needs of youth permit them to make a unique contribution. Roger Hart's (1979) work investigates children's exploration, use, knowledge of, and feelings for places. Hart found that our greatest period of geographic exploration is our childhood. Attempts to design environments for children should be preceded by an understanding of children's activities in and experience of the physical environment.

One step to shifting the role of children and youth in society to a more contributory and positive one is to provide opportunities for them to act on their conceptions in real-life situations. By making a place for youths in community participatory processes, they will be empowered to make their unique creative contributions. Young people need to participate as equal partners in making decisions about their own environmental futures. In Norway, for example, many municipalities developed action plans for children and youth based on goals set by the national government, which include statements such as, "Young people must be integrated into society, given responsibilities, and have opportunities to influence their own living conditions "(Moore, 1986).

The environmental yard, a project initiated by Robin Moore (Moore and Wong, 1998), developed an asphalt urban schoolyard into an educational resource and community open space (Figure 1.1). With the goal of involving as many of the present and future users as possible, a survey solicited ideas from children, teachers, parents, and nearby residents. Students completed a written survey that asked three questions:

- What do you like about the yard at Washington School?
- What do you dislike about the yard?
- What would you like to see added to or changed in the yard?

The results of the survey indicated that although the children valued the old play equipment, most respondents expressed a desire for natural spaces. Student and teacher groups went on field trips to observe play areas in other neighborhoods, as well as to sample the local flora and fauna. Based on the results of surveys, field trips, and children's design proposals, architecture and landscape architecture students proposed alternative layouts for the site.

Community groups discussed their needs, proposals were evaluated, and a master plan was presented to local officials that aimed to upgrade the physical environment and to reestablish the natural habitats that existed prior to the asphalt. The results of a postoccupancy evaluation from the 350-member student body, which compared the actual use of the yard with the children's perception of

FIGURE 1.1 Construction of the Washington School environmental yard was a community process. (Photo: Robin Moore.)

it, revealed that the natural settings were among the most attractive and memorable to the children. The evolution of the yard was integrated into the development of the education program. Numerous studies conducted over a 10-year period confirmed the extent of teacher and student growth resulting from the curricular involvement facilitated by the yard.

Rewards for Youth's Participation

Youths who are involved in participatory processes reap a variety of rewards, including reduced alienation, skill development, and empowerment. Community organizations empower young people by providing a strong sense of membership, a range of developmentally appropriate activities, and a structure within which everyone is accountable (Heath, 1991). Youths learn an applicable problem-solving model (Figure 1.2), learn to analyze and evaluate information, learn the skills for teamwork, learn compromise, strengthen communication skills, and develop attitudes and behaviors of the world of work (Schine, 1990).

Society also derives benefits from youth's participation in community activities. The United States depends on volunteers for numerous services, for creative solutions to community problems, for fund-raising, and for political action. Cooperative effort is essential to survival of a democratic society. Professionals will be called upon to cooperate in the development of programs, collaborate in their execution, and coordinate participation of adult and youth volunteers. Young people need not to be included as a courtesy, or because they are needy, or to keep them out of trouble, but because they belong in the community process.

FIGURE 1.2 Youths taking part in community building. (Photo: Henry Sanoff.)

Consequences of Participation

Citizen participation in design and planning has increased rapidly in the past few years to the point where it is a frequently praised practice. Federal legislation and the demands of citizens themselves have combined to make citizen participation an essential requirement in any urban project. Yet nothing in community design and planning has caused more contention. In most communities citizen participation is the principal source of confusion and conflict.

Barriers to participation in design and planning are generated by the process itself, and others are associated with false assumptions about participation. Common barriers are identified as follows:

Some professionals argue that participation is not necessary, and often undesirable for eventual users to participate in designing and planning, inasmuch as they do not have the necessary expertise and often get in the way.

The technical complexity of planning issues and problems can discourage or inhibit citizen participation, particularly without a skilled facilitator. If planning organizations preempt community involvement by defining problems as too technical or too complex for nonprofessionals to understand, they may engender political passivity, dependency, and ignorance (Forester, 1988).

Because everyone has a different opinion, you will get as many answers as the number of people you ask. Another, contradictory, argument is that people are so similar that their needs are undifferentiated.

Although people are indeed different and their preferences may vary, research has shown that ignoring these differences has resulted in dissatisfaction with the results. Yet excluding users in the design and planning process, based on the assumption that all people are the same, usually results in solutions that are totally uniform, in which everyone is assumed to have identical requirements. Both approaches have resulted in considerable user dissatisfaction.

Participation can be threatening to professionals and managers who feel it threatens their role as experts since it implies shifting decision control to users.

Professionals have expertise that is different from that of users. Users have expertise in identifying problems, not necessarily in solving problems. Collaboration is effective when all participants in the process share their areas of expertise with one another.

Involving users is more time-consuming, and therefore more expensive, than relying on professionals who have broad experience and specialized knowledge.

The time and effort devoted to involving users is a basic form of community or organizational development. Helping participants to resolve conflicts and having them identify goals that can be widely discussed are invaluable contributions to any community planning process.

The lack of adequate experience by professionals, government officials, and managers in working in collaboration with users can limit the effectiveness of participation.

An outside consultant can facilitate the participatory process and train local professionals and officials.

Often, the people involved do not represent the majority but are, rather, citizens who represent special interests.

Citizen participation has been found lacking because many affected citizens are left out of the process, the influence of those citizens included in the process is minimized, and the process is inefficient in bringing citizen input to the decision makers. Participation is unequally distributed throughout society because the qualities that lead some to participate—motivation, skills, resources—are not equally distributed (Verba and Nie, 1972). Factors that inhibit participation include overwhelming personal need, low sense of efficacy, and suspicion of bureaucracy. These are characteristics often associated with poverty.

Every effort should be made to include people who will be affected by design and planning decisions. This often requires contacting individuals directly, contacting schools to reach children, and contacting religious and community organizations and clubs.

There is a danger that the entire process turns out to reflect the aphorism that a camel is a horse designed by committee. Everything is likely to end up as a compromise.

People can be reasonable. Most people will change their views in light of new information when presented in a way that helps them see how the overall scheme fits into their own vision. In fact, the camel is an apt metaphor, as it is a unique animal capable of accommodating severe climatic conditions as a result of its unique design.

Case Study Research Findings

In a case study analysis of ten community-developed and maintained gardens and parks in New York City, Francis, Cashden, and Paxson (1984) identified the following criteria used in evaluating the projects to point out issues common to many community-developed open-space projects:

- Phase and degree of community control
- Project initiation
- Size of organizing group
- Number of key participants
- Ethnicity of organizing group
- Neighborhood ethnicity
- Relationship of group to other neighborhood efforts
- Opportunities for new group participation
- Group goals
- Funding source
- When funding was secured
- Dependability of funding
- Materials source

- Staff and workers
- Size of site
- Permanency of site
- Site ownership
- Site condition prior to development
- Site use
- Site activity
- Adjacent neighborhood/street activity
- Site accessibility of neighborhood residents
- Location of site in neighborhood
- Site users
- Perception of success or failure
- Income in neighborhood
- Neighborhood stability

An analysis of the ten case studies sites in New York City resulted in several observations about the consequences of open-space projects:

- Participants report a personal feeling of accomplishment in improving their neighborhood.
- Participants report gaining confidence and skills from their involvement.
- Participants develop friendships and a sense of belonging.
- Projects help to improve the appearance of adjacent areas.
- Projects inspire other open-space projects in the community.
- Projects can exclude teenagers from using or managing the site.
- Projects require considerable time and energy from participants.

The authors recommend the following ingredients necessary for starting and maintaining a successful open-space project:

- Clear and agreed upon goals
- Good group dynamics
- Clear definition of responsibility
- Continuity and commitment by participants
- Diversity of skills and experience of participants
- Sympathetic community climate
- Group control of decision making, funding, and development process
- Realistic fund-raising strategies
- Good knowledge of the community
- Large number of volunteers to do physical work

A review of the public involvement literature conducted by Lach and Hixson (1996) included descriptive case studies of the effectiveness of various processes and effective implementation strategies. They discovered, however, a lack of documentation related to the value or cost-effectiveness of participation. Their literature review did indicate that participants valued such issues as public acceptability, accessibility, good decision making, education and learning, time commitments, and trust. To identify value and cost indicators of public involvement, they conducted interviews with people who had been involved in participatory projects. Combining the literature review, interviews, and expert judgment, they identified public involvement value attributed to the process, to the outcomes, and to the cost.

The following are key indicators of the value of participation:

- Opening the process to stakeholders
- Diversity of viewpoints
- Meaningful participation
- Integrating stakeholder concerns
- Information exchange
- Saving time
- Saving and avoiding costs
- Enhanced project acceptability
- Mutual learning
- Mutual respect

Lach and Hixson also developed direct and indirect cost indicators of the public involvement effort. Certain costs can be linked to traditional accounting practice, such as preparation and participation time, facilities, materials, and services. Other indirect costs, such as participants' time commitment, lack of opportunity to participate in other projects, and heavy emotional demands on participation, cannot be easily measured. The intent of their research was to develop prototype indicators to be tested in ongoing and completed public involvement programs.

Results obtained from project participants indicated that the positive aspects of their involvement were that a diversity of viewpoints in the participation process was valuable and that project savings occurred in the form of saving and of avoiding costs. The authors detected a discrepancy between the perceived time commitment of participants, which seemed quite large, and the actual time spent on preparation, participation, and follow-up, which appeared to be modest. This suggests that the actual time commitment in the participation process must be carefully tracked. Such indicators as those identified by this research effort provide an initial point for discussion with potential sponsors of participation projects about the fears, as well as the benefits, of public participation.

Participatory Reform

More people participate in local planning today than ever before. This participation is supported by local authorities and provides unique opportunities for increasing

public awareness of a variety of community issues. However, the capacity of participatory design to address issues of environmental risks and poverty has diminished,
argues Hester (1996), because powerful local interests tend to dominate.

Citizens today tend to be motivated by self-interests and are shortsighted in
their efforts, which are increasingly segregated along class and racial lines. As
wealthy citizens embraced participation and environmental risks have become
clearer, an increasing number of dangerous land uses, such as landfills, toxic sites,
and polluting industries have been located in poor communities (Bullard, 1990).
Thus, participation has been used to preserve the quality of life for affluent and
powerful citizens. Those who already have economic clout are involved in politics
in ways that disproportionately increase their influence, making the practice of
democracy increasingly biased against the economically disadvantaged (Easterbrook, 1995).

Quality-of-life participation and efforts at neighborhood protection frequently rely on the methods of advocacy that were developed initially to empower
the poor. Special interest groups empowered through participatory processes
block one another's actions, creating a local gridlock. Many people tend to be
more sophisticated in their knowledge of participation processes, yet they are often
fearful. This citizen motivation is evidenced in actions based on sentiments such as
"not on our street (NOOS)," "not in my backyard (NIMBY)," and "locally unwanted land uses (LULU)."

Only by refocusing on the initial reasons for community participation can
local problems be effectively solved. This suggests that grass roots must be empowered with the authority and responsibility for positive local action, not just blocking action.

Local groups with similar goals that lack communication or cooperation
may undermine the potential for mutual benefits. This dominance of narrow special interests must be replaced by a broader civic vision that penetrates social and
physical barriers. Hester (1996) advocates a reformation of the participatory
process that stresses the conscious pursuit of a sense of community, a new form of
governance that empowers local communities, and the creation of sustainable
communities. This new approach to participation, argues Hester, should examine
the cumulative impact of actions and their ecological implications.

Mark Francis (1998) recognizes that participation has become a tool for
defending exclusionary, conservative principles, rather than for promoting social
justice and ecological vision. He proposes a new proactive role for professionals
that distinguish them from their more traditional counterparts. The new professional employs a visionary approach that allows a community to expand its vision
through participatory processes. Effective visionary action requires persistence and
risk taking. In the United Kingdom, Wates and Knevitt (1987) distinguish the differences between conventional and community architecture as follows:

Conventional Architecture: Users are passive recipients of an environment
conceived, executed, managed, and evaluated by others with professional
experts.

Community Architecture: Users are the clients. They take control of commissioning, designing, developing, constructing, managing, and evaluating their environment.

Conventional Architecture: Top-down, emphasis on product rather than process, bureaucratic, centralized and compartmentalized, secretive, impersonal, anonymous.

Community Architecture: Bottom-up, emphasis on process rather than product, flexible, personal, localized, continuous, holistic and multidisciplinary, evolutionary, familiar, people managed, and open.

Conventional Architecture: Experts occasionally make superficial attempts to define and consult end users.

Community Architecture: Experts are commissioned by and are accountable to users, or behave as if they are.

Conventional Architecture: Self-conscious about style. Most likely modern or post-modern movement.

Community Architecture: Unself-conscious about style. Most likely to be contextual, regional, with concern for identity.

Proactive practice, argues Francis, begins well before there is a paying client and continues long after the contract ends. In 1987, Francis proposed an integrated regional open space system for Davis, California, called the Davis Greenway. The greenway concept was presented in environmental forums and refined in participatory planning workshops. The idea ultimately became the open space element of the city's general plan. His proactive effort established a future vision that generated substantial community involvement and an open space constituency.

Diffusing NIMBYism

The Alberta (Canada) Special Waste Treatment Center near Swan Hills has proven a model of private and local government collaboration, not only for its transcendence of NIMBYism, but also for its alteration of the traditional methods of the siting process and the nature of interactions between key participants (Rabe, 1994). The conditions necessary to foster cooperative outcomes rely on the creation of new governmental institutions that can mediate factional conflict, the establishment of public participation processes well before final decisions must be made, and the development of competent professionals to oversee policy and build public trust.

The Alberta approach involved numerous general information meetings, sharing technical reports with community organizations. Meetings in every county and affected community (more than 120 in all) were held to respond to citizen questions, as well as to provide information about the hazardous waste situation in the area. Local political leadership was effective in building public trust by advocating the voluntary nature of the siting process, the economic development potential of a waste management facility, and how this effort was part of a comprehensive waste management strategy.

Meaningful methods of public participation are necessary to achieve any future breakthroughs. Political dialogue is needed to diffuse the adversarialism that is common in NIMBY-type situations and move toward processes of conflict resolution (Williams and Matheny, 1994). If participation is to have a significant impact, multiple participatory methods must be employed (Mazmanian and Nienaber, 1994).

To diffuse NIMBYism, methods of compensation were proposed at a very early stage in the process. This strategy is consistent with the lessons offered by game theorists who suggest that altering the payoffs and how they are distributed may result in stable, cooperative outcomes (Axelrod, 1984). Swan Hills officials contend that the economic impact of the facility has been substantial in the prosperity enjoyed in the years following facility approval.

Public opposition to unwanted facilities is often described as selfish parochialism, generating locational conflict that prevents attainment of societal goals. Robert Lake (1993) suggests a reconsideration of the assumption that siting of unwanted facilities is in conflict with societal needs. Whether it involves siting a hazardous waste incinerator or locating a homeless shelter, such strategies concentrate costs on host communities. An alternative approach is to restructure production to produce less waste, which initially shifts the costs to capital. Similarly, an alternative strategy to locating homeless shelters is to alleviate joblessness and reduce the incidence of poverty through capital restructuring.

Lake further contends that the reason NIMBYism is such a powerful political force is that it is an integral factor in the land development process, guided by the rate of return on property. The proliferation of problems associated with suburban sprawl, low-density development, socioeconomic, racial, or ethnic segregation, traffic congestion, and environmental pollution threaten profitability of land investment. Plans to address these problems often encounter opposition from consumers who invested in the land. Therefore, Lake suggests a proactive approach, such as mounting an effort for recognizing the pervasiveness of poverty to help establish political support for easing the homelessness crisis and, hence, the pressure for siting group homes and social services. Similarly, Lake suggests that support for hazardous waste source reduction may reduce pressure to impose waste incinerators on resistant communities.

Conflict Resolution

All communities and organizations experience conflict at some time during their daily efforts. One view is that conflict and disputes occur when people are involved in meeting goals that are incompatible, that people work against each other when their goals are competitive (Moore, 1986). Another view is that conflict involves incompatible behaviors between parties whose interests differ, where people are disrupting one another's actions (Brown, 1983). The assumption that conflict is based on opposing interests leads to viewing conflict as a power struggle. Assuming that people have cooperative goals leads to viewing conflict as a common problem that can be resolved for mutual benefit.

People find themselves in conflict because they assess situations differently, vary in their objectives, and/or prefer different courses of action. Such differences may occur because people have different values, or because they have different information, or because they process information differently (Lozare, 1994).

Although there may be negative consequences associated with conflict, disputes can be positively resolved if the participants can develop cooperative problem-solving procedures. Avoidance of conflict, however, undermines people's well-being and effectiveness. Managing conflict reduces the time wasted by redoing tasks and results in more efficient use of resources. Addressing conflicts encourages people to understand the viewpoint of others and to become less egocentric. People can become more confident and feel empowered to cope with difficulties by directly confronting them (Tjosvold, 1993). Having others listen and respond to their feelings build people's self-esteem. Learning to manage conflict facilitates the well-being of people as well as the effectiveness of organizations.

The absence of conflict usually means that different viewpoints have been excluded from the decision-making process. Conflict can broaden views of what is possible and allow more choices. Disagreement can be used to uncover prejudices, needs, and values and to improve skills in interaction. Groups that use conflict for learning, instead of winning or losing, become stronger.

Research has established that the probability of achieving favorable outcomes is enhanced when all parties know and practice sound negotiating techniques. Such situations help mediate differences without the use of manipulative methods. Negotiation is a procedure for resolving disputes; it is a form of joint problem solving. People in conflict, however, often need some form of help to settle their differences. Mediation is a voluntary process of helping people resolve their differences with the assistance of a neutral person. Mediation is applied to a variety of organizational, environmental, and public policy disputes. For mediation to occur, parties must have begun the process of negotiation. Thus, mediation is an extension of the negotiation process, requiring the involvement of a mediator who brings a new dynamic to the dispute. Negotiation is a psychological process involving group dynamics, in which there is often an expression of strong emotions. Problems associated with negative dynamics in the negotiation process often involve a lack of trust and poor communications. Creating an atmosphere of trust and cooperation is referred to as conciliation, an integral part of mediation.

Moore (1986) outlines 12 stages of the mediation process:

1. Initial contacts with the disputing parties to build rapport and credibility, educating the participants about the negotiation process, and eliciting a commitment to the mediation process.

2. Selecting a conflict resolution strategy to guide mediation, which includes competition, avoidance, accommodation, negotiated compromise, and interest-based negotiation.
3. Collecting and analyzing background information about the people involved through direct observation, interviewing, and secondary sources such as reports, minutes, or newspaper articles.
4. Developing a detailed plan for mediation, identifying strategies that will enable agreement, answering such questions as who should be involved, what procedures will be used, and how will participants be educated about the process and agree to proceed.
5. Building trust and cooperation and clarifying communication by responding to intense emotions, suppressing emotions, and resolving misperceptions.
6. Opening negotiation by establishing ground rules and behavioral guidelines by facilitating communication and information exchange. Communication techniques may include the following:
   a. Restating what has been said in the same words
   b. Paraphrasing what has been said in different words
   c. Dividing an idea into smaller parts
   d. Summarizing the message
   e. Organizing ideas into a sequence
   f. Generalizing the points in a message
   g. Asking probing questions for elaboration
   h. Asking questions for clarification
7. Defining issues and setting an agenda by ranking the issues in terms of importance and selecting the most important items for discussion, by identifying issues that are most likely to reach agreement, by identifying the issues that require agreement first, by negotiating more than one issue simultaneously to allow for trade-offs, and by defining issues in terms of principles, then working out the details.
8. Uncovering hidden interests of disputing parties through the use of communication techniques such as restating, listening, or generalizing, as well as questioning and brainstorming in small groups.
9. Generating options for settlement, which is best achieved in small discussion groups using brainstorming, Nominal Group Process (Delbecq, Van deVen, and Gustafson, 1975), or through the use of hypothetical scenarios in which participants in small groups determine how the problem can be solved.
10. Assessing options for settlement, which often requires an initial review of the interests of all parties, then combining, dropping, or modifying alternatives to reach a final settlement.
11. Reaching substantive agreement, which requires disputing parties to reduce the number of differences in order to terminate their conflict. This final bargaining stage requires parties to make offers, concessions, or agreements as they incrementally converge on a settlement within a prescribed deadline.

12. Formalizing the settlement, which can be a public or private oral exchange of agreement or a written agreement of promises between disputants.

Mediation is a participatory process whereby the mediator educates the parties involved in the mediation process. The primary responsibility for the resolution of a dispute rests on the parties themselves; agreements reached in negotiations are voluntary, and the mediator's responsibility is to assist the disputants in reaching a settlement.

Combining Conflict Resolution and Public Participation

Combining conflict resolution and public participation processes is a model proposed by Conner and Orenstein (1995) to diffuse a controversy when several citizens groups are in opposition to a proposed action. Conflict resolution focuses on developing understanding, trust, and acceptance between appropriate parties with the assistance of mediators or facilitators. In some instances, however, significant publics do not have organizations to represent them in discussing key community issues. Integrating conflict resolution and public participation allows the general public to be informed and involved as well as to develop consensus building with group leaders.

The 12-step integrated process is described as follows; strategies are identified as public participation (PP) or conflict resolution (CR):

(PP) **1.** Develop a profile of the community's social characteristics, key leaders, and groups.

(CR) **2.** Convene a meeting of interest group leaders to identify key issues and options.

(PP) **3.** Inform the general public through various media about the process and proposals.

(PP) **4.** Organize workshops to discuss issues and produce a synthesis for interest group leaders.

(CR) **5.** Enable interest group leaders to review proposals and public responses to it.

(PP) **6.** Inform the general public through various media about alternatives, indicating selection criteria and their assessment.

(PP) **7.** Organize workshops to respond to public concerns for group leaders to consider.

(CR) **8.** Convene a third meeting of interest group leaders to review alternatives and establish evaluation criteria.

(PP) **9.** Publish alternatives acceptable to interest group leaders and seek responses from the public.

(PP) **10.** Organize workshops to identify preferred alternatives and convey results to group leaders.

(PP) **11.** Conduct surveys to broaden participation of the general public. Convey
results to group leaders.

(CR) **12.** Convene meetings to integrate the views of interest group leaders, the
interested public, and the general public. Convey results to all public
groups involved in the process.

This process relies on effective public information to allow people to make
informed decisions. Too many information campaigns have failed because people were not prepared to receive information that did not support their world-
view. Consequently, opening people's mind to change is a crucial initial step.
DeBono (1985) suggests that people need to think in a design mode. Rather than
determining blame for present situations, where argument, negotiation, and
analysis tend to look back, people need to look forward at what may be created.
Equally significant is the need for mediation expertise to create effective working
relationships between special interest groups, technical consultants, and elected
officials.

Organizational Participation

The ability to build collaborative relationships is regarded as the basis for future
community, as well as organizational, success. In an era of organizational complexity and change, maintaining organizational health relies on cooperation and
collaboration across and within organizations. Participatory empowerment,
whereby citizens or employees have decision-making power, is also regarded as a
key factor in achieving healthy organizations. This combination of collective decision making with individual responsibility demands an atmosphere of trust. Trust
is developed essentially through interpersonal interaction that provides a basis for
dealing effectively with change (Ring and Van de Ven, 1994). Face-to-face communication is pivotal in establishing effective interaction and appropriate flows
of information, the foundation from which cooperation is possible. Out of this
cooperation will develop ideas, decisions, and strategies, all of which rely on the
development of consensus. The more group members are involved in a decision-
making process, the more likely they will develop feelings of teamwork and cooperation, thereby increasing their motivation, commitment, and contribution to the
group.

Pettigrew and Whipp (1993) emphasize the requirement for organizations
to understand their environments, pointing to the need for them to become open
learning systems in order to deal effectively with the challenges that changing environments produce. Interaction with the environment implies listening, but may
also necessitate internal adjustments within the organizational structure. Corporate CEOs are discovering that to implement change they must first know the

organization culture before introducing such techniques as quality circles, a form of teaming and participatory management. Quality circles are different from committees or task forces, because their leaders and members are trained in specific techniques of the circle process, including brainstorming and consensus decision making. The circle itself determines what problems will be analyzed and solved. The quality circle is a participative management tool designed to systematically harness the brainpower of employees to solve an organization's problems of productivity and quality. A quality circle facilitator is similar to a public meeting facilitator (Creighton, 1995).

The elements in an organization that constitute its "culture" include expectations and assumptions about how good members should behave, common language and understanding about the meaning of words and events, major policies, symbolic meaning assigned to the design and use of space, the look and feel of the organization and its members, and commonly held values about what is worth doing and how it should be done (Becker and Steele, 1995). To create an effective design and planning process, professionals must understand how the organization makes decisions, the basis on which those decisions are made, and the role it assigns to the physical environment. Culture is a critical determinant of how well an organization is able to deal with change. It is through culture, largely in terms of attitudes, values, and patterns of behavior, that it can be transformed to better deal with its environment (More, 1998). Organizing this process is referred to as strategic planning, in which its most important product may be the process itself.

Good strategic planning is a participative process in terms of reflecting an organization's vision about how it should operate and the actions needed to prosper in that envisioned environment. Fundamental to this view is the understanding that there are many "stakeholders" in the planning process and that participants have different views about what is, what ought to be, why things are the way they are, and how they can be changed. The core of this approach is that individuals or groups have a stake in what the organization does by being able to affect or being affected by an organization's operations.

Clarifying information and its underlying assumptions becomes a major objective of the strategic planning process. A participative view of the strategic planning process outlined by Mason and Mitroff (1981) involves the following factors:

Participative. Many individuals must be actively involved, because the information they possess is varied.

Adversarial. Opposition must be designed into the planning process to allow doubt to surface and be publicly debated.

Integrative. A coherent plan of action, corresponding to a shared vision of the future, is needed to guide the strategic planning process.

Supportive. Managers must be actively involved in the process so that they understand the rationale for various decisions.

This approach opens the way for people to find and pursue points of communality involving their own interests and those of the organizations for which they work. This approach can also serve to enhance the performance and experience of everyone involved in an organization. People do indeed gain satisfaction from feeling competent, in control, and free to choose for themselves. Personal involvement in shaping their workplace will aid the development of responsibility, cooperation, and self-motivation. Studies in small group behavior produced evidence for the "participation hypothesis." Verba (1961) states that "significant changes in human behavior can be brought about rapidly only if the persons who are expected to change participate in deciding what the change shall be and how it shall be made."

In a classic study reported in the Herman Miller magazine, *Ideas,* Sommer (1979) noted that allowing employees to select their own furniture from sample items assembled in a vacant warehouse resulted in a layout that was decentralized, modest, and personal, with the individual station at its core. The office had an unplanned quality, as the total environment arrangement evolved from the sum of individual decisions. Different employees had different equipment and furnishings and were more satisfied with their work setting than those in a comparable sample of employees who worked in a setting furnished from a single furniture system prescribed by expert space planners. Of particular interest here is that the warehouse building has been denied design awards while the latter has received several. One juror described his denial of an award on the basis of the plan's "residential quality" and "lack of discipline and control of the interiors." In the latter case, visual order and social control becomes the goal, not productivity or user satisfaction.

The argument that employees want everyone treated in a visibly identical fashion does not hold up when employees participate in a procedure that allows them a genuine opportunity to make informed choices. Similarly, the appearance of order is based on the premise that the designed environment is created for users that are more or less identical. Yet we have seen from the results of this and other research that there are many differences between individuals and that these differences should be reflected in the complexity and variation of processes of environmental support applied to them.

A Steelcase/Harris (1987) survey of American office workers has shown that they are permitted much less participation in decisions about their work, and workplace, than they want. Research (Brill, Margulis, and Konar, 1984; Becker, 1988) has indicated that increased employee involvement is associated with greater satisfaction with the work environment and a stronger commitment to decisions made about it.

A poll of the Lloyds of London building, conducted by Becker (1988), revealed that 75 percent of the people working there found the new building less satisfactory than its predecessor, a consequence of not involving occupants in decisions about their workplace. Eighteen months after occupancy major changes were required to one of the most expensive buildings ever built.

In the case of Xerox Corporation, a history of union-management relations had built an organizational culture of trust and cooperation. Although this collaboration reduced the level of conflict, the worker participation program was initially limited to shop floor problems that could be resolved without changing the labor contract or infringing on management decisions. As a result of declining international competitiveness, a cost study team was formed to study machines and work flow, allocations of cost, rethinking jobs and work rules, and increasing worker responsibilities. The team proposed new ways of thinking about problems and new social processes for resolving those problems that led to basic changes in structures and processes of participation—in effect, changes in organizational culture in Xerox manufacturing plants (Whyte, 1991).

There are many ways of involving employees in planning and design decisions. Some companies use surveys; others use structured focus groups to react to schematic design proposals. In some instances employees may actually help design their own workstations by selecting their furniture or laying out their own work areas. The key is to involve employees in decisions they care about and to demonstrate to them that their ideas actually contributed to the final decision. Involving employees in workplace decisions can also save organizations thousands of dollars by reducing the likelihood that money will be allocated to physical design solutions that workers consider unacceptable.

The process begins with the problems currently faced by the people who work in an organization. Instead of beginning in the conventional way with a review of the literature, stating the hypothesis, and finding a target organization to test the method, the process begins by discovering the problems existing in the organization. Working with the members of an organization and diagnosing their problems helps to focus the literature search as well as the previous experience of the researcher/professional. Gustavsen (1985) and Eldin and Levin (1991) describe this notion of the reformation of the workplace as a "democratic dialogue." Gustavsen goes on to propose nine criteria for evaluating the degree of democracy in a dialogue aimed at democratizing work (Gustavsen, 1985, pp. 474–475):

- The dialogue is a process of exchange between participants.
- All individuals concerned must have the possibility to participate.
- All participants should be active in the discussions.
- All participants in the process are equal.
- Work experience is the basis for participation.
- At least some of the participants' experiences must be considered legitimate.
- All participants must develop an understanding of the issues at stake.
- Initially, all arguments pertaining to the issue under discussion are legitimate.
- The dialogue must continually generate agreement that leads to investigation and action.

A key component in maintaining a healthy organization in the future is a continuous strategic planning process engaged in daily by all levels of the organization. Organizations will require a clear organizational vision of how they will do what they will do. Karl Marx longed for the day when workers, through revolution, would own the means of production. Instead, they are the literal owners, because the means of production in most organizations these days reside in the heads and hands of the workers themselves; if they leave, almost nothing remains (Handy, 1997).

CHAPTER

2

Participation Methods

Participation in community issues places serious demands and responsibilities on participants. Although citizens groups voluntarily organize to participate in community projects, the technical complexity of such projects usually requires professional assistance. In addition to the need to address technical complexity, sound design and planning principles must be incorporated in the development process. Without guidance, community groups may respond only to situations of crisis and may not achieve the goals that originally united them. Often community volunteers cannot draw upon personal experiences for solving environmental problems and may arrive at solutions that create unforeseen, serious consequences. Therefore, the management of participatory efforts is important.

People will join if change can and will occur. Participation can function if it is active and directed and if those who become involved experience a sense of achievement. At the same time, a reexamination of traditional design and planning procedures is required to ensure that participation becomes more than confirmation of a professional's original intentions.

Organizing citizens' efforts can take many forms corresponding to different environmental issues. The goal of participation is to encourage people to learn as a result of becoming aware of a problem. Learning occurs best when the process is clear, communicable, open, and encourages dialogue, debate, and collaboration. As more people learn about environmental issues, their decisions will have positive

37

effects on the quality of the environment (White, Nair, and Ascroft, 1994). One of the fundamental hindrances to the decision to adopt the participation strategy is that it threatens existing hierarchies. Nevertheless, participation does not imply that there is no longer a role for institutional leaders. It only means that a dialogue is necessary between grass-roots citizenry and government leadership regarding needs and resources to meet needs (White and Patel, 1994).

The professional's role is to facilitate the citizen group's ability to reach decisions about the environment through an easily understood process. Most often this will take the form of making people aware of environmental alternatives. This role also includes helping people develop their resources in ways that will benefit themselves and others. Facilitation is a means of bringing people together to determine what they wish to do and helping them find ways to work together in deciding how to do it. A facilitator should make everyone feel included in what is going on and that what each person has to say is being listened to by the group. Facilitation can also include the use of a variety of techniques whereby people not professionally trained can organize themselves to create a change in the environment. If people are to discover the principle of quality for themselves, they are more likely to do so in small groups. Significant changes in people's behavior will occur if the persons expected to change participate in deciding what the change shall be and how it shall be made.

Good planning for community participation requires careful analysis. Although it is critical to examine goals and objectives in planning for participation, there are various techniques available, each of which performs different functions. In the last several decades there have been numerous efforts to accumulate knowledge about various participation techniques, as well as the function that these techniques perform. Citizen surveys, review boards, advisory boards, task forces, neighborhood and community meetings, public hearings, public information programs, and interactive cable TV have all been used with varying degrees of success, depending on the effectiveness of the participation plan. Because community participation is a complex concept, it requires considerable thought to prepare an effective participation program.

Strategic Planning

Strategic planning is a management technique borrowed from the private sector. Poister and Streib (1989) report that 60 percent of cities with populations of more than 25,000 use some form of strategic planning. Basically, strategic planning is an organized effort to produce decisions and actions that shape and guide what a community is, what it does, and why it does it. Strategy is the act of mobilizing resources toward goals. It includes setting goals and priorities, identifying issues and constituencies, developing an organization, taking actions, and evaluating results (Checkoway, 1986). Strategic planning requires information gathering, an exploration of alternatives, and an emphasis on the future implications of present decisions. It can facilitate communication and participation, accommodate divergent interests and values, and foster orderly decision making and successful implementation.

A strategic plan is a method of developing strategies and action plans necessary to identify and resolve issues. The challenge in creating a plan is to be specific enough to be able to monitor progress over time. To be usable, a strategic plan should have built-in flexibility to allow for revisions as new opportunities become apparent. Strategic planning is action oriented, considers a range of possible futures, and focuses on the implications of present decisions and actions in relation to that range (Bryson, 1988).

The development of a strategic plan requires the creation of a vision statement to provide suitable guidance and motivation for the ensuing process. The vision should emphasize purposes arrived at through group sessions in order to establish a common reference point for the broad objectives of the community. It outlines the key areas of concern within the community and will help people make decisions that support that vision.

The foundation for a strategic plan, often referred to as environmental assessment, considers needs, priorities, issues, and opportunities. Environmental assessment, or postoccupancy evaluation (POE), is the practice of using methods such as surveys, questionnaires, observations of people's behavior, and focus groups to discover exactly what makes the environment work well for its users. A POE is a procedure that involves users in their own assessment of their everyday physical environment. POEs can be effective in correcting environmental errors by examining urban environments in use, or in preventing potential errors through the use of survey results in a project's programming stage.

Environmental assessments have also helped to persuade clients to choose design alternatives they might otherwise not have considered. Some professional firms carry out their own evaluations in order to measure building performance against the original program, to acquaint the designer with the opinions and attitudes of the client or user, and to provide the designer with useful feedback for the design of similar facilities.

Goal Setting

The results of an environmental assessment can serve as a starting point for the identification of goals. A goal is an end toward which an effort or direction is specified. A goal specifies a direction of intended movement, not a location. In this sense a goal reflects an underlying value that is sought after and is not an object to be achieved (Smith and Hester, 1982). Goal setting can be seen as the guiding process necessary for successful community design.

Goals identify what should be accomplished through the plan. Therefore, it is the participants in the planning process who are responsible for shaping goals over the course of the project. Goals begin as open-ended ideas derived from knowledge of community needs. Whereas a goal is the desired general result, an objective is a desired specific result. Objectives should respond to each goal by defining a direction. They are definable and measurable tasks that support the accomplishment of goals.

Smith and Hester (1982) propose 12 reasons for setting goals:

1. Setting goals provides a sound basis for planning, implementation, and evaluation.
2. Setting goals clarifies problems.
3. Planning based on goals elicits community support.
4. Goal setting leads to positive action.
5. Goal setting leads to creative problem solving.
6. Goals are based on the potential of a community.
7. Plans based on goals can be evaluated and consciously changed.
8. Goal setting promotes human resource development.
9. Goal setting identifies the community-wide needs and values of minorities and special populations.
10. Goal setting has long-term educational value for the participants.
11. Goal setting is a good investment.
12. Participatory goal setting demonstrates good faith on the part of community leaders.

The primary inputs to goal setting are the collective knowledge, skills, abilities, and experiences of participants in the process. Although most processes are iterative, there are three stages of development integral to goal setting that require examination. Goal identification, the first stage, requires an awareness of the problem and a willingness to confront controversial issues. Goal clarification is the attempt to understand and describe feelings and emotions that may be explicit, or unexpressed and implicit. Identifying goal priorities is a process of rank ordering according to a certain criterion. The sum of goal identification, goal clarification, and establishing goal priorities comprises what is commonly known as goal setting.

Goal setting entails documentation and analysis. It also entails people—local informants, a community of clients, all of whom have their own social, political, and economic agendas. Goal setting involves collecting stories and identifying common themes that bind people together. Local people can provide knowledge about function, values, history, and structure of community institutions. Story gathering, or qualitative research, is an approach whereby people are treated as informants, not as subjects. They are encouraged to tell what has happened to them as a way of explaining how things work, not just what things are (Peattie, 1968). Goal setting results in a mutual understanding of interests and, subsequently, interpretation of issues.

Goals may be stated in a variety of ways. Jones (1990) suggests that the PARK categories be used to organize goal statements:

- Preserve (what we have now that is positive)
- Add (what we do not have that is positive)
- Remove (what we have that is negative)
- Keep out (what we do not have that is negative)

A goal statement should contain one major thought, but not specify how it will be met (that comes later when strategies are identified for accomplishing goals). Statements should begin with an action word such as *develop, provide, maintain, reduce, continue, increase,* or *upgrade.* Equally important as writing clear goals is making sure they represent stakeholders' views.

Strategies further clarify the methods required to reach a goal. There may be a variety of strategies required to reach a goal. Action steps advance those strategies further by specifying activities that contribute to their achievement. An action plan defines what action will be taken, who is responsible for getting it accomplished, and when the action plan should be complete (Figure 2.1). An action plan is expressed as follows:

What—A document that defines the actions to be taken, the person(s) responsible, and the time frame for completion

---

SAMPLE PLANNING WORKSHEET

This worksheet will help your planners to keep track of goals, objectives, strategies, and action steps.

Area of Planning: _____

Goal: _____

Objective: _____

Strategy: _____

Action Step	Responsibility	Timeline

FIGURE 2.1 Action plan work sheet.

Why—Defines roles and responsibilities and provides a tool for tracking implementation

How—Defines actions, gains commitments and agreement on deadlines

Although participants in the strategic planning process are amenable to supporting the actions required, a sense of ownership and accountability for all enabling actions will effect successful implementation.

Strategy Selection

A group process for identifying strategic issues is referred to as the *snow card* (Greenblat and Duke, 1981) or *snowball* (Nutt and Backoff, 1987) technique that combines brainstorming—which produces a long list of possible answers to a specific question—with a synthesizing step, in which answers are grouped into categories according to common themes. Each of the individual answers is written onto a 5-by-7-inch index card called a "snow card"; the individual cards then are fastened to a wall according to common themes, producing several "snowballs" of cards.

Guidelines for using the snow card technique are as follows:

- Select a facilitator to guide the process.
- Form the group(s) that will use the technique. The group size can vary from 5 to 12 members. Several groups can be formed if a large number of people wish to participate.
- Participants should be seated around a table where the index cards can be read clearly by all.
- Participants should focus on a single problem or issue.
- Participants should silently brainstorm as many ideas as possible, then select five best items to be transcribed onto separate index cards.
- Cards are collected by the facilitator, fastened to the wall, clustered by all participants, then discussed until agreement is reached about categories and their contents.

Strategic planning cycles typically begin with an appreciation and articulation of a perceived necessity or threat. Opportunity also can capture people's attention, although it seems to do so less frequently than necessity or threat. People and organizations are attached to ideas. In fact, organizations, agencies, and institutions are all organized around ideas, many of which are outmoded. Strategic planning, if it is to be effective, is often focused on replacing the way things are being done now with other ways. Schon (1971) argues that it is more important to manage ideas, rather than people or structures, because ideas are the rallying points of collective action.

Strategic Planning Process

Several conditions must be satisfied for a strategic planning process to be effective:

- There must be a compelling reason to undertake a strategic planning process. Key decision makers must see some important benefits from strategic planning, or they will not be active supporters and participants.
- The process must be supported by important and powerful leaders and decision makers.
- There must be a process advocate, a person who believes in strategic planning and assumes the role of facilitating the thinking, deciding, and acting of key decision makers.
- The process must be tailored to the community situation.
- Key decision makers must talk with one another about what is important for the community as a whole.
- Resources needed are the attention and commitment of key decision makers.

Visioning

Visioning is a process that seeks to "create living, useful guides for public actions intended to position the community for the future" (Thomas, Means, and Grieve, 1988). Participants are asked to think about how the community should be and to find ways to identify, strengthen, and work toward a community vision (Figure 2.2). Participants are asked how they would like their community to be in 20 years and to try to put that vision into words or images. It is effective to start the process with a large group informally brainstorming what should be included in the community vision. Then, breaking into small working groups of about seven, participants should discuss the ideas and present them to the larger group. Once participants present their views, common themes are identified and strategies are developed to move the community in the direction of the vision. Although specialists may carry out specific policies and recommendations, citizens remain responsible for the framework within which decisions are made. The shared vision belongs to the group rather than to any one individual.

Community visioning projects are conducted by citizens, often referred to as stakeholders, who care about the future of their communities. The stakeholders in successful visioning processes represent the community's diversity. As the planning group for the visioning process, they set goals and develop the action plan and implementation strategies.

Successful visioning projects usually follow a similar process. The National Civic League (Okubo, 1997) has identified a ten-step process:

Revitalizing Spring Hope

Spring Hope, N.C.   *A Report From The Spring Hope Revitalization Commission*   May 17, 1984

What kind of town do we want to be?

One of the prominent issues deemed vital by the first public meeting for downtown revitalization was that the people of Spring Hope want to maintain the atmosphere of a small Southern town while embarking on a program of controlled growth.

When asked to describe the sense of a small Southern town, the people who attended public meetings on the revitalization plan last fall suggested a model image of the ideal. I have combined the ideas into what I hope is a coherent whole, to give you a starting point to base your decisions on the revitalization concepts I am discussing. Please remember that these ideas are those of your friends and neighbors, your fellow citizens in Spring Hope.

The most oft repeated image of the town is its friendliness, its supportiveness, and the caring attitude of its populus. In a small Southern town, everyone knows his neighbors, can speak to anyone met on the streets, and everyone is courteous and pleasant. On the darker side, however, and Spring Hope's citizens are not the only small town folk to have noticed this, the people of this mythical small Southern town, while outwardly friendly, are suspicious of strangers, nosy, and know each others' business. Further, while the Southern hospitality and caring is real, there is very little support for poorer folks, teens, or elderly people.

A small Southern town has a strong sense of community. Citizens identify with the town and there is a community spirit which brings them together when others need help.

A small Southern town has a quiet tempo, a slow pace. Very important, it is a place that its citizens know well. They can easily walk around town without getting lost. And they feel safe in town because the crime rate is low and surroundings are familiar.

It has active trade and commerce, yet no large or heavy industry. The town has small specialty shops and stores, enough to supply necessary items for the comfort of its citizens but not overcommercialized. It has no freeways, expressways, or traffic congestion.

It has a well-run city government with active participation by all of its citizens. It has good police protection services, but does not have overtaxed water and sewer systems, and it has a forward looking zoning ordinance to help maintain the balance between urban and small town continuity.

A small Southern town should have no substandard or tenement type housing. A small Southern town has clean air, and an appealing commercial district that is well maintained, with trees, shrubs, and places to sit and visit. The commercial district is well defined and compact. It is both pretty and clean. Its sidewalks are maintained and in good repair — as are the sidewalks in all of the quiet residential areas of town.

A small Southern town has an active recreation program. Whether under the leadership of the many churches or of the organizations and agencies in town, the widespread recreation programs have a large participation by families as well as individual family members. Facilities for active participation in sports are available to all who might wish to use them, during the day as well as at night, and especially on weekends.

Essentially, the citizens of a small Southern town have pride in their town. There is a sense of unity among the people. The atmosphere of town is relaxed, yet enthusiasm about the town and its direction is deeply a part of every citizen.

This description of a small Southern town was given to me by your fellow citizens of Spring Hope. When you think about the city's needs and the dying downtown area, think too about the values they described. Are they worth keeping? Are they worth saving for? How can they best remain a part of this town?

A new vision

Bringing Spring Hope's downtown district back to life is one of the more important issues affecting Spring Hope and its commercial prosperity. The Spring Hope Revitalization Commission, after eight months of work and four public hearings, takes pride in presenting to the citizens of Spring Hope a Downtown Revitalization Plan prepared by Peter Lassen, a graduate student of architecture at N.C. State University.

Mr. Lassen came to Spring Hope under the auspices of the Community Development Group (CDG) in the School of Design. Directed by Henry Sanoff, professor of architecture, the aim of the CDG is for local citizens, who best understand their problems and potentials, to work with the students and faculty of the School of Design in making decisions and plans important to their communities.

This study, while reflecting the creativity of Peter Lassen and hours of his hard work and dedication, was also a true team effort. Working with Lassen at the School of Design were Peter Batchelor, professor of architecture, and Robert Stipe, professor of landscape architecture. Working with Lassen in Spring Hope were the faithful members of the Revitalization Commission, Dorothy Nelson, Devon Edwards, Pauline France, J.T. Edwards, Terri Cassidy, and Beth Hildreth.

This supplement, also prepared by Lassen and made possible through contributions by the Spring Hope Enterprise, is a summary of the final Revitalization Plan submitted to Spring Hope Board of Commissioners this week. Financing for the project was provided by the Town of Spring Hope and the Spring Hope Chamber of Commerce, to whom we officially present our recommendations and on whom the burden rests for turning this fresh vision of the future into our own dreams of what Spring Hope has the power to become.

Ken Ripley, Chairman
Revitalization Commission

Kiosks: new symbol of revival

Because the commercial buildings of Spring Hope are located in a ring around the depot, the first image that visitors to town receive of the central business district is the backsides of buildings.

Thus, this first image is one of service lots and dumpsters, of loading docks and truck parking. It does not welcome the visitor but indeed shows its worst side to the very people the downtown business people are trying to attract. This negative image is reinforced by the casual contrast of passing through the town's beautiful, well kept residential neighborhoods before arriving at its center.

Driving into the central business district of Spring Hope from any of its major entry points should be an experience which provides the visitor with a basic level of understanding of the town, and some sense of delight. In addition, this drive should help instill a sense of pride in the people who live in town. To accomplish this a kiosk has been designed as a new symbol of Spring Hope to both signify the major entrances to the central business district and to provide information about current activities in town. The kiosk is a modern interpretation of a gazebo, with details and proportions based on the town's major architectural attraction, the depot. It is a light ornamental structure which will be used to display notices of significant community events. The four kiosks will be located to draw vehicular traffic into the central business district, but will also include benches and drinking fountains so that pedestrians who walk into the town's center may relax on their way to town.

The four kiosks are to be located strategically at the main driving entrances to the central business district. The first, placed to form the western entrance, is to be at the new intersection of Main and Nash Streets.

The second, at the intersection of Railroad and Walnut Streets, is intended to attract the attention of people driving into town along N.C. 581, and draw them into the town's center.

Two other kiosks, one on Nash Street and one on Branch Streets, both between Ash and Pine Streets, provide entrances to the city's major parking lots.

In addition to the kiosks, wooden benches should be placed strategically within the central business district to provide pedestrians a place to relax in the shade. The benches should be visually acceptable to the townspeople and blend with existing architecture. Similarly designed wooden trash cans should be located near the benches and the kiosks.

FIGURE 2.2   Newspaper report on a community vision.

1. *The Initiating Committee.* This group of about 10 to 15 people representing the broader community lays the foundation for the visioning process. Its members focus on the process and logistics necessary to move it forward. Their diverse interests lend credibility to the process.

2. *The Project Kickoff.* This initial event allows participants to get to know each other and to understand the purpose of the visioning process.
3. *The Environmental Scan.* At this stage it is useful to examine those forces at the state and national levels that can effect change on the community.
4. *The Community Profile.* Here the participants examine the current circumstances in the community and assess what their future will be if no intervention occurs.
5. *The Civic Index.* This is a tool developed by the National Civic League to measure a community's problem-solving capability.
6. *The Community Vision Statement.* Stating a vision is the way to develop a framework for projects and priorities for 10, 20, or 30 years into the future.
7. *Action Plans.* Participants identify projects, implementation strategies, time lines, and responsible parties.
8. *A Community Celebration.* A visioning process should conclude with a celebration acknowledging the work of all participants and announcing the plan to the community.
9. *Shifting from Planning to Implementation.* This is the transition stage when responsible parties build on the momentum of the celebration and begin their work.
10. *The Implementation Committee.* Successful visioning projects require a group to oversee and support the implementation process.

Brea Visioning Process

A visioning process was employed in the town of Brea, California, where the opening of one of the largest regional malls had had a negative impact on the city's downtown district, located just a mile away. In an effort to reactivate the downtown, the Brea Redevelopment Agency acquired almost 50 acres of land for a major rebuilding program. However, in order to ensure that the development would be part of an overall vision for the downtown that reflected broad community involvement, the city council decided to undertake a three-day workshop. The workshop, or charrette, called "Brea by Design," consisted of professional advisors who worked with Brea residents to develop a vision statement for the downtown development, rather than a detailed design solution.

The opening session of the charrette, which occurred on the evening prior to the 3-day workshop, oriented participants to the objectives of the visioning process. On the following morning the resource team conducted an "awareness walk," during which a number of participants recorded their impressions of particular views and specific locations. These observations were shared with all participants. The comments included such ideas as "We need people on the street" and "Let's have a pub like Cheers." Residents of Brea realized that walking through the town had provided them with a different perspective than driving through the downtown.

The rest of the day was devoted to small group discussions, led by resource team members, about the people the town should serve and the needed elements the town should contain. A final session organized the recommendations and noted where agreement occurred and where it did not. Recommendations from the workshop included such policies as the following:

- Establish a new identity; downtown should be a visual and symbolic focal point for the community.
- Make Brea for Breans; the downtown should appeal to residents of all ages and all backgrounds.
- The views of the hills, which provide a dramatic backdrop to Brea, should be preserved and emphasized.

The resource team then translated the ideas and recommendations of the workshop participants into a plan and policy statements such as "The downtown core should feature an effective and vital mixture of land uses, with a high degree of foot traffic and shared parking" and "A shopping center should be developed with landscape and design treatment to enhance its view from the highway." The final vision statement was presented to the city council and potential developers. When the developer was finally selected, he credited the charrette process with sensitizing him to the community's interests.

The charrette was successful in obtaining residents' views as well as informing residents about their present community. The vision statement resulting from this process provided a basis for evaluating developers' proposals.

Empowering the Vision (ETV) in Rock Hill*

Rock Hill, South Carolina, a city with a 1990 population of 47,000, is a community that has gone to extremes to save its commercial core. In the early 1970s Rock Hill's downtown area was in rapid decline. Suburban shopping centers and residential development were eroding the downtown's strength as the city's business center. In 1972 downtown leaders initiated discussions with the city regarding the future of the area. In addressing the problems of downtown, a planning study was conducted to make the area more efficient, more attractive, and more active. Over the next two years a redevelopment plan outlined specific projects, which included the construction of a covered, climate-controlled mall over a three-block section of Main Street and the creation of a Special Improvement District to repay the city for the total cost of construction of the mall.

TownCenter Mall proved successful for a decade in maintaining the downtown's retail base. By the late 1980s, however, the mall was suffering from the downtown's decline as the city's retail center. At that time, the city and the Rock Hill Economic Development Corporation, in conjunction with the South Car-

---

*Beth Bailey, urban designer, Rock Hill Economic Development, who was instrumental Rock Hill's downtown development, provided useful background material for this section.

olina Downtown Development Association, used a community-wide strategic planning process (Wheeland, 1991) called Empowering the Vision (ETV) to develop a ten-year plan to transform the city's image. ETV employed a strategic planning process that included nine basic components: the initial agreement, a steering committee, theme groups, the ETV staff, special events, charrettes, models, the general public, and a time table.

Initially, the city developed a coalition of private, public, and nonprofit organizations that would help develop a strategic plan for the city. The coalition formed a steering committee to monitor the process and coordinate implementation of the strategic plan, whose goal was to capitalize on the strengths of Rock Hill and result in growth that would allow opportunities for citizens to improve their quality of life (City of Rock Hill, 1987).

Based on research conducted by the city staff on major trends, issues, problems, and opportunities facing Rock Hill, several theme groups were created: Business City, Educational City, Garden City, Historic City, and Functional City. The theme groups were organized as the mechanism for developing a plan. More than 100 citizens participated in the groups, in which they studied their area, identified issues, and developed a plan based on their vision of ensuring quality development. Staff positions were created to assist the theme groups in the technical and graphic areas, as well as to document and communicate their results.

Numerous special events were scheduled during the two-year process, such as workshops, lectures by consultants, tours, receptions, and a conference. Different theme groups conducted site visits throughout Rock Hill and neighboring cities to assess various cultural, historic, and land use patterns. The most significant special event was the charrette consisting of intensive work sessions and meetings with theme groups in a central location. A vacant department store located in the declining town mall, one of the problems in the downtown area, was donated to the city for the theme groups to meet and set up their work. This allowed the citizens to participate and recognize the need to create a vision for a new Rock Hill that would guide the development of the central core of the city.

The architectural firm of the Morgan–Adams Group (later named The Adams Group) prepared physical models and computer-generated images to help theme group members, community leaders, and citizens obtain a clear view of the vision for a new Rock Hill. Color photographs of various parts of the downtown area were scanned and digitally altered to show the changes that would occur if the plans were implemented. Citizens participated in the theme groups, in suggesting ideas for the improvement of the cultural, historic, and economic development, and in an open house to review the details of the final plan.

All themes pointed to returning Rock Hill to a village atmosphere. A downtown Raise the Roof Party initiated the task in 1993, when a bulldozer punched the first hole in the mall wall. Removal of the main street mall cover revealed many historic buildings that, except for the mall cover, might have been removed when earlier urban renewal demolished much of the downtown (Figure 2.3). The Rock Hill Economic Development Corporation purchased 26 downtown buildings, 15

FIGURE 2.3   Demolition of covered downtown mall. *(Photo: Beth Bailey.)*

of which were relocated during the renovation and returned to their Main Street locales (Figure 2.4a and b).

Rock Hill won two major awards for the ETV process: the 1989 Planning Award from the South Carolina Association for American Planners and the 1990 South Carolina Municipal Association Achievement Award for cities with a population over 25,000. The strategic planning process has made Rock Hill more livable, strengthened the economic development aspects, and instilled a sense of unity among the various groups in the community.

Charrette Process

The word *charrette* derives from the French translation of "chariot" or "cart," reminiscent of the one used to collect architectural designs produced at the Ecole des Beaux-Arts in Paris at the end of the nineteenth century. Often, the students would be drawing while the carts were moving, giving the word the meaning of a last-minute burst of activity to meet the deadline. The charrette process, as used today, refers to the rapid pace at which these designs were finalized and the energy that ensued from that production. But a newer component, consensus, has emerged as a guiding principle throughout the charrette.

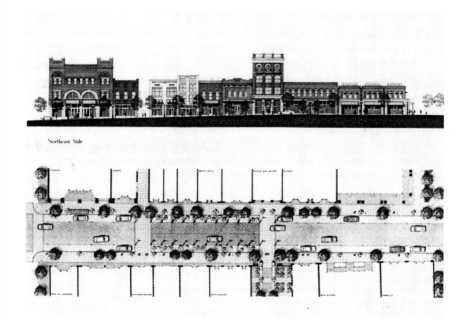

FIGURE 2.4a   Facade elevation of proposed streetscape. *(Courtesy: Rock Hill Economic Development Corporation.)*

FIGURE 2.4b   Completed renovation of main shopping street. *(Photo: Beth Bailey.)*

The contemporary charrette operates simultaneously as a product and a process. Depending on the nature of the product, the necessary tools will vary. The typical charrette process maximizes participation over a three-to-five-day framework. In addition to a structured schedule and an open process for participation, the charrette includes three defined mechanisms. The first, idea generation, requires a knowledge transfer among all affected parties. The second charrette mechanism, decision making, requires a dialogic discourse about the ideas presented. Finally, problem solving provides recommendations and proposals as process outcomes.

The charrette process has proven to be a successful goal-setting technique, a collaborative exchange and an interdisciplinary problem-solving approach. It is a successful participatory design strategy when applied to specific goal-oriented objectives of a clearly defined problem. The charrette becomes less a technique and more a collaborative planning process when used in conjunction with other participatory techniques within a defined program. In general, the two main objectives of the charrette are as follows:

1. To gain the unified support of a representative cross section of citizens who are committed to implementing the proposed solutions
2. To get the commitment of the power structure to secure the necessary resources in order to effect the changes

The following are the basic strategies of a charrette:

- Perception of a common goal or sense of urgency
- Involvement of all factions of the community
- Full citizen participation (includes those not experiencing the problem)
- Maintaining a sense of individual contribution to the total process
- Resolution of conflict and redirecting its energy toward community tasks

First of all, the community must have a sense of urgency about certain issues in order for a charrette to become an effective mechanism for change. It is important to get various factions to work together toward the common goals of the charrette. This is more likely to occur if the individuals within these factions feel a sense of personal contribution to the total process. "If they [citizens] do not perceive that they can satisfy their own goals, they will not participate" (Altman and Wandersman, 1987). It is particularly important for the steering committee to know which faction of the community has the greatest interest in solving the problems, because its members are the people most likely to formulate the solutions. Creating a dialogue within working groups will allow people who are not experiencing the problems to learn from those who are. The charrette manager must maintain control of the group dynamics: get the groups to work and, if necessary, be able to diffuse any disruptive behavior. A charrette has several essential ingredients:

- An identifiable problem
- User participation

- Involvement of professionals from within and from outside the community
- The adoption of short- and long-term goals
- A commitment to put the recommendations of the charrette into action

Categories of Charrettes

Charrettes can be altered to fit most local situations; they generally fall into four categories (Zucker, 1995):

Educational charrettes. An educational charrette can last from one day to several weeks. It generally addresses a well-defined architectural or urban design problem and results in schematic, illustrated ideas. The process usually involves university architecture students and instructors. Such programs often include community participation and serve community issues.

Leadership forums, retreats, focus groups. A one-or-two-day forum for citizen activists, elected officials, and nonprofit developers, among others, can be a useful tool to define local problems, list issues, and test alternative strategies in an informal setting. Such programs have been implemented as a series of events lasting several months.

Traditional problem-solving charrettes. A traditional design charrette is usually a one-or-two-day program; under some circumstances it may run from four days to two weeks. Practicing professionals focus on producing solutions to a well-defined problem. Results usually include a design plan for a specific building such as a homeless shelter, or a streetscape, urban park, or multiple-building project on a defined site. Traditional problem-solving charrettes often include citizens who participate in the overall process.

Interdisciplinary team charrette. This is an intense three-to-four-day interdisciplinary team process that takes a holistic approach to community issues, with an emphasis on community participation. Teams of 8 to 12 practicing professionals are drawn from various disciplines: economic development, transportation planning, public policy and management, private and public finance, sustainable development, and architecture and landscape architecture, among others. Issues addressed include economic development, affordable housing, neighborhood crime, and transportation.

Interdisciplinary problem-solving techniques allow communities to assimilate solutions at the neighborhood scale—an important social building block. Many urban problems can best be resolved at this level.

Interdisciplinary problem solving helps communities to make connections between diverse issues that might not otherwise be made in using traditional planning methods. Interdisciplinary problem solving helps to reestablish lost connections between people, connections within communities, connections across neighborhoods, cities, and regions, and connections between formerly unrelated government programs. These connections must be grounded in neighborhoods that nurture cultural diversity while maintaining local character and human scale. At the heart of these concepts are neighborhood and community; it is the place and the scale at which the other three organizing principles—human scale and human development, diversity and balance, and sustainability, conservation, and restoration—take on meaning and social power.

In the charrette, the process requires an accelerated rate of participation and an unveiling of all agendas. With all parties at the table, the transactive dialogue evolves into decision making. An individual's interests are not ignored; rather, they are considered in respect to others and are modified accordingly.

The role of modification during the process is important to identify at the outset of the charrette. The eventual goal is local consensus. The extent to which consensus demands modification is something that cannot be ignored. In his discussion of consensus decision making, Avery (1981) comments, "What occurs in consensus is not compromise, i.e., giving up of something you want, a something that is assumed to be fixed and unchangeable, but a profoundly if subtly different event: reformulation, in which what you started out wanting *itself changes*. You do not lose something of this fixed position, you change, see something better, improve your benefits in the contexts of the group exchange, the new information, the longer, better vision generated."

A charrette consensus is seen as an agent of self-awareness and knowledge through action or learning by doing. On the other hand, compromise is seen as a loss. The perception of this "loss" needs to be adjusted so that the consensus process is seen more as an evolving modification or reformulation of ideas.

Regional and Urban Design Assistance Teams

R/UDAT is an acronym for Regional and Urban Design Assistance Teams. The title derives from two American Institute of Architects (AIA) national committees—the Regional Planning Committee and the Urban Planning and Design Committee—that shared responsibility for the program when it first started. The key feature is an invited interdisciplinary team of professionals who address problems at various scales, ranging from city and regional issues to those of neighborhoods. The team, together with local supporters, then prepares recommendations and development schemes.

During the months preceding the R/UDAT process, site visits to the community are conducted to understand the issues, to collect relevant information, and to determine the appropriate team composition. The team's four-day visit usually begins with a walking and/or driving tour through the study area. Meetings are also conducted with elected officials, community leaders, planning and zoning boards, banking and special interest groups. A community meeting open to all interested citizens is conducted on the second day. The purpose of this meeting is to gather information from nonestablishment groups such as neighborhood organizations, block groups, and ethnic and minority representatives. This open meeting helps to sharpen the team's understanding of major issues. On the third day team members begin their planning in a 24-hour nonstop problem-solving work session that consists of conceptualizing, writing, and drawing. The problem-solving approach is based on a team discussion of concepts, followed by joint or individual work groups focusing on different segments of the problem. A final report is prepared and made available on the evening of the fourth day, which is the second open community meeting. Here team members present their recommendations to the community. Following the R/UDAT charrette, additional visits are made by select team members to help the community move forward with the recommendations and to develop strategies to remove roadblocks to progress.

In 1995 the town of Salisbury, North Carolina, played host to a group of 11 visiting architects and landscape architects. These professionals volunteered a week to study the Innes Street corridor in response to community concerns about unsightly development along portions of the street, Salisbury's most historically significant traffic artery. The city leaders commissioned an intensive study of this corridor by the North Carolina AIA Urban Design Assistance Team (UDAT) led by Peter Batchelor. Based on a week of on-site research, many interviews with local citizens, officials, and developers, and many debates, recommended actions included immediate strategies for enhancing and protecting the corridor from further degradation. Others included strategies that required the cooperation of several agencies, businesses, developers, utility companies, and local citizens. Although the design team offered many ideas, such as bringing back the trees that lined the street when it was more residential (Figure 2.5), it was agreed that at the

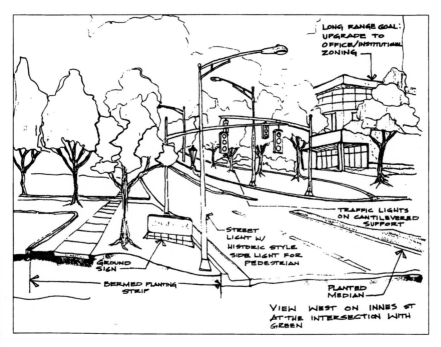

FIGURE 2.5 Drawing of a RUDAT recommendation. *(Drawing: AIA North Carolina Urban Design Assistance Team.)*

heart of the plan lay one element that would determine the success or failure of the whole: cooperation.

Based on the 100 R/UDAT projects conducted in the United States alone, three ingredients have been identified for success (Batchelor and Lewis, 1985):

- First, the process is as important as the product. All members of the community must be openly involved in the initial stages of goal setting through the development of implementation strategies. To be successful, the process must be sensitive to the people in the community, the culture and history, the physical fabric, and the political climate.
- The second requirement for achieving success is the formation of an interdisciplinary team. Today's complex urban issues require professionals with different backgrounds and areas of expertise.
- Third, citizen participation is regarded as the key ingredient for success. The citizen's movement is no longer the scattered local voice it was only a few decades ago. Cities belong to the people who live in them.

Fishbowl Planning

The basic objective of fishbowl planning is "to ensure that planning for public works projects is highly visible to all interested individuals and organizations" (Sargent, 1972). Concerned citizens are to be involved in the planning process from the beginning. Throughout the planning process, citizens serve as a check on agency planners and contribute ideas, insights, and alternatives of their own. The process was developed by Howard Sargent of the Corps of Engineers as a result of a controversy that began in the late 1960s, in which recreationists, conservationists, and the governor of Washington were in conflict with local developers, many property owners within the Snoqualmie River Basin, and the Corps of Engineers (Mazmanian and Nienaber, 1994).

The debate arose over the need for a dam and reservoir for the Middle Fork of the Snoqualmie River in northwestern Washington as a means of flood control from major storms, particularly as there was equal concern for preservation of the greenbelt of agricultural land below the river. Flood management studies conducted by the Corps of Engineers, however, did not compare costs and benefits of alternative proposals; consequently, opponents of the dam and reservoir organized a delaying action. A public hearing attended by more than 1,000 people emphasized broad public concern about the project and how this issue had polarized the community.

It was the recommendation of the governor's environmental review team that the project should not be authorized. Instead, the Corps of Engineers was to conduct an in-depth study of all alternatives in conjunction with the appropriate agencies of the State of Washington. The study was undertaken by the newly appointed district engineer, Colonel Howard L. Sargent, who viewed this as an opportunity to implement a comprehensive public participation and open planning process, which he described as "fishbowl planning." The four procedural components of fishbowl planning are workshops, public meetings, citizen committees, and a brochure of the study. The study brochure is an essential component of fishbowl planning because it provides a written record of all alternative solutions suggested by citizens or agencies. The brochure serves as a forum for debate about alternatives.

A number of workshops and public meetings did not reveal any new information or consensus, but led to participants' greater appreciation for one another's views. As a result, approval was withheld for the Corps to proceed with any of the alternatives. Continuing community interest in the problem of flooding brought a crisis intervention group to mediate between opponents and proponents. This effort resulted in a plan agreed upon by the Sierra Club, the Washington Environmental Council, the valley farmers, the League of Women Voters, and the basin communities.

The fishbowl experience did not bring about consensus on a single alternative in the Middle Fork study; rather, it was designed to improve communication between all concerned groups, with the hope that proponents of each alternative could accommodate the concerns of others. The important point is that it is not judged as a failure if consensus does not emerge. The opening of the decision-making process had in any case never been attempted before.

Community Action Planning

Community Action Planning (CAP) is an approach that empowers communities to design, implement, and manage their own settlement programs. Its key characteristics are that it is participatory, community based, problem driven, and fast. CAP has been developed over many years in the field by Nabeel Hamdi and Reinhard Goethert, whose experiences are collected in their book, *Action Planning for Cities* (1997). Traditional planning methods, such as master plans and development plans, they argue, take too long to develop, demand substantial resources to implement, and are unrelated and of no benefit to the poor majority of urban populations.

The issues may be broad in scope, but the process begins with small-scale projects that are additive in nature, promoting appropriate technologies and local enterprises. Although stakeholder participation is at the core of action planning, a focus of CAP is building coalitions between government and nongovernment groups, between competing government departments and between competing community groups. Participation occurs when people and organizations are convinced that their interests will be better served in partnerships than without them (Hamdi and Goethert, 1997, p. 31).

At the heart of the action-planning process is a series of phases and techniques that include the following:

- Direct observation allows the planning team to see the conditions of the environment under consideration.
- Interviews and focus group discussions help to generate insights into those community characteristics that are not visible through direct observation.
- Measuring is a quantitative view of environmental conditions.
- Surveying resources, a community function, identifies local people and places that are important to any proposed program, similar to generating a "Yellow Pages."
- Prioritizing is an ongoing process whereby stakeholders consider their needs and the feasibility of implementing projects.
- Brainstorming is used to allow groups to explore alternative ways of solving problems.
- Diagramming allows time line and population information to be presented in an easily understood graphic format.
- Mapping and modeling allow people to record their feelings, perceptions, and social networks and to examine existing conditions as well as evaluate proposals for improvement.
- Gaming and role-playing can be used to build awareness of planning procedures, to anticipate potential difficulties, and to allow participants to become sensitive to one another's needs.
- Group work during all stages of the planning process helps to build cooperation.
- The process begins with identifying problems and with identifying opportunities in a workshop setting.

A workshop conducted in a South African agricultural town, an area where housing is largely built through self-help and that is deficient in its basic services, was held to assist the government of South Africa to implement a reconstruction and development program. Participants included 20 representatives of community organizations and interests. The workshop was organized into four phases:

1. Deciding what was needed (identifying key problems and priorities)
2. Sorting out how to achieve what was needed (preparing proposals)
3. Assessing what would get in the way of implementation (project viability)
4. Building a plan of action (tasks, partners, schedules, organizations, etc.) and getting projects going

The workshop produced a viable community action plan that set a development process in motion. At its conclusion, a planning unit was established and four project coordinators were selected from the community to pursue the tasks identified, grouped in four areas: health, income generation, water and sanitation, and housing. Following the workshop, the project was presented to representatives of local government who believed that the community should be empowered to sustain what had been started and that minority and low-income members of the community should be included as experts.

Planning Assistance Kit

The Planning Assistance Kit (PAK) developed at the Massachusetts Institute of Technology (Hamdi and Goethert, 1997) is a series of work sheets prepared to assist community organizations in physical planning, implementation, and management of their housing (Figure 2.6). This planning guide is aimed at aiding local community development corporations (CDCs) to manage new housing projects. The guide provides communities with a tool for clarifying objectives and defining problems. It enables communities to familiarize themselves with procedures as well as obstacles, while allowing for expanding the range of options. For public authorities, PAK provides a structure and a process for participatory decision making.

Planning occurs in a workshop setting, where conflicting interest groups are brought together to define problems, to explore alternatives, and to establish

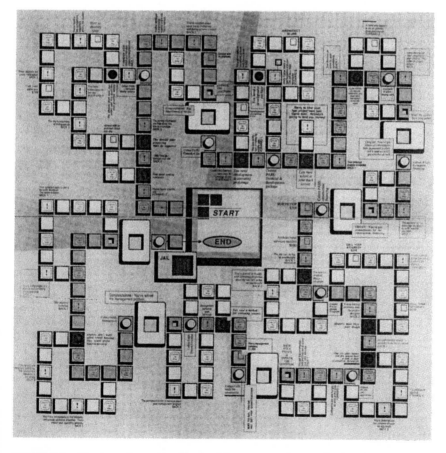

FIGURE 2.6   Planning assistance kit. *(Reprinted, by permission, from Reinhard Goethert, Action Planning for Cities, p. 211. Copyright 1997 by John Wiley & Sons, Inc.)*

priorities. A game board called "Gamepak" is used in the opening activity of the workshop, in which participants learn housing terminology while they move through several stages of the housing process. Structured as a parlor game similar to Monopoly, this exercise also allows participants to get to know one another.

The key components in the planning kit are "setting objectives" and "building programs," both aimed at the development of a proposal. PAK-I outlines procedures for setting priorities and resolving conflicts, and PAK-II introduces methods for making the community development process accessible to lay people. The use of work sheets (Figure 2.7) helps to document the process and the decisions for viewing by a wider audience.

Setting objectives includes a four-step sequence:

1. Identify and clarify concerns (what are the concerns, who is affected, and why).
2. Prioritize concerns and identify conflicts (identify interest groups and their concerns).

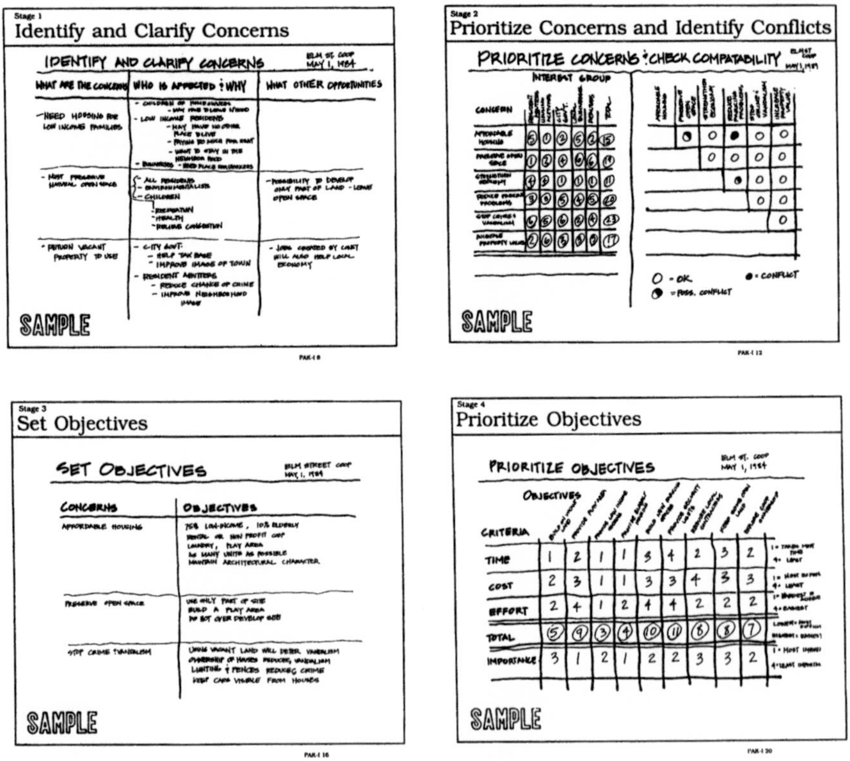

FIGURE 2.7 Typical planning work sheets. *(Reprinted, by permission, from Reinhard Goethert, Action Planning for Cities, p. 215. Copyright 1997 by John Wiley & Sons, Inc.)*

3. Set objectives (relate concerns to objectives).
4. Prioritize objectives (identify options for satisfying objectives).

Building a program initially explores strategies, options, and trade-offs by considering options, prioritizing options, identifying conflicts and opportunities, and selecting viable options. The second part of this phase, which considers planning for implementation, begins with assessing resources, identifying what is needed, and where and when to acquire what is needed. Compliance with permits, and other specific task responsibilities are delegated, and finally potential sites are evaluated to determine the best location for the project. To support the workshop activities, a directory of information about agencies and other housing resources is included in an "Infopak."

In the United Kingdom, the Prince of Wales Institute of Architecture published *Action Planning*, by Nick Wates (1996), as a tool for community design. The underlying philosophy of Action Planning is that it is interdisciplinary, collaborative, and community based. Action Planning is usefully applied to urban improvement, capacity building, new development planning, and planning under crisis, such as in rebuilding communities that have suffered political or natural disaster. Action Planning has the following characteristics: It adheres to achievable actions, is participatory, small in scale, and community based, and is reliant on local knowledge and skills. The process relies on building on existing organizational structures, available skills, and knowledge and focuses on what is achievable with visible, tangible outputs (Figure 2.8).

Action Planning is an urban management technique similar in structure to a charrette and modeled after the RUDAT process. Action Planning is an event, usually lasting four or five days, guided by a multidisciplinary team of independent specialists. Community planning weekends, as they are referred to in the United Kingdom, achieve success in galvanizing community participation and allowing collective decisions to be made in an effective way. The benefits of Action Planning include the following:

- Creation of shared visions
- Catalyst for action
- Resolution of complex problems
- Fostering of consensus building
- Heightened public awareness
- Morale boost
- Promotion of urban design capability

The Action Planning process does not finish at the end of an event. A follow-up program allows the ideas to be fully implemented. Evaluating the impact of Action Planning events is important to help focus attention on long-term objectives and improve the process. Wates proposes an evaluation form that can be modified and expanded, based on particular community needs (Figure 2.9).

	Getting Started 1–2 months* ▲	Preparation 2–4 months* ▲	The Event several days* ▲	Follow-up ongoing* ▲
Local Interests Individuals and organisations	• Concern to improve environment. • Stimulate action. • Establish Steering Group and Host (see below).	• Build momentum, enthusiasm and expectation through discussion and by focussing attention on the main issues.	• Participate in public sessions.	• Analyse proposals. • Develop support for strategies and projects. • Apply pressure for implementation. • Ongoing participation.
Steering Group/ Host/Organiser Main enthusiasts and technical advisors	• Formation/appointment. • Explore options for action. • Prepare proposal. • Stimulate enthusiasm. • Secure commitment from all affected parties. • Raise funds. • Commitment to proceed.	• Select Team Chairperson, Team members, Advisors and consultants. • Establish administration and technical support. • Gather information. • Prepare venues. • Publicise.	• Event management and administration.	• Assess proposals and prioritise. • Agree plan of action. • Publicity. • Spearhead and co-ordinate. • implementation. • Maintain momentum.
Event Team Specialists from complementary disciplines		• Homework on the locality and the Action Planning process. • Reconnaissance visit by Chairperson.	• Arrive. • Reconnaissance. • Briefings. • Topic workshops. • Design workshops. • Brainstorm. • Prepare proposals. • Presentation. • Leave.	• Revisit and assist as requested.
Support Bodies National, international and regional organisations	• Supply general information and advice. • Evaluation visit if requested.	• Supply detailed information and contacts.	• Observe. • Participate. • Assist if asked.	• Monitor and evaluate. • Assist if asked.

*Timescales.
Action Planning events can be of varying lengths but the process remains more or less the same. The length of the event and the lead times will be determined by the nature of the issues faced and the extent and capacity of existing local networks. Timescales shown above have been found to be the most effective for major urban design issues of, say, a neighbourhood or city. Shorter events work well for simpler issues such as making proposals for a single site. Shorter lead times are possible where local networks are well developed. Longer lead times can be useful for building community capacity.

FIGURE 2.8 Action planning process. *(Copyright Nick Wates, from Action Planning, The Prince of Wales Institute of Architecture.)*

Action Planning Event Evaluation Form

Title of event..

Nature of event..

Place..

Dates of event........................ Date of evaluation...

Name, title and organisation of evaluator...

Role at planning weekend (if any)..

Address ....

Telephone .... Fax................................... ....

Summarise the impact of the event on the following:

Physical environment (buildings, parks, transport, design standards)............................

....

....

Economy (work prospects, wealth)...

....

Perceptions and aspirations (self view, hopes)...

....

Local organisations (changed roles, new partnerships)...

....

The participants (members of the public, Team members)..

....

How could the event have been organised better?

....

....

What would be your advice to other communities holding such an event?

....

Any other thoughts.

....

....

....

FIGURE 2.9 Action planning evaluation form. *(Copyright Nick Wates, from Action Planning, The Prince of Wales Institute of Architecture.)*

Take Part

Take Part is a process for helping people to become aware of the problems and potentials of their shared environment. It also helps people to work together to make planning and design decisions with professionals and to implement their projects.

Take Part was developed by Anna and Lawrence Halprin, Jim Burns, and Paul Baum and in some respects resembles a musical score (Halprin and Burns, 1974). Whereas music is a closed score, in which the performer must do what the composer intends, Take Part scores are more open. They welcome the feelings and creativity of the participants, so that the "performances" of the participants become important elements in determining the results.

There are three categories of people in a Take Part team to help participants. The "workshop conductor" is like a conductor of an orchestra, helping people to work together and achieve the best results. The "facilitator" is the same sort of person, helping people in small groups just as the conductor helps the entire workshop. Because a workshop frequently involves 100 or more people, several facilitators are needed. The third category is the "recorder," who documents exactly what people discuss and recommend during a workshop. The recorder can work with small groups, like the facilitator, or large groups, recording and then reviewing the discussion with the participants to make sure that it is accurate. In this way a body of complex and interrelated insights and data is developed for the designer and planner to work with.

Usually, a workshop begins with an "awareness walk" or trip to the project area. Through these trips, people with little previous awareness of each other learn a common language and bond through a shared experience of the physical reality and of each other's perceptions. Many projects of different sizes and degrees of complexity have been undertaken with Take Part processes (Halprin and Burns, 1974). Sometimes a project is a single building, such as a school, or it can be something more complex, such as the downtown of a large city.

Participatory Action Research

Participatory action research (PAR) is proposed as a new paradigm for effectively utilizing the knowledge generated by the environment-behavior community through the integration of design, planning, research, and participation. This is an outgrowth of traditional research approaches that are not capable of dealing with goals, values, and problem solving. Similarly, the behavioral research model, which consists of an institutionalized separation of research and application, does not facilitate collaboration between researchers, designers, and planners (Seidel, 1982). The specialization of knowledge makes it impossible for one group to plan and determine optimal solutions on behalf of the world community. Similarly, the problems of poverty and social development are complex and require multidisciplinary collaboration.

It may no longer be possible to plan effectively for people, given the changing nature of the economy, the political landscape, and the speed at which these changes occur in cities and urban areas of the world (Friedmann, 1992). This awareness stems from Lewin's (1946) concept of action research, a model that not only integrates theory and practice, but requires that one must act on a system in order to understand it and that the designer/planner will consequently be involved in influencing the outcome. Action research is a proactive strategy in which research utilization has political and social relevance. By designating people and their concerns as the starting point, research takes on a more activist role and can be described as participatory research. Participatory action research involves practitioners in the research process from the initial design of a project, through data gathering and analysis, to final conclusions and actions arising out of the research (Whyte, 1991).

Participatory research, however, has been defined differently by its proponents. Participatory research is seen as the development of a community's potential, as collaborative problem solving, and as a synonym for "user participation" in planning and in the decision-making process (Lineberry, 1986). Gaventa (1993) suggests, "Participatory research attempts to break down the distinction between the researcher and the researched, the subjects and objects of knowledge produced by the participation of the people-for-themselves in the process of gaining and creating knowledge. In the process, research is seen not only as a process of creating knowledge, but simultaneously, as education and development of consciousness, and of mobilization for action."

Ramasubramanian (1994) describes participatory research as an approach that

- develops the capacity of the participants to organize, analyze, and discuss concepts to the level required by the particular issue in which they are involved,
- develops a process to incorporate the participants in the research and decision-making process, which includes the basic assumptions, the research design, and the methods of evaluation, and
- returns the research findings to the participants.

The long-term goal of participatory research is to empower people to effect social change. This new outlook is not unique to design and planning, but has been taken up by professionals of many disciplines in regard to the distinction between *research for the people* versus *research by the people*. Conventional design and planning practice usually undervalues the expertise of users and denies their involvement in decision making. Lack of design or planning training, however, does not interfere with citizens' ability to make meaningful judgments of environmental alternatives early in the decision-making process. Expensive models are not needed to engage them in the process and to elicit their feedback to incorporate in final decisions (Kaplan, 1987).

A participatory action research model (Wisner, Stea, and Kruks, 1996) reflects the view that people who use the environment, who are the traditional subjects of research, should be active participants in the research and equally active participants in changing the environment. This idea is based on the belief that user groups have an expertise equal to, but different from, the expertise of the professional. Participation thus becomes a central component of the research approach. Users are then involved in evaluating research results and, subsequently, in developing recommendations about how to address problems that have been identified.

In practice, the participatory research process of intervention is initiated by a community development agency, an extension service of a university, or a church group. The researcher/practitioner needs to be well informed about the community, both historically and sociologically, through records, interviews, observations, and some form of participation in the life of the community. The organizational aspect of a PAR begins by informing the larger community of the purpose of the project and identifying the key individuals who will play an active role in its development. The researcher/professional acts as a facilitator and technical resource person as the community decides how to formulate the problem to be investigated, what information is needed, what methods should be used, what procedures should be followed, how the data should be analyzed, what to do with the findings, and what action should be taken (Park et al., 1993).

The degree and nature of participation in all phases of participatory action research is a critical factor. Empowering participation implies that participants are in charge of the inquiry by actively helping to create and codetermine in every phase of the research process (Eldin and Levin, 1991). Yet empowering participation in action research does not imply that everyone in the community or organization is to be involved in every phase of the research process. PAR is a representative form of participation in which all stakeholders' interests and viewpoints are included. The criteria for creating an effective dialogue include the following (Gustavsen, 1985):

- All concerned must have an opportunity to participate.
- Initially, all participants are equal.
- Participants should be active in the discourse.
- All participants must understand the issues at stake.
- Initially, all arguments should be considered legitimate.
- Agreement should arise continuously from the dialogue as a basis for investigation and action.

This action approach offers designers and planners concerned with user needs a new set of social science tools. These new tools not only provide the professional with a deeper understanding of the human condition, but offer an opportunity for engaging in an effective dialogue with people who use the environment.

This approach is in contrast with the use of more casual methods of inquiry that typically reveal what is already obvious, or traditional social science approaches that tend to generalize people's requirements (Argyris and Schon, 1991).

Clearly, this suggests an expanded role for the professional to include the function of instructor and facilitator of the decision-making process, in addition to being an advocate for the principles of good design and planning. Professionals can easily change their behavior to accommodate this new role. It requires a shift in the allocation of time from project development to the front-end or pre-design/planning stage in which more reliable information can minimize the time normally wasted in second-guessing client/user needs, requirements, and preferences. This new role will subsequently increase the professional's social standing, esteem, and respect in the community. A process that is rooted in open and meaningful communication is essential to learning. Through mutual learning changes can be brought about. These changes will evolve, as it may not be necessary to produce finished and unalterable solutions, but to extract solutions from a continuous dialogue with those who will use the professionals' work.

Case Study of a Town Relocation

The U.S. Army Corps of Engineers identified the town of North Bonneville in the state of Washington as the best location for a powerhouse; consequently, its residents faced eviction and relocation (Comstock and Fox, 1993). The residents of North Bonneville were independent and self-sufficient in their personal and family lives, yet unified by the common threat to that relationship. Unwilling to relocate to Portland, Vancouver, or Seattle, the residents rallied around a common goal of relocating as a community, where they could maintain their social relationships. The Corps of Engineers, on the other hand, did not believe that it was authorized to replace towns, but only to compensate individuals for the cost of relocation.

In a search for assistance in maintaining its identity, the town contacted Evergreen State College in Olympia, Washington, an institution that enabled faculty and students to pursue problems in an in-depth, interdisciplinary context. The residents of North Bonneville discovered Russell Fox, a faculty member interested in empowering citizens through participatory research, and his students, who were looking for projects that would involve citizens in the planning process. Together they embarked on a four-year participatory research project, beginning in 1973.

The students quickly discovered that although the town's residents had extensive knowledge about their community and strong feelings about their pending relocation, they were uninformed about the complex political and social forces that could influence their future. After a discussion of the town's problems and its commitment to active involvement in the planning process, it was agreed to create a plan for the relocation of North Bonneville and to develop the capability of the residents to use this information in pursuing their goals.

The first phase of the project included the information needed to plan for the relocation of North Bonneville. A report produced during this phase included such information as the town's historical and regional context, demographic and economic data, sociological and cultural patterns, physical infrastructure and community facilities, geographical and natural features, and other external factors affecting relocation.

Students lived in the community while gathering data and discussed the use of this information with the residents. Through informal discussions and community workshops, the students shared their findings with the residents. As a result of this participatory process residents became aware of the discrepancy between their sense of community and how differently the Corps of Engineers viewed relocation. The residents realized that their goal of maintaining the social relationships of their community was different from the government's goal of building a powerhouse. They discovered that the government perceived their community as physical structures and people as abstract individuals.

A relocation planning study documented the knowledge of the residents and a clear sense of their identity as a community. Through research on their community and their newly acquired planning skills, the residents were able to create a better community in a new location. At the appropriate time, the townspeople demanded of the private planning firm the right to participate in planning the new town so that they could incorporate their knowledge into the design. The residents also refused the Corps's offer to plan the new town, realizing they would have no control over such a process. Finally, the people of North Bonneville gained federal legislation to require the Corps to pay for the design of the new town, to be carried out under the community's control.

This project demonstrates how participatory research provided a basis for a successful political struggle by a community. During the participatory research process the people of the town, with the help of the students, learned about themselves and their environment and were able to put this knowledge to use in creating a new community. The students guided the research process, taught technical skills to the community, and organized information provided by the residents. The data gathered and skills learned gave the community the self-confidence to challenge the Corps of Engineers. This town of fewer than 500 people challenged the U.S. Army and won.

Runyon Canyon Master Plan

When the city of Los Angeles acquired Runyon Canyon, the Department of Parks and Recreation received a burned-out, 133-acre wasteland, the result of a 1984 fire that caused mud slides, floods, erosion, and serious injuries. With the city's history of environmental degradation, the attitudes toward the canyon—disregard, fear, and abuse—would have to change if its native ecology was to be restored. The firm of Community Development Planning and Design, headed by Randy Hester

(*Landscape Architecture*, 1987b), convinced the Department that the master planning process had to be educational as well as participatory.

To help the public overcome its fears, the planning team took citizens on site tours to provide them with knowledge of the landscape, which helped to gain community support for restoring the canyon's native ecology. A score sheet was developed to allow citizens to evaluate the damage and potential, thus creating an inexpensive database. The model consisted of a three-step transformation that accrued over a 12-step participatory planning process (Hester, 1987b). "Place knowing" means a user can name, locate, describe, and attribute some use to a place. "Place understanding" is knowing why a place is the way it is and how it might change. "Place caring" is an active state, based on an emotional bonding, that involves a sense of ownership and responsibility. This approach can achieve a sense of caring and increased understanding, reversing the cycle of placelessness and abuse.

Listening, the first step, enabled the planning team to learn from local school officials that a generation of children was growing up with undeveloped gross motor skills because the neighborhood playgrounds and open spaces were inadequate. As a result, the master plan included natural areas where a child could explore, climb, and learn about animal habitats. The team employed focused techniques to engage different citizens groups throughout the process. More than 400 citizens participated, representing such diverse interests as native plants restoration, homelessness, historic preservation, children, crime prevention, and property values.

Participation Techniques

The techniques described in this section all require sufficient planning time and clearly stated participation goals. They evolved as a result of the criticism of citizen involvement as being time-consuming, inefficient, and not very productive (Rosner, 1978). It is because of narrow time and financial constraints that structured participatory techniques have proven to be successful.

There are a wide range of techniques available to designers and planners. Some of these techniques have become standard methods used in participatory processes. For example, participation rarely occurs without the use of interactive group decision-making techniques in workshops. At the same time, field techniques such as questionnaires, interviewing, focus groups, and group mapping have been used effectively by designers and planners to acquire information. In general, many of the techniques facilitate citizens' awareness to environmental situations and help activate their creative thinking.

In conjunction with the need for achieving effective dialogues between people is the need for technical assistance. Qualified and sensitive professionals must often provide technical assistance to allow people to participate more effectively in developing plans or objections to plans. The forms of technical assistance vary, including local community design centers, on-site project offices, and private and public sector community design professionals.

The key to making community design work effectively is a range of techniques for enabling professional and lay people to collaborate creatively. Participation rarely occurs without the use of interactive group decision making, which usually occurs in workshops, and interviewing and mapping allow large numbers of people to participate. The techniques are classified in five major categories: awareness methods, indirect methods, group interaction methods, open-ended methods, and brainstorming methods.

Awareness Methods

Exhibits. People need to know what an issue is about to be able to decide whether they want to participate. One way to inform and stimulate people to participate is to set up exhibits in public places, such as in a shopping mall or at a street fair.

News media. Sending a news release to a newspaper or a radio or TV station is one way to interest media in doing a story. Often a news release is used to persuade an editor to do a story, especially in larger communities where there is competition for the attention of the media. Press kits offer a more detailed and authoritative source of information useful for reporters. They should contain summary information about the decision process, as well as key technical studies. Newspaper inserts are an effective means to inform the public about the process and to keep people adequately informed. Newsletters are also effective in sustaining interest throughout an extended decision-making process. They can provide more information than can be communicated through the news media.

Walking tours. Another approach to facilitate users' awareness to environmental situations, particularly where people have adapted to intolerable conditions, is a planned walk through the area of study. This walk allows participants to rediscover a familiar situation or to become acquainted with a new situation. This approach may include a map or plan, designating specific stops to record impressions, and a list of specific tasks. This technique is most effective as an introduction to the participatory process. A map of an eight-block study area, locating specific stops, appeared in the Smithfield, North Carolina, newspaper prior to an open community workshop. Townspeople filled the streets on this self-guided walking tour to rediscover the positive as well as negative features of the town (Figure 2.10).

Indirect Methods

Surveys and questionnaires help to gather information, attitudes, and opinions from a sample of the user population. In Ohya, Japan, a mapping survey allowed citizens to identify and locate areas of environmental degradation; in Raleigh,

Discovering Selma

You have now completed your walk through downtown Selma.

What are your favorite buildings in this area? Do you often come here? If not, what do you feel would make you come more often?

(Ed. Note: This walking tour study of downtown Selma was prepared by five NCSU School of Design students for use by local citizens who wish to provide input for revitalization of downtown Selma.)

Thank you for taking part in the first step towards evolving future directions for downtown Selma.

The process that we are beginning is rooted in active citizen participation in sharing information, establishing needs and priorities, and formulating implementable plans that can fulfill those needs and priorities.

Familiar features of our everyday environment sometimes can be surprisingly unfamiliar. Most people can quite easily walk past a building every day without even noticing it. In this first step - a walking tour through Selma - we will be improving our awareness of the town. We will observe the buildings and their details, the open spaces, the roads and the linking paths, the parking spaces, and the roadsigns. We will use all our senses (smell, touch, taste, sound, and sight) to record our feelings about the places. We will then be able to discover the qualities, problems and potentials of the town. We will use our discoveries and experiences to make decisions about what should be done to benefit Selma, its citizens, and its visitors.

We will share our experiences at a community workshop, to be held at the Selma Elementary School cafeteria at 7:30 p.m. on Tuesday, September 28, 1982. Please note the time and the date, and try to attend it.

The workshop should last approximately 3 hours. If you cannot come to this meeting, it would be very helpful if you could get your comments and answers back to Dan Collins, the city manager, at the Town Hall, before September 28.

Some suggestions

The walking tour starts at the crossing between Pollock Street and Railroad Street.

Locations of the steps on the tour are indicated on the map. It is suggested that you follow the sequence shown on the map.

Please take your walk on any day before September 28, between 9 a.m. and 5 p.m.

Please cut this sheet out and take it along with you. Use it to make observations, comments, sketches, and plans during the walk. (Take some extra paper, it may be required.) This is your record to be used in the workshop.

Please bring these record sheets with you to the community workshop on September 28, 1982.

Have an enjoyable and informative walk. See you at 7:30 p.m. on September 28, 1982.

Starting point
Pollock St. X Railroad St.
Walk along Pollock St. towards Anderson St. At what point do you feel that you are entering the downtown area?

Step 1
Have a general view of the surroundings. Does this view lead you into downtown Selma?
Look towards the row of buildings on the other side of Anderson St. Are these buildings being used in their full potential? How else might they be used?
Continue walking down Pollock St. and turn right into the parking lot behind the church. Observe the back of the buildings on your right. What do you feel? Why? Would you like to make any change on what you see?

Step 2
Observe the open space

around you. What would you like it to be used for?

Walk back to Anderson St. along the alley. Would you walk here at night? Why?

Take your left and go up the alley across the street on the left of the sea food store. As you walk up the alley, observe your feelings. Would you make any changes in the surroundings? If so, which changes would you make?

Step 2
Stand at this point and look around you. Observe the view towards Pollock St., the back of the buildings, the trees and the grass. What are your impressions of this area? What would you like it to be used for?
Look at the large wooden house. Would you like to see it being used? What kind of activity/use would you suggest for this house?

Go down the alley towards Raiford St. What do you feel?

Step 4
Look at the row of buildings across the street. Notice the canopy and the details on the facades. What do you particularly like about this view? What do you particularly dislike about this view?

Turn left on Raiford St. While walking, observe all around you. What do you feel on approaching the corner between Raiford St. and Anderson St.?

Step 5
Look at the old Person-Vick building diagonally opposite.
What features of this building do you like most? What features of it do you dislike?
Suggest some appropriate activity/use for this building.

Now look at the old Selma bank building behind you. Suggest some appropriate activity/use for this building.

Continue your walk along Raiford St. Noting particular note of the graphics along the way. What are your impressions about them? What are your feelings about the traffic on this street?

Step 6
Look towards the theatre. What do you think about its location?

Walk down Waddell St. and turn right into the parking lot behind the bank.

Step 7
Would you like to sit down and spend some time in this place? Which of its attributes do you like most? Which of its attributes do you dislike? Would you like this place to be used for any other activity?

Continue along the alley paying particular attention to the back of the buildings. Do you like to use the rear entrances of the stores on your right?
Cross Anderson St. and go down the alley on the right of the Courthouse building. What are your impressions about this building?

Step 8
What do you feel about this space? Would you like it to be used for any other activity?

Continue along the alley into Railroad St. Look to your left towards the railroad station. Notice also the area between you and that building. What do you feel about this space? Would you walk up to the railroad station from downtown?

Step 9
Stop at the corner of Railroad St. and Raiford St. Look at the entire length of Raiford St. What do you feel about this view? Would you make any changes on what you see? If so, what changes would you make?

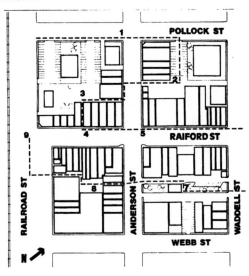

FIGURE 2.10 Walking tour insert in the *Johnstonion Sun* newspaper.

North Carolina, a mapping study identified boundaries of citizens' perceived neighborhood. This approach yields easily quantified, rapid results. The limitation of this approach is that it reflects the position of those who prepare the surveys rather than those who respond to the questions. One-on-one interviews, however, can provide much more information. Although interviewing does not yield a scientific sample, it does provide qualitative and detailed information, information that often cannot be obtained any other way.

Group Interaction Methods

Face-to-face interaction, often referred to as a workshop, characterizes all group methods. Focus groups usually consist of six to ten carefully selected people with a facilitator who guides the discussion to relevant issues. A charrette, on the other hand, is an intensive participatory process lasting several days or longer, depending on the complexity of the problem. This is a process that convenes interest groups in a series of interactive meetings aimed at solving a particular problem. Phases of the charrette process may include workshops or working sessions that engage participants in the development of ideas, recommendations, and decisions. A "design-in" may also be used as part of this process or as an independent method. This is a hands-on approach whereby professionals and citizens work together with plans, photographs, and/or models to explore alternatives.

Open-Ended Methods

Informing a large audience about proposals, generating interest, or securing approval can take the form of a community meeting, also referred to as a public hearing or a public forum. Public meetings allow community leaders to present project information at any time during the process. The tight structure of such meetings, however, does not permit ample time for discussion. Although this is referred to as community participation, only the most aggressive personalities tend to participate and often dominate the discussion. Public reactions in open meetings are often determined by a vote through a show of hands.

Participatory cable television. Although many communities broadcast city council meetings over local channels, television can be used in a more participatory way. The city of Roanoke, Virginia, developed an electronic town meeting called a "design telethon," in which several television events were held in the Roanoke Design 79 series. The city consulted the architectural firm of Centerbrook, which developed a series of district maps that were presented on the air, with proposals being phoned in and discussed. At the close of the first one-hour broadcast, there was a recap of the ideas collected and the architects returned to their office to consider each one. The next show included development alternatives that had been published in a local newspaper. Votes for preferences were sent in, and the plan was refined. The third show presented the final plan in model form. A total of 59 individual projects were proposed. Within three years the citizens of Roanoke approved bond issues for all but seven of the projects (Sanoff, 1994).

Planning ballot. A planning ballot was conceived as a way to broaden active citizen participation by providing a way for people who could not attend or speak out at public meetings, to express their feelings. The Yerba Buena Planning Ballot conceived of by the San Francisco Design Center (Sanoff, 1978) was made up of three parts: three propositions outlining plan alternatives; thirteen policy statements dealing with how the project should be planned, financed, and administered; and a section containing a map of the project area and a selection of land uses from which people could devise their own plans. A detachable part of the ballot could be mailed or placed in one of several ballot boxes located in the project area. Together, the three parts of the ballot provided people with a way to organize and express their preferences for the most important facets of a large, complex urban renewal project.

Brainstorming Methods

Teamwork is beneficial in creative problem solving, but nowhere more so than in idea generation (Lumsdaine and Lumsdaine, 1993). The best-known method for doing this is brainstorming. Classic brainstorming is a verbal method of problem solving used with small groups of three to nine people, with three rules to follow:

1. Generate as many solutions as possible.
2. Wild ideas are encouraged.
3. No criticism is allowed—judgment is deferred.

There are, however, other brainstorming methods, sometimes referred to as brainwriting, for groups larger 12 members. These methods can also be used by a group of people who cannot meet in the same place at the same time:

Gallery. Each member is given an easel and a large pad, with time to write down all his or her ideas about the problem. Time-out is called. Participants circulate among the easels, then return to their own to make additions and modifications. Idea hitchhiking occurs. Notes are collected and given to another team for evaluation. This method is particularly effective for people who are uncomfortable when speaking in front of a group.

Pin Card. People sit around a large table and write ideas on note cards. The cards are then passed around, and participants can add their ideas and improvements to the original idea. Cards are then collected to be evaluated by another team.

Nominal Group Technique (NGT). The problem is presented, and participants silently write down their ideas in a five-minute period. Ideas are then pooled, discussed and voted on, and ranked in order of preference. This technique combines the idea generation and idea evaluation phases into one session (Delbecq, Van de Ven, and Gustafson, 1975).

Cranford Slip Writing. This method is used to collect ideas when large groups of people want to be involved in the process. After the problem definition has been presented, each participant is asked to write down 20 ideas, each on a separate slip of paper. These are collected and given to another team to organize and evaluate the ideas generated.

Ringii Process. This is a Japanese process in which an idea is circulated in written form. An idea is written on a slip of paper; each participant makes notes and sends it along to the next person. The originator gets it back, digests the suggestions, and rewrites the idea. This process can be done in several rounds. It avoids any expected personal conflicts.

Delphi Method. This is a technique that begins with written brainstorming and continues until consensus has been reached on the best ideas. Here participants can remain anonymous; no direct interaction occurs, because the idea collection is done by questionnaire or on-line computer. After the ideas are collected, they are listed and the list is circulated for evaluation and ranking by each participant. This process is continued until a consensus is reached (Delbecq, Van de Ven, and Gustafson, 1975).

Interactive Brainstorming

Verbal and written brainstorming techniques can be combined to take advantage of the best features of each approach. Groups of about 20 people can participate in interactive brainstorming, and these methods feature periods of idea writing and the oral sharing of ideas.

Idea Trigger. After an initial period of silent activity, in which each participant writes ideas on a notepad with two columns, members take turns reading their lists. As a member reads from his or her list, other participants note any new or hitchhiking ideas they have in the second column. After going around the group once clockwise, the process is repeated, moving counterclockwise around the group. Once the second cycle is completed, the ideas are collected for later evaluation (Lumsdaine and Lumsdaine, 1993).

Panel Format. When a larger group is present, say from 20 to 30 people, a panel of 5 to 10 participants can be formed, who then verbally brainstorm in front of the rest of the group. Members of the group at large write down their own new or hitchhiking ideas as they listen to the panel. After the process is completed, the ideas of both the panel and the "audience" are collected for later evaluation.

Group Process

A collaborative, affirmative group process is a way for people to share ideas and to improve the quality of each other's work. The recommended size of an affirmative group is eight persons, each of whom presents a proposal to which each of the others responds. The rules of the process are as follows:

1. No leader, only a referee/timekeeper (who also presents).
2. Each person has 5 to 10 minutes to present his or her idea or project. Each other person has 1 to 2 minutes to respond.
3. Each responds only affirmatively, in the form: "If I were you, (presenter's name), I would . . ." (Responses that resemble previous ones should not be inhibited—repetition is useful to the presenter.)
4. The presenter does not reply, but records each affirmative response in writing, and as fully as possible. This list of responses is the valuable result.
5. After everyone has responded, the presenter replies to all the affirmations together and subsequently attempts to incorporate all or most of them in the next version of his or her design.

The referee/timekeeper's role is to do the following:

- Ensure that each response begins with the words "If I were you . . ." (A difficult habit to learn, but very helpful—it often involves changing from destructive to constructive language.)
- Keep everyone to the time allowed and to the sequence of speaking.
- Prevent the presenter from replying to responses until the end of a round (another difficult habit to learn—to overcome defensiveness).
- Ensure that the next person does not begin responding until the presenter has written the previous response.
- Limit the times of presenting and responding so that the total time is not excessive.

Several years ago, John Chris Jones developed this seemingly mechanical procedure and found that it improves the quality of comments and of subsequent idea development, provided that the rules are imposed firmly enough to enable people to overcome the nonaffirmative, aggressive, or defensive habits that often prevail in committee-like groups.

Digital Technology

Digital media may have a significant and strategic role to play in facilitating communication and collaboration in a variety of settings. Creating an effective human interface to complex information is the aim of telecommunications services. Videoconferencing is a one-to-one communication, which means that all participants have equal status and no one person is in control of the conference. People can see each other, talk to each other, show each other relevant documents, and change those documents together. CU-SeeMe is a real-time, desktop videoconferencing program developed at Cornell University that provides the ability to transmit and receive digital audio and video on personal computers. It allows individual or multiple users to participate with sites at different locations from a desktop computer (Figure 2.11).

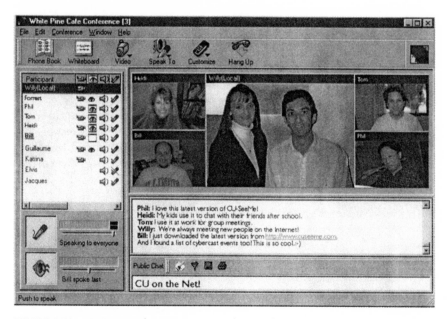

FIGURE 2.11   CU-SeeMe Desktop image. *(Screenshot provided by White Pine Software. CU-SeeMe is a registered trademark of White Pine Software.)*

Simulation modeling, combining video, CD-ROM, and computers, uses technology immediately useful for participation practice. Computer simulations of buildings allow viewers to walk through, fly over, and alter interior and exterior features. CD-ROM is used to store and access the information. Similarly, videos of physical models allow participants to view a building or streetscape from many different points.

SimCity (Bremer, 1993) is a CD-ROM city simulator game that allows the player to design and build small rural towns or large megalopolises. Designed by Fred Haslam and Will Wright, SimCity is a building game aimed at maintaining large cities without sacrificing quality of life. In SimCity, the player is the planner and mayor of an unlimited number of cities. Initially, the player has to identify long-term goals in order to plan a workable strategy. The game consists of a number of scenarios with different challenges. Disasters such as fires, riots, tornadoes, and monsters from outer space are included in all the scenarios. Cities can be expanded, or new cities can be started by generating a new landscape. The City window is the main work area for shaping a city and the land beneath it. A City toolbar allows the player to modify the landscape, center on different areas of the city, and build the city infrastructure as well as many other features. Maps of cities from all over the world are available to allow the participant to improve on a favorite city.

The VisionDome, a collaborative virtual environment, is an interactive digital display that enables group interaction around a shared application. The public, planners, and public officials can walk through a proposed urban development, experiencing the environmental impact. The VisionDome delivers a full-color, raster-based, interactive display, with 360-degree projection and a 180-degree field of view. The tilted hemispherical screen is positioned so as to fill the participants' field of view, creating a sense of immersion in the same way in which large-screen cinemas draw the audience into the scene. The observer loses the normal depth cues, such as edges, and will perceive 3D objects beyond the surface of the screen. The dome itself allows freedom of head motion, so observers can change their direction of view and still have their vision fully encompassed by the image (Figure 2.12). The VisionDome allows groups of 8 to 14 people to view three-dimensional models in an immersive environment, facilitating focus groups or collaborative interaction.

The Center for Housing Innovation initiated the Net Energy Communities (NEC) project to create computer-based decision support for public participation in neighborhood planning and design (Kellett, 1998). NEC develops four tools: Site Modeller, Elements of Neighborhood, Scenario Modeller, and Scenario Calculator. Together, these tools help charrette participants define site-specific issues and circumstances influencing their development choices, increase the generation of acceptable alternatives, and measure alternative scenarios against common indicators of energy, environment, community, and cost.

NEC's Site Modeller builds digital models of project sites using quantitative, qualitative, and visual information, including location base maps, air photos,

FIGURE 2.12   VisionDome. *(Photo: Jay Tomlinson.)*

explanatory diagrams, movies, pictures, Geographic Information System (GIS) wireframes, and land use suitability models. Elements of a Neighborhood is a compilation of neighborhood design elements derived from case studies. Organized by land use, such as open space, housing, commercial property, and streets, case studies are illustrated with air photos, movies, scaled site plans, and design drawings. They are measured by attributes of planning, design, energy, environment, and cost. NEC's Scenario Modeller (Figure 2.13) allows participants to understand and visualize proposed scenarios by assigning selections from Elements of a Neighborhood to areas of a site. Scenario Calculator will compile quantitative data and evaluate measures for these scenarios through a series of comparative pro forma reports.

Participation Games

Participation can take place through other types of involvement, such as design and planning games for organizing group decision making. Jerome Bruner (1967) suggests that one of the key factors in the learning process is participation—particularly by the use of games that incorporate the formal properties of the phenomenon for which the game is an analogue. A game is a simulation of a real situation, allowing participants to act out situations and experience the interactions of a community activity. Games are educational because their purpose is to create an environment for learning and prepare people to act (Duke, 1974). Gaming is a participatory approach to problem solving that engages a real-life situation compressed in time so that the essential characteristics of the problem are open to examination. This technique permits learning about the process of change in a dynamic environment requiring periodic decisions. Essentially, a complex problem is identified, its essence is abstracted, and the end result is a process referred to as a simulation. Games consist of players, placed in a prescribed setting, with constraints within this setting represented by rule systems and methods of procedure.

Games used for teaching in the community produce outcomes such as learning of principles, processes, structures, and interrelationships; empathy and understanding for predicaments, pressures, and real-world problems presented by role players; and a strong sense of efficacy (Abt, 1970). Games used for skill development by businesspeople, police officers, and diplomats help to develop skills in persuasion, bargaining, and strategic planning. Game use in social planning is helpful when players try out different forms of social structure, resource allocation, and communication within a simulated environment to test the effectiveness of ideas, costs, and rewards of various options (Duke, 1974). The use of games by groups to explore values, ideas, and behaviors as a communication function gives participants a better understanding of themselves and others. Games used in conflict resolution facilitate communication between dissimilar or

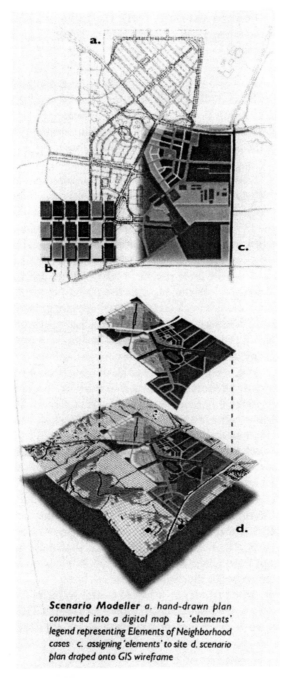

Scenario Modeller a. hand-drawn plan converted into a digital map b. 'elements' legend representing Elements of Neighborhood cases c. assigning 'elements' to site d. scenario plan draped onto GIS wireframe

FIGURE 2.13 Scenario Modeller showing hand-drawn plan converted into a digital map and GIS wireframe. *(Courtesy: Ronald Kellett.)*

opposing groups (Greenblat and Duke, 1981). Design games get people involved in the play and in their design and planning results. There are several reasons for this, but three are central:

1. Participants take a role and argue the problem from that posture.
2. Games organize complex details into an overview model. This allows a player to grasp details that might otherwise be lost.
3. Games require trial decisions, and this commitment sharpens the thought processes of the participants who are required to act.

A familiar feature of games is that of winning and losing. The behavior and interaction of participants in a game can possibly involve competition, cooperation, conflict, or even collusion, but are partially described to allow for spontaneous behavior. The basic format of this chapter, however, is group discussions that are collaborative in nature and that require consensus decisions. Bargaining and voting methods create situations that have only two sides. These methods are increasingly more unrealistic and usually force people to take extreme positions in order to influence votes. Moreover, losers in any situation become disgruntled. Therefore, all the gaming exercises in this book are based on the premise that there should not be winners or losers in the decision-making process. Every participant should be a winner. The consensus process, then, replaces the traditional process of voting.

All of the techniques included here have gone through the test of experience. Each method aims to accomplish specific tasks, ranging from increasing people's awareness to particular environmental issues, to teaching concepts and relationships, to clarifying value differences between decision makers. Values are those beliefs we hold to have some intrinsic worth. Value differences between individuals often account for their inability to achieve agreement in group problem-solving situations. Quite often so-called differences of opinion result from basic value differences not made explicit. Values clarification methods encourage people to examine their own beliefs.

In each design game the individuals make choices, hold positions, and debate them. In making choices individuals have to examine their feelings, self-concepts, and values. The final goal of the exercise is a plan of action for an entire group of people—a goal that usually requires some compromising. Participants in these design groups learn about each other's value differences and use the game props to clarify and reconcile those differences.

Each design game provides a variety of materials, including lists of objectives, activities, activity symbols, and environmental settings. The range of possibilities has not been exhausted. It is appropriate to add or eliminate items from any list of objectives, as well as to provide an opportunity for participants to include their own choices of objectives or settings.

The games included in this book help to facilitate an understanding of strategies for solving a variety of environment problems and imparting information in a meaningful way. Each game has a structure that helps to focus the group process, control extraneous variables, and increase the probability that certain learning will occur for the participants. Although games help participants to understand the complex interweaving of environmental and social forces, they can also provide insights into situations so familiar that their characteristics are not perceived. Games help sharpen perceptions.

Another form of design game requires the direct involvement of community residents in an organized decision process. Specific community issues, however, should guide the development of this process. The quality of leadership through the decision procedure will affect the success of this approach. Leadership is necessary to ensure that all participants contribute to the fullest of their abilities.

The process should reflect the willingness of people to work together, yet not force their involvement beyond their competence. Attempts at involving community residents in all stages of the design process may lead to early withdrawal, particularly if progress toward implementation is slow. An effective process for involving people must be carefully designed. The random involvement of people without a clear sequence of events and without clearly understood roles can result in chaos.

There are several factors that contribute to the success of any type of participation. Initially, there must be a shared view of the goals of the project and what the participants want to achieve. As the process moves ahead, the goals may change, yet the structure should be adhered to because open-ended processes that permit people to join and drop out usually end in frustration. Creating a steering committee or citizens council at the outset can ensure continuity of the process. Their role includes the maintenance of open communication between all participants at all times. Open dialogues often protect against hidden agendas that may emerge. The process requires that there be a clear beginning and end and that participants understand their responsibilities and their interconnection with each other and with the designer or planner.

The role of the professional in this process is not only to be the facilitator, but also to be the technical specialist who makes recommendations and develops the necessary documents. Because the design process is open to lay people, clear and readable communication systems must be employed. Steps to designing a game include the following considerations:

- Define the problem area to be simulated.
- Define the objective and scope of the simulation.
- Identify the people and organizations involved.
- Define the motives and purposes of the participants.
- Identify the resources available to the participants.
- Determine the transactions to be simulated and the decision rules to be followed.
- Formulate the evaluation method.
- Develop the prototype.
- Test and modify the prototype.

Workshops

Workshops are the settings for many types of participatory techniques. The term *workshop* means that citizens engage in experiences that provide an opportunity for learning about human relations. Learning is most functional when it grows out of personally involving experiences that require reflecting, developing, and testing of new insights and approaches to problem solving. These processes become clear when participants are required to resolve their differences as they pursue a common goal.

Workshops achieve a high level of interaction between people sharing a common purpose. A workshop is a planned event in which participants learn from each other as they explore issues. An important component in the development of a workshop is that of building group cohesion. Opportunities should be provided for group members to become so involved with each other that they begin to see each other as persons and become interested in each other. It is the intent of this experience to facilitate learning that might otherwise be haphazard and diffuse. In order to accomplish this, it is necessary to organize the experience so that there is a focus to the group process. It should also increase the probability that certain learning will occur for the participants. This experience, however, does not dictate what a participant should learn.

Development of characteristics such as listening and problem solving are skill-building aspects of the goals. They include methods of interpersonal communication, group problem solving, sensory awareness, giving and receiving feedback, and team building. Techniques employed to direct learning include activities such as making or building something, discussions, summarizations, board games, interviews, inventories or checklists, role-playing, and tasks.

An appropriate combination of goals and techniques will produce an atmosphere appropriate for learning. Workshops can vary widely in topics, time lengths, and goals, and it is necessary that all three be carefully chosen. Because the workshop participants will be using various activities to heighten their sensitivity to the environment, the meeting space and graphic quality of the materials are important factors that can contribute to a successful session.

The quality of a meeting space should reflect an awareness of the environment by ensuring adequate ventilation and light, movable furniture, and a setting that makes participants generally comfortable. Arrangements that set the audience apart from the speaker are not desirable, as it is important to establish a feeling of informality and encourage interaction.

Generally, it is useful to promote an upcoming workshop, especially one open to the public, with mail flyers, press releases to the newspaper, and television and radio coverage. Participants attending workshops should receive an information packet including the program and workshop schedule. It is also useful to document the workshop through photographs, slides, videotapes, or audiocassettes, and to record all decisions.

Certain activities are basic to any environmental workshop. First, it is necessary to clearly state the workshop's goals, schedule, and events. Participants will become involved if they know what to expect. As an opening activity it is desirable to provide the participants with a personal experience that relates to what they will encounter. This overview may take the form of a simple lecture, the presentation of environmental issues, or a slide show introducing basic concepts of awareness, understanding, and action. The focus should be on active participation in activities that involve all the senses, allowing discovery and encouraging exploration. Each participant should carry new information and fresh insights from the workshop.

Group performance is more effective when it is clear to the members why the group was formed. It is important that there be a leader who will clarify the members' roles and the group objectives of the workshop. Appropriate role definitions will help to reduce barriers between members, encourage free communication, and decrease the tendency for high-status individuals to be unduly verbal. Workshop participants need to understand the context of their discussions and see the potential of their collective creativity before the process starts.

Workshop participants should be divided into groups of five to nine people, inasmuch as groups of fewer than five may lack the knowledge or critical judgment needed to analyze the problem and arrive at a decision. As groups become larger than nine people, the opportunity to participate declines and dissatisfaction occurs. Workshops can be conducted with many parallel groups in one or several locations simultaneously; however, it is necessary to allow opportunities for groups to periodically present their conclusions.

Antagonism and conflicts arise when groups create together, just as they do in "real-life" situations. In both situations negative forces can emerge, which can either destroy personal relationships and group cohesiveness or become positive forces for dynamic change and interchange. The core of the issue is to recognize conflict and to make it acceptable and visible, rather than attempt to squelch it or deny its validity. Conflict, when looked upon as an important resource, can become useful rather than destructive. A group leader or facilitator can help members share activities and learn to work together.

A major source of conflict in community workshops can be the feeling of participants that their viewpoints are not being heard, and for this reason they may become belligerent and antagonistic. It is the responsibility of the group facilitator to see that conflicts, when they arise, are settled constructively. One of the important ways of resolving conflict is for the leader to listen to what is said and then to repeat it—making sure of what the person or the group has said. This is called the language of acceptance, which means that one person accepts another person for what he or she is and how he or she feels, even though the first person may not agree.

A recorder working with each group is also an important contributor to the successful operation of the process. The recorder's function is to keep notes on what everyone in the group says, so that in feedback sessions all individuals have the assurance that they are being listened to and that their input is being valued. Summaries constitute one method of group feedback that helps to resolve conflicts. After each session the group leader can summarize important points, making certain that everyone's point of view has been accurately stated. This ensures that the process evolves on a basis of common agreements and that people can identify and accept accomplishments before proceeding to the next activity.

In participatory sessions, opinions, biases, and judgments have their place, but their purpose is to allow choice and encourage input rather than to prevent ideas from flowing. Summaries during a session allow the group to perceive what has been happening and to determine how to continue. Agreements can be reached, or disagreements can be made visible so they can be constructively resolved. This information should be diagrammed in a series of easily understood drawings and models. On the basis of the objectives agreed upon in the workshops, a series of program alternatives can be developed. Alternatives should be discussed in meetings with appropriate groups and may be presented to the larger community for approval. The intention is to reach agreement on which of the solutions best responds to the concerns of all participants. This final workshop is a necessary step prior to implementation of the project. Workshops are an effective means for achieving face-to-face interaction between citizens as they share in decisions that determine the quality and direction of their lives.

A planning workshop with parents and teaching staff of the SUNY Stony Brook children's center focused on the site development of a new campus children's center. Several groups consisting of four participants each, with the aid of preassembled site planning kits, explored alternative locations for their new facility. Scaled wood blocks were constructed to provide a three-dimensional concept that would be easily grasped by the participants (Figure 2.14). The wood blocks corresponded to all the required functional areas and classrooms. Work groups manipulated the pieces into various combinations of age-group classroom arrangements until they reached consensus about the appropriate solution. During the two hours devoted to this exercise, participants considered many issues

FIGURE 2.14 Work group using the site planning kit. *(Reprinted, by permission, from Henry Sanoff, School Design, p. 25. Copyright 1994 by John Wiley & Sons, Inc.)*

that would influence the design of the facility, including solar orientation, circulation, age-group clustering, and parking. Not surprisingly, each group arrived at similar solutions. They all divided the site into locations for four separate buildings, to reflect the characteristics of their present facility. A rift that had occurred between the university administration, parents, and teachers, resulting from poor communication and unclear expectations between parties, prompted the choice of a collaborative workshop. The site-planning workshop improved relations between all groups and provided a new channel of communication for parents and staff to share their child-related expertise.

Study Circles

In contrast to typical public meetings and workshops, a community-wide dialogue on public issues can be accomplished by the use of study circles grounded in the historical town meeting tradition. They consist of small groups of 5 to 15 people who agree to meet several times to collaboratively discuss a community issue. Study circles are voluntary and highly participatory. Each member has an equal opportunity to participate so that the group can assimilate the experience of all its members. People are invited to share their ideas and learn from each other. In the process, they can explore new ideas because agreement is not an objective of the discussions (McCoy et al., 1996).

In the past, most study circles have taken place within schools, colleges, community groups, and religious institutions, where important issues were considered. Recently, however, there is a growing interest in community building through the use of a community-wide study circle program.

Community-wide study circle programs tend to be broad-based discussion sessions involving numerous study circles. Extensive collaboration between community organizations allows for the involvement of citizens from all parts of the community. These programs generally develop out of a sense of urgency resulting from a local or generally pending crisis and often evolve into successive rounds of discussions.

On the personal level, study circles allow participants to "take ownership" of an issue. Participants form new friendships and new community connections. They also often learn that they are not alone in their desire to confront an issue.

For organizations that sponsor study circles, this participation broadens their connections to the community, and develops new working relationships with other organizations. For the community, a study circle can result in outcomes that include everything from new playgrounds to programs for addressing community problems. Study circles can also lead to new collaboration between community sectors.

Organizing a Study Circle

The basic steps for organizing a study circle are outlined by the Study Circles Resource Center (SCRC), a project by the Topsfield Center (McCoy et al., 1996):

- Organize a working group of community leaders.
- Involve the working group in a study circle process.
- Involve the working group in program planning.
- Identify and recruit sponsors.
- Recruit and train discussion leaders.
- Develop a time table to coordinate all study circles.
- Generate media coverage to promote the study circle program.
- Recruit study circle participants.
- Inform all participants about proposed actions.

A community-wide study circle program is usually initiated by a working group of community leaders who approach the issue from different experiences and perspectives. A study circle derived from the working group will allow participants to understand the process and the value of a dialogue between different community organizations. It will also help to solidify the working relationships within the group.

The working group is responsible for planning the program, which entails recruiting study circle participants and leaders and identifying sites in the community. Planning the program also requires the identification and recruitment of sponsors who can lend their resources and credibility to the program.

Once sponsors have been recruited, pilot study circles can help to solidify their commitment and their understanding of the study circle process. Pilot study circles can also help to recruit a pool of potential discussion leaders. The recruited discussion leaders will require training through the support of a local college, university, or human relations organization. Media coverage of the study circle program can help to generate greater community visibility and to explain why people should take part in the program.

Lima, Ohio, was where it all began—with a large-scale, community-wide study circle program. When the Lima working group, which consisted of the mayor's office, Ohio State University at Lima, and a task force of clergymen, began the study circles in 1992, they did so out of a belief that they would be fostering a way for the community itself to develop solutions to racial tensions. But the organizers had no idea what those solutions would be. Lima's study circles have led to more than changes of attitude. With more than 1,200 Lima citizens participating, numerous projects, programs, and cooperative efforts have resulted. These include youth mentoring projects, collaborative school-business efforts, a new playground, a new soup kitchen, and a neighborhood "peace zone." These projects emerged from the pooled ideas of small groups of people who found a voice through study circle processes and gained the confidence to become problem solvers and community builders.

Postoccupancy Evaluation

The physical environment affects our health, our work, our leisure, our emotions, and our sense of place and belonging. When the environment works well, our lives and our communities are enhanced. Although the environment is intended to support our individual needs, it is necessary to gain knowledge about diverse human needs and how the physical environment satisfies them. Evaluation is the systematic assessment of environmental performance relative to defined objectives and requirements. The assessment process is a means of providing satisfactory environments for the people who own, manage, and occupy them.

A postoccupancy evaluation (POE) is an assessment process that can be applied to any type or size of environment or facility. The type of POE utilized for a particular situation is a function of the amount of time available, the resources, and the depth of knowledge necessary. Preiser, Rabinowitz, and White (1988) describe three distinct levels in carrying out a POE—*indicative, investigative,* and *diagnostic*—each consisting of certain phases: planning, conducting, and applying the POE.

An indicative POE is a short-term process that seeks to identify major successes and failures. The methods of collecting information consist of questionnaires, walk-throughs, and interviews, usually conducted with a committee representing the client's organization. Questions ordinarily focus on issues related to performance, spatial adequacy, and image. A walk-through assessment of the entire facility or physical setting relies on direct observation to verify issues that may have emerged from the questionnaire. Interviews and a summary of findings conclude the process.

An investigative POE, according to Preiser, Rabinowitz, and White (1988), is a more extensive investigation that relies on a literature search to establish evaluative criteria, as well as comparisons with analogous situations. The phases of the investigative POE are identical to those of the indicative POE.

The most detailed and comprehensive approach is the diagnostic POE, in which the data collection methods include questionnaires, surveys, observations, and physical measurements. These studies are long-term in nature and tend to focus on a building or physical setting type, rather than a particular environment.

Prior to initiating a POE, there are several preliminary steps that require consideration in preparation for on-site data collection. First, the client is briefed on the nature of the process, the type of activities involved, and the shared responsibilities. Research methods and analytical techniques are determined at this stage. In addition, background information, such as building documentation, the client's organizational structure, and the liaison individuals, is necessary to establish a POE plan. The plan will include the development of specific information-gathering methods, sampling methods, authorization for photographs and surveys, and data recording sheets. Initially, an observation of the building or environment under working conditions for several hours will be sufficient to prepare a data collection plan.

The primary tasks in conducting a POE are the collection and analysis of data. Timing, too, is important, in order to minimize disruption of functions in the client organization. Therefore, coordination with the user groups can facilitate the distribution and collection of data-recording forms and other printed materials necessary for a manageable evaluation process.

Data collection and analysis precede the interpretation of the results into useful findings. Reporting and presenting the findings of the POE are integral to the client's understanding of the results. POE findings typically describe, interpret, and explain the performance of a building or environment. After extensive discussion of the findings, a recommendation for future action is made.

Postoccupancy Evaluation Methods

The success or failure of an evaluation often depends on the skill with which an evaluator selects and uses information-gathering methods. Friedman, Zimring, and Zube (1978) have classified the methods used in data collection into four categories—direct observation, interview, simulation, and pencil-and-paper tests, all of which directly or indirectly involve user participation.

> *Direct Observation.* In this method, data are collected from direct contact with real-life situations and from behaviors that occur naturally. The observer, unobtrusively, records ongoing events and all activities in a particular setting.
>
> *Interview.* This method is the most commonly used in assessing people's reactions to physical settings. Interviews can be structured, whereby the type and order of questions are decided in advance, or they can be unstructured, whereby the interviewer asks questions of interest while visiting a site.
>
> *Simulation.* In this method, people's comments are evoked from representations of settings, rather than from the settings themselves.
>
> *Pencil and Paper Tests.* Questionnaires and other written instruments may be useful and efficient methods to survey users. Both open-ended and fixed response questions can reveal users attitudes and preferences.

Tasks in the Evaluation Process

When planning an evaluation, it is necessary to identify the tasks needed: *initiate, plan, execute,* and *use* the evaluation. To begin, it is necessary to identify who initiated the idea of the evaluation and the motivation behind the request. Next, the key issue or any unresolved problem should be clarified to begin the planning process. This will aid in determining the kind of information needed, the scope of the evaluation, who will conduct the evaluation, and who will participate. The execution phase consists of selecting the appropriate tools needed for the type of data to be collected. Finally, a forum for the discussion of outcomes can raise the awareness of the benefits of the evaluation. To bring the process of evaluation to proper completion, actions must be taken to honor whatever commitments were made to the participants of the process.

Key questions have to be posed before finalizing an evaluation plan. This is a convenient way to inquire into the details that must be considered. Baird and others (1996) identify a sequence of questions corresponding to the phases of the evaluation process:

1. Who initiated the idea for an evaluation?
2. What is the main motivation behind the request for an evaluation?
3. Who is required to authorize the evaluation?
4. What are the key issues?
5. What are the anticipated benefits?
6. What kind of information is needed?
7. Who will manage the evaluation process?
8. What is the required scope of the evaluation?
9. What method will be used?
10. What constraints are there?
11. What resources are needed?
12. Is the evaluation plan subject to approval?
13. What techniques will be used to collect data?
14. What data are needed?
15. What information can be extracted from the analysis of data?
16. Does the information gathered answer the key issues?
17. Do any parts of the evaluation have to be reworked?
18. How will the results be communicated?
19. How will the outcomes of the evaluation be discussed?
20. Who will authorize action?
21. What actions will be authorized?

A key issue is whose judgments should be sought in an evaluation. There is a tendency to regard expert opinion as always more reliable and correct. For many aspects of the environment, the experts are the people who know most about using it—the users.

An application of a postoccupancy evaluation was conducted during the remodeling phase of the Durham Arts Council (DAC) housed in a vacated city hall building (Sanoff, 1983). After five years of occupancy the Council secured funds to make the spatial modifications that would suit the work flow of the organization. In a preliminary study of users' satisfaction with their current environment, often referred to as a postoccupancy evaluation, a survey was conducted with the DAC staff, members of affiliate organizations, and independent artists who rented studios, totaling 14 people.

Understanding the organization and its purpose was the focus of the study. An assessment of the adequacy of its current environment revealed that DAC places the greatest emphasis on the provision of service to the community through art classes and cultural events. Staff members' perception of the organizational goals was identical to its chartered goals. Council members were also asked to record their typical activities on a daily log, to rate the adequacy of the places where they were performed, and to describe the flow of information between council members and the nature of the social environment.

The results of the study showed that many of the workplaces were described as being too small, although the social environment was described as friendly and cooperative. Positive environmental conditions related to light, temperature, and ventilation contributed to people's satisfaction with their jobs. Similarly, places that were too warm or poorly ventilated were reported to have a negative impact on job performance and satisfaction. Because the building's occupants had identified many serious malfunctions in their work environment, a procedure was developed by the design team to permit the users to redesign their work spaces. Work groups were organized and provided with floor plans of their existing three-story building, along with a sheet of graphic symbols corresponding to all their spatial activities.

Participants examined their work space needs, estimated area requirements, and prepared a plan layout for each of the three floors of the building (Figure 2.15). The three participant groups proposed opposing solutions, which they compared and evaluated, along with the design team, and arrived at a solution to reconcile their differences. This approach permitted the building occupants to share their experiences and spatial concerns with each other through a process of collaborative planning. Results from all groups were summarized, as shown in Figure 2.15, and served as a point of further discussion. Finally, a layout was prepared (Figure 2.15) that satisfied the space and adjacency requirements as well as other related concerns voiced by the participants. The solution was accepted as a natural evolution of the designer/client collaborative effort, rather than as the architect's ideas that had to be accepted or rejected.

Visual Preference and Appraisal

An increased awareness of environmental effects is important to our psychological well-being in a place. It raises questions and issues, which, although constantly affecting our relationship with the environment, sometimes remain unnoticed during our daily experience. One might question the need for awareness of these effects. It is in the physical world itself, the world that we create and change according to our needs and values, that we find reasons.

Urban environments, for instance, are constantly changing and growing, often indiscriminately. Buildings are demolished to give place to new ones, and

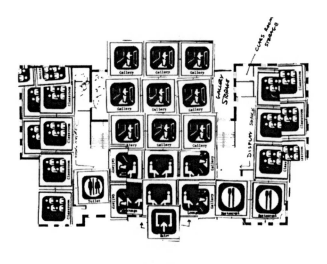

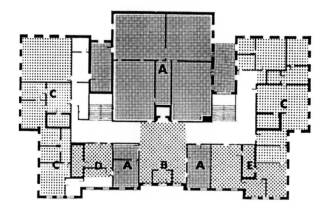

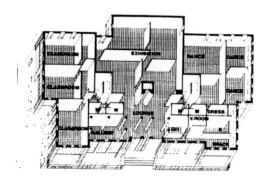

FIGURE 2.15 Transformation of floor plan from participants' ideas to the architect's drawing.

neighborhoods are modified to create more space for cars. Those who do not have a say in the decision-making process make decisions, under the guise of effecting progress, to facilitate their acceptance.

However, such changes have many more effects than we may realize. When buildings are demolished and neighborhoods modified, familiar environments become unfamiliar, altering our feelings of comfort and safety. We lose the ability to orient ourselves and spend more time determining where we are in relation to where we want to go. More significantly, we cease to identify with places and things that surround us because their formerly unique characteristics have been homogenized for the sake of practicality and economics. At the extreme, large-scale urban projects are so interjected into existing cultural and physical situations that marked and distressing forms of antisocial behavior result. The necessary destruction of the Pruitt-Igoe complex in St. Louis is still one of the most convincing examples of environmental psychosis to date.

In short, continuous and indiscriminate changes, at the least, contribute to the creation of environments lacking the character of their local makers and users and often introduce inappropriate and destructive forces. As evidence of contemporary dissatisfaction with urban environments in particular increases, the need for understanding and knowledgeably modulating the interaction between people and place becomes more critical. Variety and change, nonetheless, are necessary ingredients of a pleasurable, memorable, and healthy environment. Becoming aware of perceived environmental effects is a necessary first step in striking the delicate balance between familiarity and monotony and boredom, and between variety and confusion and disorientation. With an understanding of how physical surroundings affect us psychologically, we can become more aware of our effects on these environments, and on ourselves, when we allow them to be changed.

Nonverbal environmental messages, which are part of our experiences, are conveyed by many parts of our immediate surroundings. Some of the places that stand out visually in the environment are familiar to us, either because they have been part of our everyday experiences or because they are similar to places we have experienced in the past. If we are open to learning, these are the places that "tell" us about people and their activities and evoke either good or bad feelings, reflecting our present sensations and associations with our past. The ability to identify features in our environment relies on our recognizing visual elements that stand out in the landscape because of their size, height, color, or any other aspect that contrasts with the surroundings. It means that we see characteristic elements against a background, which can range from a building in the streetscape to a park in the neighborhood. The ability to identify parts of the environment allows us to recognize the familiar and to appreciate the new.

A place has meaning for us as individuals when it relates to, and has in fact become the setting for, events of our personal life. Some meanings are shared by a group, or even by a whole community, when they relate to events of its communal life.

Often when we think about symbols and meaning in relation to the environment, we restrict ourselves to monumental structures, particularly religious and civic buildings (Rapoport, 1982). Because all building forms convey messages reflecting the inner life, actions, and social conceptions of the occupants, it is necessary to reevaluate the meaning and desirability of existing buildings as suitable for new uses.

Various approaches can be used to heighten people's awareness of building image. In the town of Kinston, North Carolina, a public workshop was held in which residents could evaluate the desirability of four alternative vacant buildings for housing a future community arts center. Through the use of a series of comparative drawings, it was possible to convey changes to the character of each building after it had undergone specific design modifications (Figure 2.16). Arts council members rated each alternative using a prepared list of adjective opposites. The results of the ratings were compiled to allow for a fruitful discussion. From the participants' viewpoint, this technique was effective because they were able to examine future building images, to acquire an expanded vocabulary for describing the built environment, and to engage effectively in a discussion of the options available to them. The major limitation to this technique is that it is difficult to anticipate which option the participants will prefer.

Another technique that has been used to develop an understanding of people's environmental preferences is a questionnaire exploring variations in spatial character (Figure 2.17). Staff members of the Durham Arts Council were asked to describe each of several photographs and to rate, in order of their preference, that which best fit their idea of an arts center (Sanoff, 1991). The exercise was particularly illuminating inasmuch as the council members initially believed that their building, the former city hall, was adequate in appearance. When comparing their facility with others that more effectively conveyed the image of an art center, council members quickly altered their view about their facility and instructed the design team to explore modifications to their building that would be more expressive of an art center.

As a result of the success of this comparison technique, three major art center spaces—an entrance lobby (Figure 2.18), an exhibition gallery, and an office—were selected for exploring differences in spatial character and sensitizing the participants to the range of possible options. Photographs were selected from a wide range of choices, based on how representative they were of different spatial features. A list of opposite pairs of adjectives allowed the participants to rate each of the photographs.

Streetscapes

Environmental character as it pertains to streetscapes can equally engage community members in exploring various types of street improvements. Design proposals can be generated and compared with drawings (or photographs) of the present streetscape (Figure 2.19). This method is effective with small working groups, allowing them to

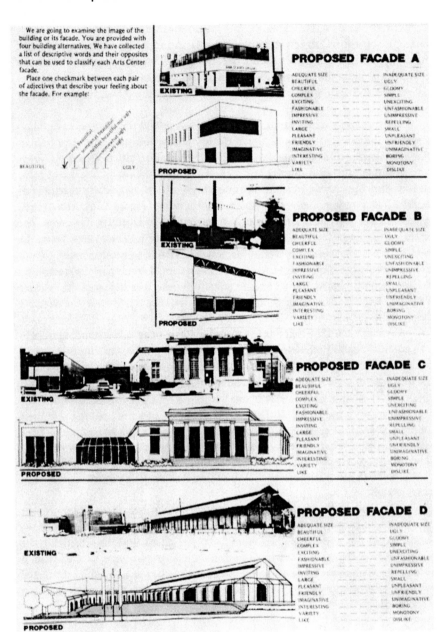

We are going to examine the image of the building or its facade. You are provided with four building alternatives. We have collected a list of descriptive words and their opposites that can be used to classify each Arts Center facade.

Place one checkmark between each pair of adjectives that describe your feeling about the facade. For example:

FIGURE 2.16 Proposed modifications to existing buildings.

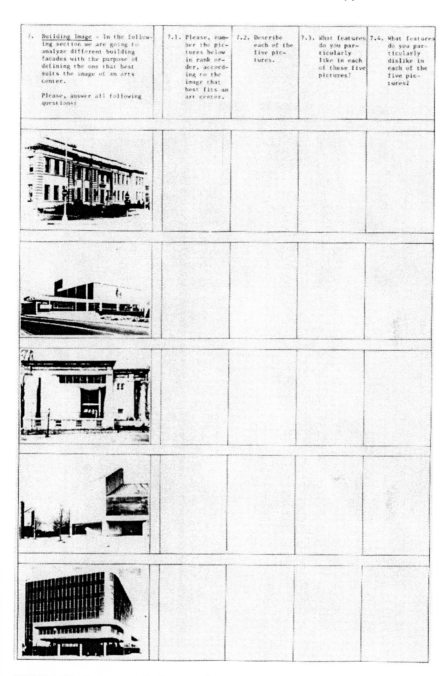

FIGURE 2.17 Rating system for the image of an art center.

8. Visual Quality — The purpose of this section is to assess the adequacy of different settings to the performance of specific activities in the center.

Three different activities were chosen.

8.1. Entrance Lobby

a) List the picture numbers in rank order according to the image you have of an ideal lobby space.

_____
_____
_____

b) Choose one adjective in each pair to describe each of these five pictures. Circle the picture number to show your choise.

EX:	1	(2)	3	(4)	5	Ugly	Beautiful	(1)	2	(3)	4	(5)
	1	2	3	4	5	Cheerful	Gloomy	1	2	3	4	5
	1	2	3	4	5	Comfortable	Uncomfortable	1	2	3	4	5
	1	2	3	4	5	Dark	Light	1	2	3	4	5
	1	2	3	4	5	Imaginative	Unimaginative	1	2	3	4	5
	1	2	3	4	5	Inviting	Repelling	1	2	3	4	5
	1	2	3	4	5	Noisy	Quiet	1	2	3	4	5
	1	2	3	4	5	Spacious	Cramped	1	2	3	4	5
	1	2	3	4	5	Variety	Monotony	1	2	3	4	5

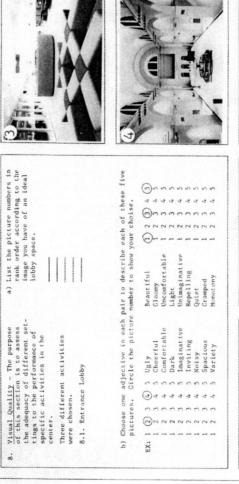

FIGURE 2.18 Method for visual quality rating of different entrance lobbies.

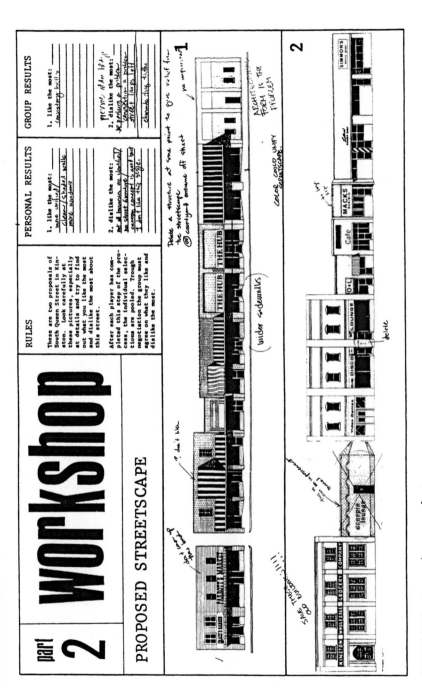

FIGURE 2.19 Annotated streetscape drawing.

generate a variety of likes and dislikes by annotating the drawings. Responses from the participants can enable designers to proceed effectively to the next stage of design development with solutions that are within the range of acceptability.

Awareness Walks

Awareness walks and trails attempt to add significance to a particular place and to encourage the observer to get the most from a given area. The walk typically provides historical background and may be associated with an illustrated guide. In the features observed, a walk may indicate planning problems or social issues, as well as offer aesthetic appreciation and enjoyment of what has been preserved. A trail often challenges the visitor to explore, demands a questioning approach, and invites the participant to appraise the quality of what is observed and experienced.

Historic architecture has been the major focus of much guided touring, and specialist groups have provided opportunities for guided walks through significant buildings and sites. The protection of buildings of historic interest and the conservation of the special character of neighborhoods and towns have stimulated considerable interest in the development of walks and trails. More recently, walks and trails have been developed in the belief that residents as well as visitors should be aware of the aesthetic assets of a particular place. Assisting the community in discovering itself has provided considerable incentive for walk and trail development. As a tool for understanding of and exploration in the environment, a walk or trail manages perceptions of the environment and directs the senses to specific sites.

Halprin (Halprin and Burns, 1974) has used awareness walks with community groups as an introduction to the planning process, inviting them to take part in a downtown walk with specific stopping points. A walking route can also be related to longer journeys by car or by public transport. Although the range of purposes for a walk is limitless, it is necessary to stress that those producing a walk or a trail should have a clear idea about its purpose, which can be education, enjoyment, or stimulating an interest in the planning or improvement of an area. Winders and Gray (1973) advocated that the aim of trails should be to

- Arouse interest in the townscape and in the ways in which it has evolved
- Discover the processes that are currently shaping the urban environment
- Encourage a critical evaluation of the visual quality of the urban scene
- Develop the skills necessary for an analysis of the urban environment

Goodey (1974) describes a variation of the awareness walk as "the sensory walk." Experiencing a townscape through a sensory walk serves as a foundation for descriptive or analytical activity. The sensory walk is an opportunity to become acquainted with the familiar and to reexamine the environment through the senses and emotions. The organization of linked activities begins with being open to what the environment offers. Freeing the senses can be encouraged by removing one sense so that greater reliance is placed on another. For example, a blindfolded person experiencing the environment may absorb sounds, smells, and textures differently than a sighted person. A sensory walk is initially unstructured and entails observing surfaces, edges, textures, and colors.

Goodey (1974) constructed a townscape walk for Abingdon (in the United Kingdom), requiring participants to carry out specific activities at a number of identified locations along the route. With the aid of a map, participants were instructed to take various roads and discuss immediate impressions of the locale. Next, they were to search for a place to sit and absorb the smells, sounds, and other sensations of the area.

A townscape walk is a method for recording visual experiences. The purpose of the walk is to engage participants in looking at the everyday environment, "to get a feel for it," and to evaluate the impact of the environment emotionally and aesthetically.

Visual Appraisal

An approach for developing a deeper understanding of the visual environment is a self-guided tour. Unlike other assessment strategies that rely on conventional social science techniques for describing and judging the environment, a checklist offers individuals and groups a procedure for taking a structured walk through a building. This is an impressionistic approach that increases people's awareness of the environment by focusing on visual factors. The results of such a walk-through encourage responses about views, walkways, barriers, orientation, wayfinding, and appearance.

Tom Markus, in his book *Buildings and Power* (1993), describes the distinct elements of our experience of a building: form, or what things look like; what people do in the building; and how we sense where we are—in what relation to other spaces inside and outside the building. Observers using a checklist appraise visual quality in terms of four key elements—*context, massing, interface,* and *wayfinding.* Any building or group of buildings is amenable to such appraisal. Through a series of checklist questions and a numerical rating scheme, scores are assigned to the factor being appraised. The process uses notes, drawings, and photographs to supplement the factors described in the checklist. (Bishop, 1987).

A numerical score from 1 to 7 (1 = highly inappropriate, 7 = highly appropriate) is assigned to each question in the checklist. Individual scores are then averaged, and an overall project score is assigned. An appraisal report includes the following:

- Description of the building(s) appraised with supporting illustrations (photographs, sketches, maps, and diagrams)
- Appraisal of the building according to the four-factor analysis using the checklist, with responses and numerical scores for each question provided.
- A paragraph describing the success or lack of success with which each factor is achieved or satisfied.
- Analysis of numerical ratings by computation of average scores for each factor of the appraisal, and computation of the overall score for the building(s).
- Concluding comments based on the overall appraisal of the building(s).

Four-Factor Building Assessment

The four-factor building assessment is an approach that allows the assessor to focus on 4 key elements of building assessment: *context, massing, interface,* and *wayfinding.* A series of checklist questions and a numerical rating scale are used to assign a score to each factor being assessed.

For each question in the checklist, a numerical score from 1 to 7 (1 = *highly inappropriate,* 7 = *highly appropriate*) is assigned; then the average score for the factor is calculated by adding all the individual scores for each factor and dividing by the number of questions answered. To assign an overall score for the building, based on the four-factor analysis, the average scores for each factor are added and the total is divided by 6.

Factor 1—Context: The building's setting

(Complete the response for each question shown below and assign a score from the choices provided by asking yourself how well the building suits the context.)

Score: highly inappropriate—1 2 3 4 5 6 7—highly appropriate

_____ 1. How well does the building suit the pattern of the surrounding streets?

_____ 2. How well does the scale of the building suit the site it sits on?

_____ 3. How well does the scale of the building suit the scale of the surrounding buildings?

_____ 4. How well does the scale suit the character of the neighborhood?

_____ 5. Do the public and private areas relate well to one another?

_____ 6. Do the land uses adjacent to the building seem to fit harmoniously with the building?

_____ 7. Does the type of building and its intended use fit well with the type and uses of adjacent buildings?

_____ 8. Does the appearance of the building fit in well with the type of buildings surrounding it?

_____ Average Score (total/8)

Write any comments or concerns you may have about how well the building suits or fails to suit the context of the surrounding area.

_____

_____

_____

Factor 2—Massing: Buildings are organized in form into some type of massing. Massing of the parts gives both form and meaning, as well as variety, to the building.

(Complete the response for each question and assign a score from the choices shown below by concentrating on the subdivisions of the building's form and deciding on the appropriateness of the designer's choice of massing.)

Score: highly inappropriate—1 2 3 4 5 6 7—highly appropriate

_____ 1. Concentrate on the subdivision of the building's parts as viewed from the outside. Do the parts integrate well with each other and form an effective and pleasing appearance?

_____ 2. Do the subdivided parts of the building appear to have a specific function? Is the function of each part easy to identify?

_____ 3. Is it clear as to what various subdivisions of the building might mean to visitors? Would a visitor know where to go on entering the building?

_____ 4. Are the various parts of the building planned carefully in relation to one another and to the characteristics of the site?

_____ 5. Is there sufficient relationship between the parts of the building for it to appear as one unified structure?

_____ 6. Is there enough variation in the structural parts and massing to provide interest and variety?

_____ Average Score (total/6)

Discuss the subdivision of the building into identifiable parts and how successfully the concept of massing has been employed.

_____

_____

_____

Factor 3—Interface: The interface is the crucial meeting place where the inside of the building connects with the outside.

(Complete the response for each question shown below and assign a score from the choices provided by deciding how well the building satisfies the problem related with Factor 3—Interface.)

Score: highly inappropriate—1 2 3 4 5 6 7—highly appropriate

_____ 1. How clearly or effectively does the exterior of the building indicate its interior function(s)?

_____ 2. How effectively does the inside of the building connect with the outside of the building? Are the connections appropriate and functional?

_____ 3. Are the exits and entrances easily accessible?

_____ 4. Are the various openings related to thoughtful planning of the interior? (Consider entry of light, view, privacy, noise, heat, glare, atmosphere, etc.)

_____ 5. Are the exits appropriate in regard to safety?

_____ 6. When you move from the exterior of the building to the interior by means of the main entrance, is the experience pleasant, interesting, or special in any way?

_____ 7. Are the clues to what is public and what is private space clear to the visitor?

_____ 8. Have the designers, in your opinion, handled the problem of interface well in their design of this building?

_____ Average Score (total/8)

Write your comments about how well the design of the building has addressed the problem of Factor 3—Interface.

_____

_____

_____

Factor 4—Way finding: Way finding is the ability for people to discern routes, traffic patterns, or passageways in and around the building.

(Complete the response for each question shown below and assign a score from the choices provided by asking yourself how appropriate way finding is in linking the building to its surroundings and how functional the way finding is.)

Score: highly inappropriate—1 2 3 4 5 6 7—highly appropriate

_____ 1. Are sufficient routes, pathways, streets, and passageways provided to and around the building?

_____ 2. How effectively do the routes link the building to the surrounding buildings or structures?

_____ 3. What are the flow patterns of traffic or people? Are there busy periods, quiet periods, one-way flows, regular movement patterns, traffic jams? Are the routes arranged to consider these factors?

_____ 4. How effective are the nodes (meeting points) for traffic around the building, and what happens there?

_____ 5. Do all the routes make sense? Are they understandable and convenient?

_____ 6. Are all the circulation routes within the building easily understood by newcomers, visitors, service people?

_____ 7. How well are the interior circulation routes marked? Are the markings clear and easily understood?

_____ Average Score (total/7)

Write your comments about the clarity of circulation in and around the building.

_____

_____

_____

_____ Overall Score (sum of average scores for each factor/6)

Write any concluding comments you may have based on your overall assessment of the building.

_____

_____

_____

_____

_____

Community Design Evaluation Guide

A framework for communicating and evaluating community design issues has been developed by Greene (1992), in which he describes four basic principles: function, order, identity, and appeal. These principles, Greene suggests, are a synthesis of multiple sources and represent attributes that are significant enough to have universal application to all environments.

- Function is the ability of an environment to satisfy the needs of all its users.
- Order means the clarity of the environment from the users' viewpoint.
- Identity is the ability of the environment to connote special visual images.
- Appeal is the ability of the environment to offer pleasure to its users.

The community design evaluation guide (Figure 2.20) can be used to evaluate proposals or to make assessments of existing developments. Participants in this assessment can include both professionals and nonprofessionals. Repeated assessments of existing environments, both at night and during the day, can evoke different reactions that are useful starting points for discussion. A five-point rating scale allows for comparisons between participants' observations in the assessment process.

Glossary of Participation Processes and Techniques

The projects discussed in Chapters 3, 4, and 5 employ a wide range of participatory processes and techniques. They require different resources and respond to different objectives identified by the community group. Each technique is briefly defined in the following list, and its deployment is noted at the beginning of each project.

Charrette. A process that convenes interest groups in intensive, interactive meetings lasting several days

Community action planning. A process that empowers communities to design, implement, and manage their own community programs

Focus groups. A structured interview consisting of several individuals, permitting discussion of ideas

Game simulation. A technique of abstracting the essential elements of a problem without the normal constraints

Group interaction. A process in which interpersonal techniques are used to facilitate discussion and problem solving

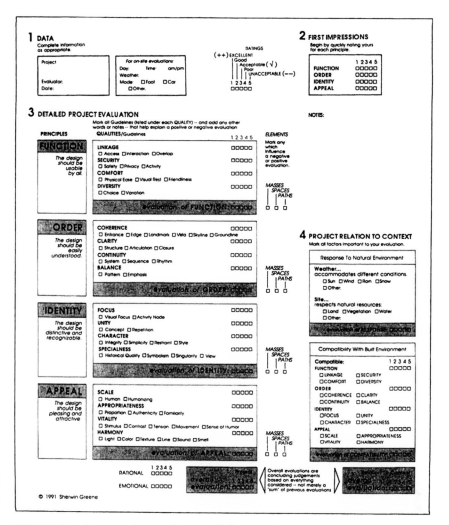

FIGURE 2.20 Community design evaluation guide for proposal or site evaluations. *(From Greene, S. 1992. "Cityshape: Communicating and Evaluating Community Design." Reprinted by permission of the Journal of the American Planning Association 58, 2, p. 181.)*

Participatory action research. An empowerment process that involves participants in research and decision making

Public forum. An open meeting held by an organization or agency to present information about a project at any time during the process

Strategic planning. A process for developing strategies and action plans to identify and resolve issues

Visioning. A process to think about how the community should be and find ways to identify, strengthen, and work toward that end

Workshop. Working sessions to discuss issues in order to reach an understanding of their importance

3

Participation in Educational Facilities

The more people feel themselves involved in architecture, the more likely we are to get the buildings we think we deserve. An enlarged architectural conscience brought about by the greatly increased participation of more people as partial clients is more likely to lead to good architecture than the most scrupulously applied aesthetic controls. If architecture is to flourish and progress in an age when change is constant and development rapid and relentless, it must, with renewed vigor, use society as a partner in the creative process. Only then can the primary unchanging function of architecture be achieved: to provide decent surroundings for people and to help them to a wider vision of life.

(Sir) Denys Lasdun, "Process of Continual Cooperation,"
The Times (London), June 1961

Inadequate school facility planning carries fiscal, human, and academic costs. Whether a school building is old or new, problems in design and planning can take a devastating toll. Schools that lack ventilation can make students drowsy or cause tempers to flare. Open classrooms with noise and visual distractions can draw attention from the best-prepared lesson plans. Congested hallways can needlessly fuel student and staff hostilities. Drab interiors, poor lighting, and the lack of pleasant social gathering spots make school less than inviting as a place to work and learn.

On the other hand, a strong facility-planning process can reap benefits beyond a pleasant environment. School and community pride and faculty morale are raised when the planning process involves the right questions, the right stakeholders, and a clear sense of purpose. The ways in which communities design their schools will help determine the effectiveness of the investment in the schools, as well as the overall livability of the neighborhoods in which they are located.

In working with more than a dozen communities over the past 25 years, with school districts large and small and budgets large and small, the author has found a number of common problems resulting from the planning process. School facility planning amounts to more than simply ensuring the safety of bus drop-off points and student locker sites, although these matters obviously are important. Instead, school leaders should set their sights on what it takes to build a "responsive" school, rather than a building or campus that simply warehouses children and faculty.

Building a responsive school requires that those who actually dwell in the space be part of the planning process—whether they are students, faculty, or community members. Failure to involve everyone can cripple the outcome for years to come. At the Wallace O'Neal School, faculty who had not been fully included in discussions about planning still resented it ten years down the road—and that fact undermined morale. The school found that although it wanted to build community spirit, quite the opposite occurred because of a lack of an inclusive planning process. Teenagers at one modern high school were asked where they went to be alone. A majority responded that they went to the toilet for privacy because, they contended, there were "few places where you can be by yourself," making it difficult to find suitable places to "concentrate on what you are doing."

For decades, educational leaders have discussed the components of a successful educational program, yet they have regarded the physical setting as an institutional backdrop, giving it scant attention. Widespread misconceptions reinforce the view that the quality of school building has no impact on academic performance. Consequently, there is a gap between the educators' view of improving quality and the process of planning schools.

School buildings ought to be an expression of the fact that exploration and discovery are important parts of obtaining knowledge. Current learning styles and teaching methods suggest the need for a new form of learning environment characterized by various activity settings and small-group activities. To obtain and maintain educational quality, however, requires changes in the facility planning process.

Considering the billions of dollars needed to repair the nation's frail and aging buildings, an opportunity to make changes in the school-planning process can improve student achievement. In spite of a body of research that clearly links school building conditions to student performance, school leaders and their governing boards have paid little attention to the significance of such statistics. Perhaps this neglect stems from the lack of suggested policies or procedures contained in the research or the lack of case studies related to the performance of school buildings from the users' viewpoint. Historically, this lack of systematic feedback resulted in the repetition of many standardized school buildings. Even today, new teaching methods have not influenced the physical nature of the classroom.

Outmoded educational specifications and standards are responsible for malfunctions and dissatisfaction with most school buildings. The use of standardized solutions guided by state and local regulations is no longer acceptable in light of the variety of new learning methods that demand different spatial configurations. School leaders need an evaluation system capable of sensing evolving needs.

As users of a school building, teachers, students, parents, and volunteers are the best evaluators of the physical environment. They should participate in any assessment. An evaluation system should be the basis for making physical improvements to school buildings, inasmuch as evaluation is a method of identifying needs. Assessing classroom environments can begin by questioning students and teachers about how they perceive and use their environment.

A 1988 study by the Carnegie Foundation for the Advancement of Teaching found that student attitudes about education directly reflect their learning environment. Activities within schools have educational and social aspects, and quality in both of these areas is important for the operation and development of schools. Not only do teaching spaces serve to deliver the curriculum, they are also places where students spend time, and as such should receive attention as well. Social areas in a school are important in creating an overall atmosphere with which students can identify, allowing them to feel ownership of the environment in which they study and play. To assess the social function of a classroom, for example, a rating scale can be devised using descriptive statements that students classify into categories to detail the actual and ideal classroom. The statements can refer to student needs and performance, considering such factors as privacy, personal space, personalization, social grouping, and participation. (See the sample rating scale on page 171.)

In a research study in California, students in open and traditional elementary school classrooms described their actual and ideal profiles of school. Students in the traditional school described their ideal classroom as one that would provide them with "lots of comfortable places" and as a place with "lots of interesting things to do." They also preferred not to spend the entire day at their desks. Open-classroom students described their actual environment as one containing variety, with "lots of comfortable places." They also pointed to the existence of a few places "where you can be by yourself" at times when they need to concentrate. Teachers and administrators can gain useful information about classroom performance in response to their educational goals by using such an assessment method.

In education, as in other institutional systems, decisions about facilities tend to be made by a few people who are not direct building users, often ignoring the direct involvement of those who do use the buildings. Involving a building committee alone does not always solve the problem of gaining schoolwide support for a project once the design work is completed. Only a process that allows for face-to-face contact between users and those who influence the decisions can result in a sense of ownership in the process and the project. Such widespread community participation in designing schools is valuable for the diversity of perspective it brings to the process. Because communities are diverse by nature and include people who reflect differences in age, culture, ethnicity, gender, aspirations, and ability, the design process is enriched by a range of viewpoints.

Personal contact between school leaders, teachers, staff, and students in an organized school planning process can also result in considerable savings in time and money. Basically, it requires asking simple questions of who, what, where, how, and when. As in managing a professional sports club, planning a participation program requires thinking about goals and objectives, options and plays, resources and timing, strategies and performances. And as in sports, planning for a successful participation program involves a great deal of thought and analysis prior to the first public performance.

Arguments persist that a participatory process requires more of an architect's time, which consequently results in higher costs. Nothing could be further from the truth. Actually, direct participation requires less time than conventional methods normally used by architects. Involving all participants in a planning workshop is more efficient than relying on information gathered in a piecemeal fashion.

At the University of Oregon, involving users early and substantively in the planning process of a new science complex allowed for substantial acceptance in the complex process of allocating space, according to university vice president John Moseley. Moreover, the users' success in developing an equitable model for spatial organization led to a high degree of ownership in the project. This made it easier for administrators to cope with problems that arose during the design and development stages. Widespread participation of faculty and staff allowed for decisions by consensus.

Carolyn Gaston, principal of the New Futures School in Albuquerque, New Mexico, reported that the participatory process used in developing her new school helped to enhance the self-esteem of the students and a sense of ownership in the school. Gaston related a story of how one student accidentally squirted ketchup on the cafeteria wall. The girl immediately got a cleaning rag from the cafeteria staff and cleaned the wall without any prompting. "You would be hard pressed to see that occur at any school, anywhere," reported Gaston, smiling proudly.

The Adams Group architects confronted a unique challenge in designing a major renovation for the First Ward Elementary School, the oldest in the Charlotte-Mecklenburg, North Carolina, district. For starters, they were dealing with people unaccustomed to making design decisions. And because of funding deadlines, a final plan and the projected construction costs had to be prepared in less than six weeks. After several intense planning workshops, the parents and staff had completely redesigned the campus. Participants went through a goal-setting process in which the outcomes were learning activities that supported each goal. Teachers working in small groups pinned photographs of different learning activities, supplied by the architect, to a campus plan and explained the reason for their choices.

The information gained from the sessions generated points of consensus as well as points of conflict. Areas of conflict included the location of various functions. Alternative plans and models were prepared for discussion with the teachers, who were asked to record their likes and dislikes on a visual rating scale. Difficult decisions and painful compromises had to be made, but the open process resulted in no losers, only winners—a natural by-product of creative collaboration. During the building construction process a "tile workshop," conceived by the architect as a way for parents, teachers, and students to personalize their building, produced 85 clay tiles that became a permanent part of the building (Figure 3.1).

An assessment of the effectiveness of community participation in the First Ward school's renovation process revealed changes in the attitudes and behavior of students and staff. Principal Pat Holleman indicated that the most important change resulting from the participatory process was the "closeness of the staff."

FIGURE 3.1 Tile workshop. *(Photo: Graham Adams.)*

Positive, marked changes were also noted in the spirits of the students. Attendance improved, and standardized test scores went up ten points in three years.

Other useful assessment techniques were applied in the expansion of the Broughton High School campus in Raleigh, North Carolina. Diagramming user flow patterns was a revelation to the students and faculty, who were not aware that space planning could minimize many existing conflicts. Real-time studies disclosed how teachers, students, and staff used the campus environment. By stationing observers at various locations on campus, people's movements were recorded at specific time intervals and transcribed onto a series of maps that described daily traffic patterns, congestion peaks and lows, and points of conflict. Students drew maps of the campus to show which street and building features were recognized as important and ought to be considered in proposing modifications to the existing facility. For the students, the original historic building adorned with a clock tower gave the school its meaning, a factor that influenced the architects' planning.

Participation of a building's users can occur during several stages of the facility planning process. Each stage requires the direct involvement of teachers and students in responding to open-ended questions and in discussing the performance of spaces for learning. Initially, an evaluation of current facilities can incorporate the knowledge and experience of students, staff, and teachers. This information can be integrated into the predesign stage in which building users set goals and priorities. An evaluation can begin with interviews, followed by a walk-through evaluation of the existing facility. Although some efforts have been made to assess classroom environments, most studies have stressed features such as lighting, temperature, acoustics, and floor space per child. School boards tend to focus on cost per square foot as an objective measure. How teachers and students perceive and use the classroom is a missing factor.

Considerable information related to the technical performance of school buildings is available, because technical elements such as structure, safety, sanitation, and ventilation can be measured by instruments. These evaluations have occurred for some time. But social and behavioral elements of performance that focus on the extent to which educational goals link activities to the physical environment have received little attention. The accommodation of various building use patterns, teaching methods, and learning styles reflect how satisfactorily a school building performs for its users. After students and faculty have occupied a new or renovated school building, their responses are important for making future improvements, as buildings are not perfect upon completion and require continuous modifications.

Self-Assessment

In a more general way, a self-assessment process was developed for citizen groups, teachers, and policymakers to interview, observe, and discuss ways and means of making middle schools more responsive to the developmental needs of young adolescents. This self-assessment process was developed in conjunction with the

Center for Early Adolescence (Dorman, 1981), a national advocate and resource center for parents and policymakers. The goal was to develop an action-oriented process for school improvement. The assessment process was developed to take a comprehensive look at middle-grade schools to see how the physical facilities, the school climate, and the teaching program accommodate the academic and developmental needs of young adolescents. The assessment program consisted of a series of schedules for interviews with the principal, teachers, counselors, students, and parents. In addition, an observation form was developed to gain a more comprehensive understanding of the school environment. It required observations of the physical facilities, in which such items as places for socialization, spatial flexibility, and opportunities for students to personalize their school were noted (Figure 3.2). Observations of the classroom centered on the ability of students to direct their own studies and modify the classroom to suit their own needs.

To stimulate more participation among school community members, design aids were developed to increase their awareness of the architectural implications of the school environment. Unless a teacher understands why one room arrangement

PHYSICAL FACILITIES	Yes	No
Building is neat, clean, and in good repair. There are few, if any, signs of vandalism or graffiti.		
Student work is displayed on bulletin boards, walls, tables in classes and other areas throughout the building.		
Pictures and displays depict various racial and ethnic groups.		
Pictures, posters, and displays show both boys and girls engaged in a wide variety of activities, for example: girls as doctors, policewomen, construction workers; boys as nurses, social workers, secretaries; girls playing baseball and boys cooking.		
Announcements are posted by students and staff about activities and concerns.		
The building itself is flexible, including some large open spaces, some small rooms. Some spaces are multifunctional.		
Furniture throughout the school is movable.		
There are quiet places for individuals, pairs, and groups of students to withdraw, relax, and think, such as student lounges or reading lofts.		
There are identified places where students can be noisy and engage in physical activity.		
There is plenty of room in corridors and classrooms for movement from one place to another.		
There is outdoor space for projects such as science gardens and building projects. It is being used.		
Students contribute to the upkeep and appearance of the school. For example, they may build furniture, clean their own tables in the cafeteria, pick up trash, decorate bulletin boards.		
There are doors or curtains on the stalls in the bathrooms and dressing rooms.		

FIGURE 3.2 Observation schedule: Physical facilities. *(Reprinted, by permission, from Henry Sanoff, School Design, p. 49. Copyright 1994 by John Wiley & Sons, Inc.)*

may be superior to another, all the physical changes in the world will have little or no impact on the nature of the learning process within the classroom. Design aids included photographs of different school settings associated with activities generated from educational goals deemed relevant by the teachers. Mixed groups of teachers, parents, and policymakers discussed and agreed on commonly accepted objectives and activities that were matched to the photographs. Similarly, photographs of different school settings were rated by community members for the positive or negative features they evoked.

A self-assessment process is usually conducted by a team of 6 to 18 school staff, parents, and a variety of other professionals, usually selected by the principal. In some instances students participate in the assessment by interviewing other students. Numerous schools across the country have participated in school improvement projects. The schools vary in size, physical facilities, location, and socioeconomic makeup of the student body, yet these factors have not been deterrents if educators wanted to improve their schools. Many schools have reported that while in the process of doing their assessments, spontaneous changes were occurring. For example, there was more positive interaction between teachers and students; more interest in the school among students, parents, and staff, and more specific behavioral objectives set by teachers. An assessment gives teachers a sanctioned method to participate in setting priorities for the school. The result is staff members who feel empowered to make their school a better place and who are committed to reaching agreed-upon goals.

In this situation, the architect is one of a number of experts involved in the process. The school assessment process is where the expertise of all people involved in the school environment contributes to the social, administrative, and physical changes.

Community College Child Development Center*

Charrette Process
Community action planning
► Focus groups
► Game simulation
► Goal setting
► Group interaction

Participatory action research
Public forum
Strategic planning
Visioning
► Workshop

---

*The success of this project is due to Joan Sanoff, Department Head, Early Childhood Education, Wake Technical Community College, who participated in the program and design development and urged the college administration and architect of record (Haskins Rice Savage & Pierce) to produce a high-quality building. James Utley also contributed to the design of the project.

An earlier version of this section appeared in *School Design*, by Henry Sanoff, published in 1994 by Van Nostrand Reinhold (now John Wiley & Sons).

The administration of Wake Technical Community College in North Carolina requested programming and design consultation for a proposed 75-child facility and training center for its Early Childhood Program. This program previously occupied classrooms in a variety of campus and off-campus buildings. A component of the education program is a practicum in which students are involved in observing and conducting exercises in children's centers throughout the county. For more effective student education, it was proposed to construct a new teaching facility with an integrated child development center.

A participatory process was initiated to guide the planning group through design development prior to selecting the building architect. Because this facility was intended as a demonstration site for the county, the department head, the teaching staff, and the educational consultants to the program were eager to follow a planning process in which research findings and their expertise and educational philosophy would be linked to design decisions. This was particularly important because the project architect was not identified at the inception of the project and the planning team would need to be sufficiently informed about the design process to be effective advocates for their ideas.

Typically, institutional client groups planning such a facility initiate a formal needs assessment that includes the following steps (see Figure 3.3 for the entire process):

1. Campus survey of student child care needs
2. Survey of campus early childhood centers
3. Site visits to early learning facilities
4. Consultation with early childhood experts
5. Departmental planning

These steps constitute the *research* phase of a collaborative design process. The research phase of this project comprised a needs assessment, visits to other children's centers, and the establishment of educational goals, which include desired staff-child ratios and other factors inherent to a high-quality center. Although research is typically initiated by the client, a professional consultant can often provide guidelines for more systematic fact-finding procedures. Surveys and visits to existing facilities, if properly organized, can reveal valuable insights into their functions, since casual visits often reveal obvious results and are often uninformative.

The purpose of this project was to create a demonstration child development center to serve as a learning laboratory for college students enrolled in the early childhood education program. It was also intended to create a building that demonstrated the use of space appropriate for children of different ages and levels of development. For young children, ranging from infants to toddlers to preschoolers, playrooms were designed to accommodate a variety of activities within learning centers. The learning centers were spatially organized to provide for active areas, constructive exploration, and fantasy play, allowing for free and uninterrupted movement.

114

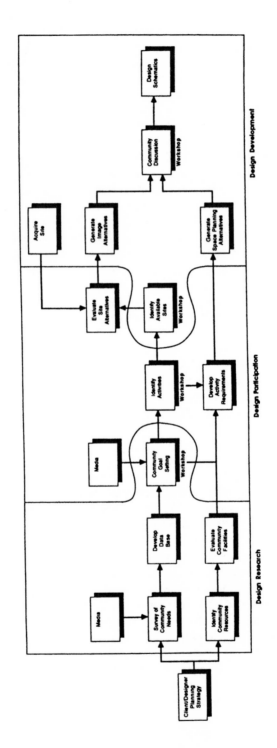

FIGURE 3.3 Stages in the design process.

Early in the planning process, representatives of the user/client group embarked on a program of visits to other early childhood centers. The visiting team "walked through" each facility and reported on its basic features. Walk-throughs consist of a briefing session, open-ended interviews with teachers, and observations of plan layout patterns of different facilities (Preiser, Rabinowitz, and White, 1988). Visitors noted the positive and negative features of the facilities. Visits to children's centers were organized to include an interview schedule and specific features to be observed, in order to familiarize teachers with the issues they would encounter during the facility development process. They also provided the teachers with the direct experience of observing an early childhood center in action.

Because the playroom is the basic planning unit of a children's center, prior familiarity with its components can enable teachers to enter into a productive dialogue with the designer. A workshop consisting of a three-dimensional modeling exercise allowed teachers to plan a playroom corresponding to developmentally appropriate objectives. Working in teams of three, teachers were assigned a task to create a playroom for a specific age group, such as infants, toddlers, or preschoolers. Found materials, including cardboard, wood blocks, Styrofoam, construction paper, and plastic, were provided along with instructions to the teachers for measuring and cutting the materials needed to construct a three-dimensional model (Figure 3.4).

FIGURE 3.4 Teachers model-making workshop. *(Reprinted, by permission, from Henry Sanoff, School Design, p. 31. Copyright 1994 by John Wiley & Sons, Inc.)*

The model-making activity was preceded by an exercise in which developmental objectives and corresponding learning centers for specific age groups were discussed and agreed upon by each team. Participants discussed model results, then connected playrooms together to resemble a building for different age groups. At this juncture, the participants discussed issues of playroom adjacencies, building flow, and location of services in an exercise lasting four hours. Walk-throughs and three-dimensional modeling are effective methods for preparing the user/client to participate actively and constructively in the planning stages of an educational facility.

Facility planning began with focusing on the child as the basic unit of development. This involved the collection of behavioral data relating to each activity in which infants, toddlers, and preschoolers would be engaged. Because the conceptual framework used for the design of the facility was the learning center, teachers identified the developmental objectives by age group for each activity that would occur in the learning center (Sanoff and Sanoff, 1988).

A water play center, for example, the objectives of which would include sensory and perceptual acuity, concept formation, and eye-hand coordination (Sanoff and Sanoff, 1988; Weinstein and David, 1987), would feature such activities as pouring, measuring, mixing, and floating objects. Activity data sheets recorded the relevant activity information and equipment needs that served as a design program and resource for future decisions. Because the planning of a children's center also reflects a particular ideology about child development, a space planning exercise engaged the teaching staff in decisions related to playroom layout. A planning guide of 45 square feet of usable space per child limited the number of learning centers that could be included in a playroom, and, accordingly, scenarios were written by teachers about a typical child's day.

The constraints encouraged the teaching staff to use trade-offs effectively, as they were required to select appropriate learning centers for different age groups. Graphic symbols corresponding to each learning center (Figure 3.5) enabled the planning of children's movement patterns in the playroom. This element was the first step in providing environmental information to foster the teacher's mental image development. Spatially planning learning centers on a "game board" that corresponded to a playroom permitted the determination of which centers were to be fixed and which were to be flexible. The spatial layout process required teachers to consider planning concepts, adjacency requirements, circulation, and visual and acoustic privacy between learning centers. Most important, the process reinforced the concept of a learning center as a planning unit.

The teachers worked through a playroom layout by manipulating the graphic symbols for each age group. They outlined a children's flow process, beginning with entering the facility, then greeting their teachers, removing their coats in the cubby area, and moving to various learning centers. When planning the infant room, for example, teachers identified the diaper change area as the focal point, providing surveillance of all other activity areas. To avoid the unsightly clustering of cribs, the teachers proposed decentralizing the sleeping area into several crib alcoves. This process entailed small-group discussions that required consensus in all

SPATIAL LAYOUT GRID

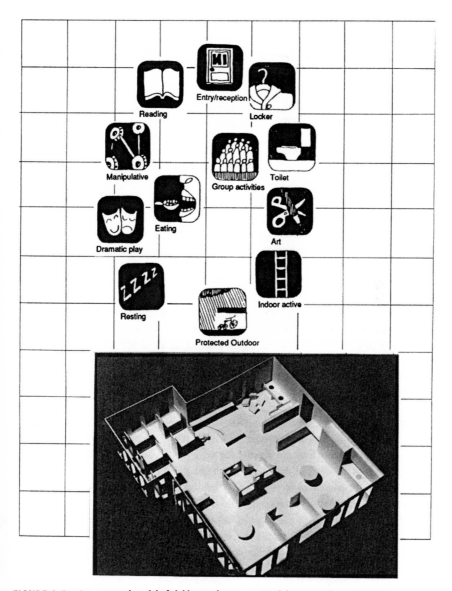

FIGURE 3.5 Diagram and model of children's playroom. *(Model: James Utley.)*

decisions. When agreement was reached, the symbols were fastened to the game board to constitute a record of the group's decisions. The designer constructed three-dimensional cardboard models of each playroom, using movable walls and furniture corresponding with the flow patterns in the diagrams developed by the teachers. This stage of the process permitted the teaching staff to visualize the three-dimensional implications of their decisions. The simplified models of the play-rooms limited the amount of information presented at one time, conveying only the most significant issues in order to avoid information overload. Teachers could reconsider earlier decisions, particularly when they saw conflicts arise that were not easily predictable in the two-dimensional diagrams.

Although circulation between learning centers was considered in the development of the graphic symbol diagrams, the physical model conveyed the need to establish clear boundaries between centers to prevent distraction, while permitting the teacher an unobstructed view of all children's activity areas. The models included information not shown on the diagrams, such as furniture and equipment, but the teachers easily manipulated the movable pieces as they referred to the activity data sheets.

When the teachers reached agreement about the best playroom arrangement, the designer developed detailed diagrams elaborating on their planning decisions. These diagrams combined learning centers into playrooms for different age groups. Although abstract in nature, the diagrams allowed teachers to gain an understanding of "conceptual relationships." Teachers were better able to clarify their intentions regarding the way in which the educational program would be enhanced in the design of the playrooms. This exercise also provided the participants with the tools to evaluate plan alternatives and, most important, a procedure for further playroom modification after the building was constructed and was in use.

The results of the participatory exercises helped to generate design guidelines, as well as to modify the requirements of the building program. Several statements described the fundamental environmental characteristics of an effective child development center:

- The environment must be comfortable and inviting for children and adults. It should reflect an atmosphere conducive to children's growth.
- Materials and equipment should be easily accessible to children in order to encourage independence and self-esteem.
- An effective means of organizing the environment is to develop learning centers, whereby the playroom is divided into areas that focus on specific activities.
- It is advisable that quieter activity areas be placed in close proximity in order to promote a quiet atmosphere. Learning centers demand visual clarity and well-defined limits if children are expected to interpret cues on appropriate areas for certain types of play.

A quality playroom would include the following learning centers:

- Creative expression/art
- Literature/language arts
- Dramatic play/housekeeping
- Block building

- Self-image, personal hygiene
- Science and exploration
- Cooking
- Water play
- Carpentry
- Manipulative activities
- Music and movement
- Personal space

More specific guidelines that influenced the final solution included the following:

- Protected outdoor play area adjacent to each playroom
- Southern orientation for playroom and adjacent outdoor area
- Daylight to be provided by rooftop glazing and glazing orientation

The teaching staff was involved in organizing all the building components into a facility design, using graphic symbols that corresponded to the major building parts, such as playrooms, kitchen, offices, corridors, and lobby area. Age group adjacencies were considered, with opportunities for different age groups to have visual contact with each other. This effect was ultimately achieved in many ways, including the provision of low windows in each playroom to allow children to see into the adjacent room. The parents' "drop-off" was the initial step in the flow process, which also examined connections between indoor and outdoor activities. The planning concept that emerged from the discussion was that of a "central spine" to which playrooms would be connected. The spine would be more than a corridor, but similar to a street where parents, teachers, and visitors could see into the playrooms to observe children's activities. To emphasize the street concept, it was necessary to fill the area with daylight through the use of overhead skylights (Figure 3.6). Each of the playrooms, too, would have a central spine leading to a covered outdoor play area. Spatially well-defined learning centers were located on either side of the playroom spine. These playrooms included fixed areas for art and water play and centers that could change their focus at the discretion of the teacher. Well-defined centers imply the need to be distinctly different from adjacent centers. This differentiation was characterized by physical features such as partially surrounding dividers or storage units, implied boundaries through the use of columns, changes in floor level or ceiling height, changes in floor covering, and changes in light levels. Learning materials, furniture, and equipment also contributed to the distinctiveness of the activity centers.

Teachers' Response to the Process

The diagrams and three-dimensional models provided a clear, sequential procedure whereby all decisions could be traced and subsequently modified. The teachers, however, found difficulty in comprehending the consequences of many spatial

FIGURE 3.6 Interior of children's center. *(Reprinted, by permission, from Henry Sanoff,* School Design, *p. 36. Copyright 1994 by John Wiley & Sons, Inc.)*

decisions. Although they were able to follow the process of playroom organization, they had difficulty visualizing the implications of alternative playroom arrangements. Continual reference to models and perspective drawings aided the teachers substantially in contributing their expertise to the design of the building. The teachers remarked that this process provided them with a better understanding of the principles of spatial planning and the role of the designer. They experienced the "ripple effect," in which the resolution of minor changes in adjacency relationships evolve into major revisions in the spatial layout of the playroom or of the building. The diagnostic procedure of examining flow processes and linking objectives to learning centers enabled teachers to develop a conceptual understanding of playroom and building layout principles.

The interaction between teachers and the designer described in this project is clearly a departure from the traditional approach to facility development. Conventional practice usually denies the expertise of the user (nonpaying client) and his or her involvement in design decision making. Moreover, traditional designers focus on the formal and visual issues and give less attention to the behavioral factors that may equally influence the form of a building. The teachers' expertise lies at the level of children's behavioral interactions within the playroom, but this factor is often ignored by designers and left to the teachers to resolve after they have occupied the facility.

A structured process enabled professionals to lend their expertise to the initial programming stages of the design process. Use of activity data sheets, graphic symbols, and form diagrams permitted the designer to integrate knowledge about children's behavior and their requirements into a format that was conducive to making space planning decisions. Integrating the expertise of the staff in this guided process established clear linkages between child development goals and the types of places where these goals could be fulfilled. The teaching staff's continual involvement in the building design process encouraged the exchange of ideas and concepts with the designer, which increased the staff's ability to act as effective design team members. The active part of the process usually terminates with the schematic design of the children's center, which is the result of the team's involvement.

It is evident from this experience that the dynamics of a participatory process and product are different from those of a more traditional design process. Not only is there a shared sense of ownership in the product, but participants are empowered by an understanding of the decisions that led to the physical form. This approach has the further promise of enabling a teaching staff to make spatial modifications after occupancy.

The effectiveness of a collaborative process is contingent upon the involvement of the designer from the inception of the project. When the designer is an integral part of the process, the building design proposals are clearly understood by the user-client group of teaching staff, parents, and administrators. On those occasions when the programming document is completed prior to the selection of the designer, significant communication problems can occur between the user group and the designer. In this instance, the architect of record was appointed by the college administration after the program and preliminary design had been completed by the consulting design team. Although considerable effort was made by the design consultant and the teaching staff to explain the rationale for the programming and design decisions, the architect had difficulty in grasping many of the nuances of the proposed design solution. Similarly, the teaching staff did not understand the technical drawings, as they were prepared for construction purposes. This situation created communications gaps in the working relations with the client, because the architect often urged quick approval to expedite the production process.

The language of the program should reflect the concepts developed by the teaching staff and conveyed in terms of educational goals and children's activities.

The language of the architect—the floor plans and elevations—are the interpretation of verbal concepts and are often unintelligible to the user group, especially if they are not developed simultaneously with the program. The implications of this experience is that ownership in the design process, achieved through active involvement in design decisions, permits the user/client to exercise free and informed choice. The separation of the program development and design stages not only limits participation of a wide range of experts, but also jeopardizes the ability of the product to fulfill the expectations of the program.

Davidson Elementary School*

▶ Charrette Process	Participatory action research
Community action planning	▶ Public forum
Focus groups	Strategic planning
▶ Game simulation	▶ Visioning
▶ Goal setting	▶ Workshop
▶ Group interaction	

The amount of time young people spend in school is so significant that it is important to recognize that much of this time is devoted to living as well as learning. Consequently, the quality of this living is an important matter. The quality of student life and the quality of education are directly affected by the quality of the school environment. A "school environment" may refer to physical provisions as well as the patterns of a school's operations. Students' perceptions of their environment, either as supportive or hostile, interesting or boring, are also integral to an understanding of the school environment.

There is a gulf between what are known to be the needs of children and their experiences in schools. Decisions about schooling are more often made on the basis of budgets and buses than on an understanding of the physical, intellectual, psychological, and social needs of young people. Schools that encourage the development of young people do not look the same nor do they have identical programs. Safety and academic achievement are necessary for all schools, but they are not sufficient in themselves to produce responsive schools. Because young people vary in physical development, intellectual capability, and interests, the need for diversity is an important characteristic of a responsive school. In such a setting students and teachers are engaged in different learning activities, for which a variety of teaching methods are used. Small-group work, lectures, individual projects, and

*An earlier version of this section appeared in *School Design*, by Henry Sanoff, published in 1994 by Van Nostrand Reinhold (now John Wiley & Sons).

experiential learning, combined with flexible scheduling, are features that respond to the need for diversity.

The school district located in the Charlotte-Mecklenburg area of North Carolina was undergoing an educational reform that had a substantial effect on the design of school buildings in the county. The result of numerous workshops and teacher in-service training programs in 1991 created a climate conducive to team teaching in the county's elementary schools. The growing population and the inadequacy of older schools in the area prompted the school administration to construct four new elementary schools in 1992, on four different sites. The Davidson site was the only one containing an existing school building, located in a well-organized community, with an appearance commission, a historic district commission, and active citizen's groups. The school planning administration selected the firm of The Adams Group (architects) because of its experience in producing effective results working with a variety of community groups and a previous award-winning elementary school addition (Sanoff, 1994). Davidson Elementary School already had a committee structure examining excellence in education, as well as a group of teachers and parents anxious to be involved in the process of designing their new school.

The Davidson Elementary School was designed to accommodate the teachers and parents' vision of an appropriate environment for 600 children, kindergarten through fifth grade. The goal of community involvement was perceived to be instrumental in achieving any changes in the traditional school delivery process, which normally bypasses the teacher's expertise and results in a building produced by formula. In Davidson, the new school was also perceived to be the center of the community, particularly because the community would fund the gymnasium.

To begin, an assessment process was developed that included extensive interviews with teachers at each grade level, as well as workshops aimed at identifying educational objectives for different grade levels and the complementary teaching methods for achieving those objectives. Integrating findings from the educational literature with the expertise of the teachers is believed to be an approach for producing school environments relevant and satisfactory for their diverse users.

The process developed by the design consultant began with an introductory meeting with the Davidson Elementary School principal to outline a strategy for parent, teacher, and student involvement. The first step consisted of individual interviews with each of the school's 30 teachers to review the educational specifications provided by the Division of School Planning. The specifications consisted of a quantification of spaces and a listing of classroom equipment for each grade level. The obvious limitation of the educational specifications was that they presumed a set of educational objectives and a style of teaching. During the interview process, many discrepancies were found between teachers' requirements and the "ed specs," such as the location of teachers' workrooms, location of the counselor's office, and general requirements for proximity between academic and administrative areas. Teachers preferred several small workrooms adjacent to their classrooms, to allow for parent tutoring and sharing ideas with other teachers, rather than the required work area designated for clusters of classrooms that would be remote from the individual classrooms. The teachers also discussed teaming and the opportunity for them to collaborate more effectively. In respect to spatial concerns, they were fearful that the long, noisy corridors in their present school might be repeated.

The interviews were followed by a walk-through evaluation by the teachers of the existing two-story school building. The walk-through revealed many negative features of their building, such as noisy corridors, desks located in the corridors for tutoring purposes, and play areas separated by parking.

The combined interviews and walk-through evaluation disclosed the features of the building that were valued, as well as giving voice to the aspirations for the new building. A parent-staff-teacher workshop followed the more individual activities. The workshop was intended to created a dialogue between teachers about their educational objectives, the variety of teaching methods generated from those objectives, and the types of places or physical settings that would be supportive. This workshop was designed to prepare the participants for the second meeting that would engage them in the site design of their new building.

Group Interaction

Prior to planning and designing appropriate environments for elementary school students, the objectives for that environment must be discussed, considered, and decided upon by the teachers, administrators, and students. The relationship between the activities students engage in, the places that accommodate those activities, and their relationship to the objectives is the basis for designing. The objectives found in the educational literature describe concepts that are paramount to the development of the young student. These objectives (Dorman, 1981) include personalization of the learning environment, student control of movement, provision of adequate meeting and social gathering places, environmental flexibility to accommodate different student activities, and the ability for students to facilitate projects and studies in their areas of interest.

Although there is agreement within the education profession that these objectives may be crucial to the development of preadolescents, there is a lack of agreement about the relationship of these objectives to the places in which they ought to occur, and to the variety of possible spatial arrangements. The interpretation and philosophy of an educational program has a significant impact on how educational objectives are evidenced and realized in the learning environment. For example, "personalization of the learning environment" is an important objective because, as the educational literature points out, the preadolescent needs to have a stake in his or her environment (Sommer, 1979). An important aspect of personalized space is the presence of designated places where students can gather, free from danger, to engage in stimulating activities, conversation, and exploration of ideas. Such places may take the form of outdoor courtyards, outdoor tables and benches, or interior places such as student lounges or corners of a larger room.

After recording observations and interviewing students and staff, the school community members were ready to consider features of the physical environment through small-group discussion sessions that stressed consensus decision making. This process, described as "relating objectives for learning to education" (Sanoff, 1994), allows parents and teachers to discuss, clarify their differences, and seek common understanding. The opening discussion was devoted to establishing commonly agreed-upon objectives. The teachers were divided into six small groups of five people each, based on their teaching focus. They selected objective statements from a prepared list generated from the educational literature. Participants were asked to make their decisions based on group consensus to ensure that all voices were heard in the deliberations. In addition to the work groups' clarifying their ideas and intentions about classroom education, there was strong support for the school's interaction with the Davidson community. Developing a sense of community emerged as an important focus for the teachers.

The ability to link teaching methods to physical settings was a new experience for the teachers, as their teaching methods were always constrained by the existing classroom. The use of photographs corresponding to the physical settings allowed participants to explore and discuss a wide range of traditional and nontraditional settings used to accommodate various teaching methods. Most important, the photographs described a variety of outdoor settings, suggesting the need for a more integrated indoor-outdoor environment for learning.

This exercise was instrumental, in successive interviews with groups of teachers, in using the model of linking objectives to teaching methods. Teachers were able to expand the physical characteristics of the ed specs to include the objectives for each grade level, the corresponding experiences planned to achieve those objectives, and the teaching methods that might be employed. This concept allowed teachers to envision the classroom as a spatial setting that should accommodate a variety of teaching methods.

The opportunity to use the outdoors for a variety of activities, for small- or large-group activities, for reading, art, eating, and gardening, expanded the teachers' awareness of opportunities for their new school building. This discovery found its way into the building design in the form of an outdoor area adjacent to each classroom, covered porches, and a variety of different courtyard spaces.

Children, too, were involved in offering their ideas and perceptions about the new school through their art and poetry. The art teacher and office staff of the Adams Group met with all the students in the school, for two successive days, in an art exercise in which the students were asked to draw a picture of their ideal or dream school. The students produced different types of drawings, including floor plans, sections, and elevations. Images such as towers, clocks, and clerestory windows appeared in the drawings. One of the interesting ideas that emerged from these sessions was that the media center could open to the outdoors, a feature that was included in the building design. The students also stressed the need for daylight in the classrooms and other areas of the building. In addition, teachers, parents, and students were asked to write a wish poem, stating their desires for their new school.

All participants were asked to complete the phrase, "I wish my school . . ." (Sanoff, 1994).

The results from each grade, along with the parents' and teachers' responses, were summarized and presented on large sheets of newsprint paper. Many of the wishes stressed the exploration of teaching methods, including team teaching and an environment that supported innovative teaching methods. There was also an interest in particular physical features, such as an atrium, bright colors, and extensive use of outdoor learning environments. Parents and teachers wished for a school that was "beautiful, unique, and interesting." The results of the wish poem, students' drawings, and all subsequent work was on exhibit in the school as an ongoing record of events, as well as serving to inform those who were not participating of the events that had occurred.

The final workshop consisted of a building image study and site planning exercise in which 35 teachers, parents, and school-planning officials worked collectively. The building image study began with a slide show depicting ten different school buildings, each representing different regional characteristics and design features. Each building was rated by the participants, and an overall priority list was established. The purpose of this exercise was to increase the participants' level of awareness to the possible variations in the visual character of school buildings. In effect, the exercise intended to expand their vision of building images beyond their everyday experiences with school buildings (Figure 3.7).

The final event was the site-planning exercise, in which participants were given a scaled drawing of the new site, located several blocks from their present school, and scaled building components representing all the spaces in their school building. All building components had labels fastened to the Styrofoam pieces. Each of the six groups was asked to develop a building plan located on the site, considering bus drop-off, parking, soccer field, cluster patterns of classrooms, outdoor space, and appropriate orientation and daylight. At the completion of the two-hour exercise, representatives from each team presented their solution for discussion and debate. The participants (Figure 3.8) then displayed all of the solutions for review.

Similarities between solutions occurred in the deliberate use of open space and courtyards and the clustering of kindergarten, first-, and second-grade classrooms, separated from the third-, fourth-, and fifth-grade classrooms. Team teaching appeared to guide many of these design decisions. Although group members had some dissatisfaction with their solutions, they all agreed that they had a better understanding of the complexity of issues requiring simultaneous consideration. They readily admitted to being more sensitive to the role of the architect and were willing to leave the resolution of problems to the architect.

The design team and the designer met after the workshop to synthesize the workshop results and to arrive at several alternative concepts that would satisfy the requirements developed through the interviews and workshops. One scheme was

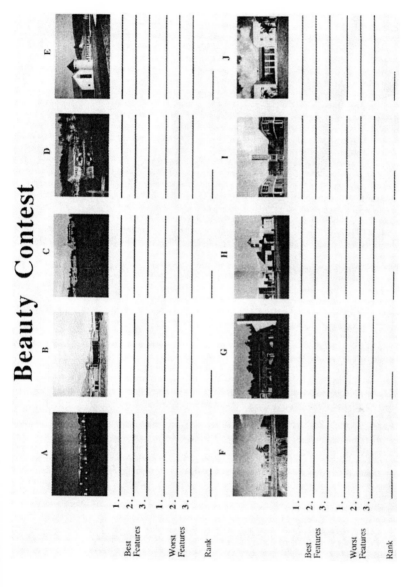

FIGURE 3.7 Rating school building images. *(Reprinted, by permission, from Henry Sanoff, School Design, p. 60. Copyright 1994 by John Wiley & Sons, Inc.)*

127

FIGURE 3.8   Parent-teacher work groups presenting site plans. *(Photo: Henry Sanoff.)*

developed and proposed to the client group by posting large-scale drawings in key locations in the present school building. Teachers were requested to write their comments, directly on the drawings, about the proposal's positive and negative features.

After several days of allowing the teachers to discuss the proposal and to comment, the drawings were retrieved and reviewed by the design team, only to find the comments very minor in detail (Figure 3.9). All the teachers seemed to identify elements of their design ideas in the architect's submission. At this point, and until preliminary drawings were completed, the involvement of teachers was limited to personal interviews clarifying details of classroom design.

The building design contained features that were not typical of traditional schools in the area. Such features were, namely, clustered classrooms to facilitate team teaching and nongraded classes corresponding to the curriculum changes occurring with all Charlotte-Mecklenburg schools, single-loaded corridors with classrooms oriented toward the south, and an outdoor play area for each classroom. This arrangement allowed each classroom to have a relatively private outdoor area.

A plan review conducted by the North Carolina State Department of Public Instruction raised questions about these and other unusual design features, some of which might increase the operating cost of the building. The Davidson school

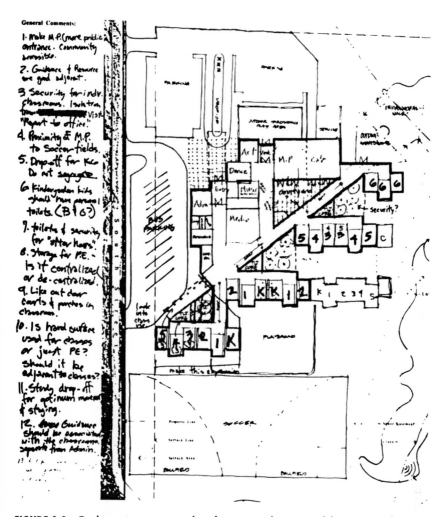

FIGURE 3.9 Teachers written comments about design proposal. *(Reprinted, by permission, from Henry Sanoff, School Design, p. 62. Copyright 1994 by John Wiley & Sons, Inc.)*

proposal was very different from any other school plan the Department had reviewed. Inasmuch as the original intention of this project was to create a building that satisfied the needs of the teaching staff and administration, as well as the historic concerns of the community, it was agreed to allow the community to make the final decision. A review with the teachers and principal indicated strong support for the cluster arrangement and the opportunity for greater teacher collaboration. The superintendent's office, too, supported the building concept and believed it would enhance its curriculum goals (Figure 3.10). Citizens of Davidson

FIGURE 3.10 *Charlotte Observer* newspaper headline.

were equally supportive of the design solution, particularly because they were providing the funds for a gymnasium to be used by the community as well. The
Adams Group commented, "If the teachers and administrators had not been
involved in the process, it is pretty clear that the state and county plan reviewers
would have been very forceful to have the architects change the plan. It was only
the intervention of the teachers and administrators, and the arguments they made
for the curriculum, that allowed the slightly higher cost for heating to be over-
powered by the gains of the curriculum."

Postoccupancy Evaluation

Construction was completed on the Davidson Elementary School in January 1994,
at which time students and teachers took occupancy. A two-person team, using a
walk-through evaluation, systematic observations of classroom and public space
behavior, and a student-teacher questionnaire, conducted ɛ postoccupancy evaluation (POE). The thrust of the POE was to validate initial design assumptions
about student ownership of the building and its positive effects on their learning.
Ownership was operationally linked to the students' ability to personalize their
environment. In addition, learning through social interaction with peers and
teachers was a factor that influenced the design of areas inside, as well as outside,
the classroom.

To this end, observations were conducted of children's behavior in eight
different classrooms. The results indicated that classrooms of younger children

exhibited versatility in seating arrangements, well-defined activity areas within the classroom, and continuous use of the adjacent outdoor area. Classrooms of the older children were arranged in such a way that the focus was on the teacher. Interestingly, all classrooms were designed to discourage an arrangement of rows of desks facing the teacher.

Thirty-six teachers and 60 students from fourth to sixth grade were surveyed. Both teacher and student questionnaires focused on the classroom and adjacent areas and how they contributed to the learning process. Distinctions were made between the influences of the teacher and the classroom environment. It was apparent from the results that the teacher's attitude toward education directly influenced students' ability to personalize their environment. Classroom territory was extended into the hall by the exhibition of student artwork and projects. However, although teachers generally agreed on the importance of providing a variety of work spaces within the classroom to allow for spontaneity of group activity, the students believed that teachers exerted considerable control over their use of the classroom environment. Consequently, personal space was perceived by the students to be limited to their desks. Yet teachers were enthusiastic about the way in which the classrooms were designed to facilitate group activities, and with the overall design of the building. Students, too, had very favorable comments about their new environment.

Although the students and teachers had occupied this building for four months prior to participating in the evaluation, it was apparent that the teaching staff needed more time to settle into the building. This additional time would allow teachers to more effectively manipulate the total learning environment to accommodate their educational objectives. Consequently, a walk-through was conducted two years after occupancy. From the results of this walking tour it was readily apparent that teachers and students had assumed ownership of the building. Creating soft spaces carved out of the wide circulation spine extended classrooms. Teachers, with the help of students, organized special activity nodes, some of which were furnished with soft, comfortable seating (Figure 3.11). Classrooms had also expanded outdoors to include gardens and a variety of student projects. Bold colors accented special places where community artists contributed their paintings and sculpture to the school. The school had become the center of the community.

The intent of this project was to narrow the gap between what we know about the education of young people through the literature and what we observe happening in everyday school environments. Observations of school buildings and classroom behavior provided insight into space use that often denies the existence of variations in types and styles of learning. Moreover, buildings produced without the involvement of those who will use them can further exacerbate the rising alienation found in many schools. It is evident that a sense of ownership achieved through participation has far-reaching positive effects, especially when the viability of traditional school building standards is questioned.

FIGURE 3.11 School interior showing activity nodes. *(Photo: Jackie Carr.)*

A University–School District Partnership

Charrette Process

Community action planning

► Focus groups

Game simulation

► Goal setting

► Group interaction

Participatory action research

► Public forum

Strategic planning

► Visioning

► Workshop

The idea for an exemplary middle school, developed collaboratively by the Wake County Public School System (WCPSS) and North Carolina State University, emerged in 1988 from discussions between multicounty governments. This school, along with the model elementary and high schools planned in adjacent counties, respectively, would give the multicounty area a full K–12 complement of innovative, exemplary schools.

During the next several years, WCPSS and university administrators discussed the feasibility of establishing a middle school and an affiliated teacher development/outreach program at the university campus annex. In the fall of 1993, a planning committee, composed of approximately 15 WCPSS teachers and administrators and 15 university professors and administrators, with a programming consultant, was established. Aided by a small planning grant, the committee was charged with developing an educational program and governance agreement for the school and the teacher development/outreach program.

The committee met as a whole ten times over a two-year period and held a community workshop that was attended by more than 150 people. Six formal task forces, numerous ad hoc groups, and several meetings augmented its work with key people from community agencies as well as each of the colleges at the university.

The Centennial Campus Magnet Middle School (CCMMS) will involve an entire population of students, teachers, and parents frequently engaged with faculty, students, and facilities of each of the university's ten colleges, as well as its corporate and government partners on the university campus. CCMMS will thus be the first middle school in the country to combine the resources of a respected school system, a major university, and a technologically advanced campus comprised of business, industry, and educational and government agencies. This setting nurtures the following unique aspects of the school and its outreach programs:

■ Extensive interaction between students and adults, including community members, industry and government researchers, and NC State professors and students

■ Exploration of adolescent concerns and real-world issues through a curriculum that integrates skills and concepts of various disciplines

- Use of cutting-edge technologies as a resource in all teaching and outreach areas
- Maximized linkages with other educators, parents, and youth-serving professionals in developing and disseminating innovative teaching/learning strategies
- Broad opportunities for ongoing research, evaluation, teacher preparation, and professional development

The Centennial Campus Magnet Middle School will house 600 students. Because of Centennial Campus architectural standards, no trailers or utility buildings may be added to accommodate more students. The school will consist of grades 6 through 8, with approximately 200 students in each grade. A pupil assignment plan in keeping with WCPSS magnet school policy will be devised prior to the opening of school to ensure that the student body is racially, culturally, and socioeconomically diverse and balanced for gender. The target date for the school opening is August 2000.

NC State has partnerships with off-campus agencies that can contribute to the school. Among these are the North Carolina Museum of Natural Sciences, the North Carolina Biotechnology Center, and other state-funded agencies. CCMMS is best understood as an innovation undertaken on behalf of the other schools in the system.

Much of the expertise represented in NC State programs and services will be available to CCMMS. In addition, NC State has numerous physical resources to share in the partnership. A partial listing includes the following:

- High-tech research and development laboratories
- Small-scale manufacturing facilities
- D. H. Hill library and access to libraries of other universities
- Multimedia production studios
- Research farms and forests
- Animal stocks
- Marine stations
- International exchange programs
- Design studios
- An outdoor education/challenge ropes course
- High-speed voice, video, and data connections to the information highway

Further, there is a fast-growing group of corporate and government Centennial Campus partners, including the National Weather Service, with whom links may be developed. Some of these partners are physically located on campus; others are off-campus research partners with whom technological linkages may be established.

The approach to the development of a building program has been to conduct a review of empirical literature, identifying reliable findings about the impacts of the designed environment on educational performance. Research findings suggest a number of recurring problems in the physical environment of a school. These problems are often associated with the overall building complex and its direct effect on the quality of the physical environment. Once identified, these problems have been restated in the form of building organizing principles, as follows:

- Territoriality and personalization
- Activity pockets and short passages
- Common areas
- Wayfinding

The concept of territoriality applies to ownership and control by individuals, small groups, larger organizations, and even countries. Territories vary in scale, ranging from objects to rooms, homes, small-scale geographical areas, and whole nations. Territories are often marked or personalized and display the presence of an owner or occupant. Individuals or groups mark boundaries, sometimes with personal items, to demonstrate territoriality.

Territories permit people and groups to display their personalities and values through the vehicle of the physical environment. People put their personal stamp on places not only to regulate access to others but, simultaneously, to present themselves to others, to express what they are and what they believe and, thereby, to establish their distinctiveness and uniqueness.

The school community comprises a number of different groups, all seeking to fulfill their basic human needs through ownership and a sense of belonging to the school environment. Visitors to school will feel more welcome if there is a public zone tailored to their needs. This zone, with identifiable boundaries, allows visitors to orient themselves without feeling threatened or threatening. Community members visiting the school should be allowed to personalize this zone.

Similarly, a student entry zone is a distinctive place that students can control and personalize. It is a place where there are recognizable entry points into classrooms and other learning spaces. Students should distinguish and decorate these areas with the products of their school activities. Although such markers can symbolize territorial control, all too often boundary definition is evidenced merely by occupancy of a place.

Public spaces surrounded with pockets of activity or small, partially enclosed areas that contain activities will make it natural for people to pause and become involved. Building thoroughfares or indoor streets should replace unfriendly corridors where nothing ever happens. The edges of the indoor street should be lined with windows, places to sit, and with entrances to learning spaces.

An indoor street that passes rooms with windows opening onto it is more pleasant to walk along than a corridor with blank walls. The traditional corridor tends to make people lose the sense of where they are and to feel that all the life in the building is on the other side of the walls. Passages should feel like rooms, with plenty of daylight and windows along the walls. Long corridors can be given a "human" feeling by breaking down their scale through intervals of light and dark.

A common area created for each social group can be located at the center of all the spaces the group occupies, and in such a way that the paths that go in and out of the building lay tangent to it. There are three characteristics of a successful common area:

1. It must be at the center of gravity of the building complex or building wing that the group occupies. It must be at the physical heart of the organization so that it is equally accessible to everyone and serves as a center for the group.
2. Most important, it must be on the way leading from the entrance to special rooms so that people always pass it on the way in and out of the building. It is crucial that it not be a dead-end room that people would have to go out of their way to find. For this reason, the paths that pass the common area must lay tangent to it.
3. It must include the right components: usually a kitchen and eating place, inasmuch as eating is among the most communal of activities, and a sitting space, so people feel like staying. It should also include an outdoor area conducive to carrying on a discussion.

In many buildings the problem of disorientation is acute. People have no idea where they are, and they experience considerable mental stress as a result. In order to be clear, a building complex must have a main circulation space where entrances open to other building components.

The Academic House

The Centennial Campus Magnet Middle School, composed of three houses of approximately 200 students each, will contain four teams of 50 students and two teachers. Each of the four teams will have its own classroom or learning environment composed of several learning centers. The creation of identifiable clusters of space that students can call their own will give them a sense of group identification, and grouping students and teachers together into small interdisciplinary teams will reinforce opportunities to develop personal relationships.

The 50-student core learning environment is the setting for a problem-centered, integrated curriculum supported by a team-teaching approach. The interdisciplinary team is a means of bringing teachers and students together to establish genuine learning communities. All team members teach the same students, and the students on the team have the same teachers in the basic academic program. Teachers and middle school students also share the same basic physical area of the school and the same schedule.

Learning environments, therefore, must allow for a multitude of teaching and learning strategies. Students move from independent to cooperative learning where smaller multiuse spaces support small-group instruction and group projects. Two-teacher teams will facilitate much of this work, and specialty teachers will work closely with teams in an integrative fashion. For this reason, project rooms are provided to enable fine arts and practical arts activities to be incorporated into the team curriculum. In addition, the space will accommodate NC State faculty and students, as well as community professionals, who will work extensively with middle school students.

Research on classroom design has found that creating small learning centers within classrooms reduces visual and auditory interruptions in the classroom, makes learning materials more accessible, increases privacy, leads to questions of increased substantive content, less non-task-oriented movement, less loud conversation, longer attention spans, a greater degree of engagement with learning activities, more teacher involvement with students, fewer teacher interruptions, and more exploratory behavior, social interaction, and cooperation among students. Learning centers within classrooms can redirect traffic, demarcate boundaries, and create small areas for privacy, all of which facilitate a learning environment.

In developing a program for the CCMMS, the intention of creating an attractive, innovative building that facilitates the school's unique goals and curriculum required the knowledge and participation of 30 experts in various aspects of middle school education. A programming process began with

- Individual interviews
- Data sheet recording
- Data sheet review

The programming team interviewed education specialists, using the format of a data sheet on which was gathered information about activity objectives, user information, proximity information, and design requirements (Figure 3.12). Although the interviews were informal, the data sheet served to focus the discussion on building-related information. Adjacency diagrams were prepared from the data sheets and, together with the interview results, were submitted to the specialists for approval.

A final workshop with the university-school district task force allowed for a discussion of the completed building program and space needs. This was the last approval step prior to the documents' submission to the school board for final approval. Although there was widespread community support for the CCMMS, the site selection and project delivery process involved the university and WCPSS in discussions lasting more than a year. When it was agreed that WCPSS would own the school and the university would lease the land, the building process followed the standard procedures for school construction. The North Carolina firm

Centennial Campus Magnet Middle School Project

Square Feet

USER INFORMATION

• Each "double classroom" team will have 2 teachers and 50 students
• Teaching assistants, NC State faculty, students, community professionals, observers, elective teachers, and parents will also use the space periodically

ACTIVITY OBJECTIVES

• To provide a secure, nurturing environment for students engaged in classroom and outdoor activities
• To provide a place for students to work in small groups and as individuals on school projects
• To facilitate individual research and exploration on state of the art interactive media equipment
• To provide a multi-purpose place for elective teachers to work with students on integrated, curriculum-based projects
• To encourage students' social interaction

PROXIMITY INFORMATION

• Classrooms must have direct access to outdoors
• Classroom should be adjacent to science classrooms, multi-purpose spaces and outside areas
• Each House must have ADA accessible toilets located near the entry for student convenience
• Teachers' team planning offices should be directly adjacent to classrooms with a visual connection between both areas
• Students should have direct access to cubby or locker storage areas in the classroom

DESIGN REQUIREMENTS

• Provide ample wall surface for team presentations
• Create visual separation between learning centers
• Introduce architectural forms that reflect group size and respective activities
• Provide clearly articulated learning centers clustered around large group (25 students) activity space
• Movable partition or dividers may be used to separate classroom into two smaller components
• Provide a water and gas source within each classroom
• Daylighting should provide ample light upon work surfaces
• Provide daylight controls for computers and AV presentations
• Incorporate acoustical treatment to diminish noise transmission within classroom
• Provide area for unobtrusive observation
• Provide clusters of storage cubbies in various parts of the room

NOTES

This classroom space is where the students will spend the majority of their school time. It is important that this space meets a variety of functional, aesthetic, social and academic requirements. The classroom space should be flexible enough to accommodate a wide range of teaching methodologies and variant group sizes. Specific learning centers should be identified to determine the classroom layout. The room should be equipped to support a variety of science activities that do not require specialized lab equipment.

FIGURE 3.12 Typical data sheet.

of Boney Architects was selected through a joint university-county review process and given the programming document to guide the design of the school. Participants involved in the initial programming process were identified to collaborate with the architect in the design review process. The initial ideas about classroom

Centennial Campus Magnet Middle School Project

ACADEMIC HOUSE	12,050 Square Feet

SUMMARY	
• Classrooms 4 @ 1700 square feet	6800 sq. ft.
• Conference Room	150
• Group Meeting Room	1700
• Project Room	850
• Resource Classroom	850
• Science Classroom	1200
• Team Teachers Office	500

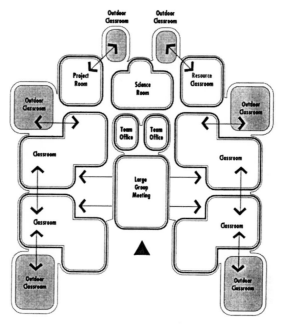

FIGURE 3.13a Academic house diagram.

design (Figure 3.13a), the outdoor environment, and the academic house generated from the collaborative planning process were well integrated in the architect's
design solution (Figure 3.13b). Building construction began in mid-1998, with
completion scheduled for the year 2000.

Centennial Campus Magnet Middle School

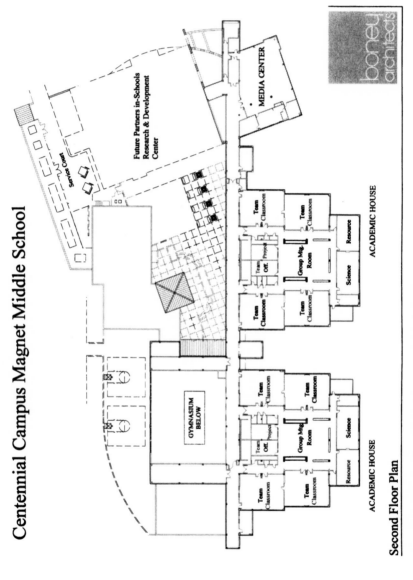

Second Floor Plan

FIGURE 3.13b Academic house plan. *(Courtesy: Boney Architects, North Carolina.)*

Minnesota Center for Arts Education

▶ Charrette Process
  Community action planning
▶ Focus groups
▶ Game simulation
  Goal setting
▶ Group interaction

Participatory action research
Public forum
Strategic planning
Visioning
▶ Workshop

This section describes an intensive research-based design process to examine the current and emerging needs of the Minnesota Center for Arts Education and to define the capital projects required to address those needs. In contrast to current educational facility planning models, a rigorous on-site data collection process formed the basis for stating justifiable needs and their corresponding costs. For three days, staff, students, parents, and clients of the resource programs division articulated deficiencies, needs, and dreams and designed what they considered to be "ideal" spaces. The workshop began with a walk-through evaluation consisting of student and faculty interviews. An assessment of each space recorded on a Spatial Data Inventory Form determined the adequacy of space, lighting, acoustics, temperature, flexibility of use, aesthetic appeal, functional requirements, and floor area. An analysis of these data affected the development of the spatial requirements needed for subsequent stages of the process. Working in small groups, 200 participants developed 39 proposals for their new facility, using a site plan of the campus, a floor plan of each building, a listing of required areas for each space, and their graphic symbols. Proposals included changes in the present use, expansion of existing buildings, additional floors, and the creation of new buildings. A content analysis of the walk-throughs, interviews, and recommendations generated by the participating teams influenced the development of three proposals developed by the design team, one of which received unanimous support from students and faculty.

In 1990 the state of Minnesota purchased a 33-acre campus of the former Golden Valley Lutheran College for use by the Minnesota Center for Arts Education (MCAE). The present campus consists of a main administrative/classroom building, a secondary classroom building (GAIA), and three dormitories (Alpha, Beta, and Gamma) surrounding an existing pond. Although some remodeling had been done to convert the junior college campus to an arts high school and outreach educational resource center, the facilities remained totally inadequate.

In the fall of 1994, the North Central Association, which is the organization responsible for the accreditation of Minnesota schools, visited the arts high school as part of its accreditation review cycle. One of the committee's major findings was the inadequacy of school facilities, in both quality and quantity. Although lauding the staff for making creative use of the limited spaces, the committee concluded that physical constraints and the forced sharing of space for incompatible functions were restricting curricular focus and potential and displacing students from the classroom. Spatial limitations required that all major performances be conducted off-site, which is expensive and logistically difficult, creating safety hazards and exacerbating conflict. Several research studies have concluded that educational building conditions are hurting student performance (Goldberg and Bee, 1991). Similarly, a recent Carnegie Foundation study (1988) found that student attitudes about education are a direct reflection of their learning environment. Current educational planning models have not effectively accounted for the social, economic, and political factors affecting the appropriate design of school buildings (Moore and Lackney, 1993). Consequently, new models of the facility planning process are required to accommodate needed changes in school buildings.

In the spring of 1995, the Minnesota Center for Arts Education undertook a research-based design process to examine its current and emerging needs and to define the capital projects required to adequately address those needs. The architectural firm of the Adams Group and design research consultant Henry Sanoff were selected to lead the process because of their significant experience in the participatory design processes they employ to obtain information used in developing capital recommendations. For three days, all Center staff, students, some parents from the parent advisory committee, and clients of the resource programs division articulated deficiencies, needs, and dreams and designed what they considered to be "ideal" spaces.

Environment-behavior research has relied heavily on detailed case studies because they answer the "how" and "why" questions and because of their unique ability to deal with the full range of evidence. Case studies allow the investigation of phenomena in real-life contexts where multiple sources of evidence are needed for the assessment of multicausal events (Sanoff, 1994). Assessment of building performance is necessary to correct unforeseen problems as well as to justify new construction or the remodeling of existing buildings. There are several categorical approaches to building evaluation. Each approach differs as to the time, resources, and personnel required to execute a successful assessment (Preiser, Rabinowitz, and White, 1988). The main tasks are to generate new ideas to aid in a programming process and to provide data for an open-ended search to increase knowledge about a setting (Sanoff, 1989; Wener, 1989). In addition, for the MCAE, the major benefit of a postoccupancy evaluation (POE) is its effectiveness in establishing a justifiable project cost, particularly when many state agencies are competing with each other for the same resources.

The POE framework includes the client-user, the physical setting, including the functional requirements and user satisfaction, the immediate environmental context, and the social/historical context. On the basis of the distinct POE levels of effort—*indicative, investigative,* and *diagnostic* (Preiser, Rabinowitz, and White, 1988)—the indicative level strategy was employed. This type of POE provides an indication of major failures and successes of a building's performance and can easily be carried out in a short period of time. One approach to generating information quickly is described as a walk-through evaluation that provides an audit of building performance. A walk-through evaluation and interviews constitute the first part of the on-site visit, which concludes with a summary of indicators of successful and unsuccessful building features.

An assessment profile generated from touring interviews with relevant users expands participation opportunities when integrated into the design process. Clearly, different types of expertise reside with people affected by design decisions and with those who influence design decisions. Building users such as teaching staff and students are experts in identifying unsuccessful building features. Their involvement resulted in a greater meeting of social and functional needs and increasingly effective utilization of available resources. Eliciting teacher and student involvement is more effective in seeking satisfaction than simply responding to building ailments identified during the POE process. This collaborative effort is aimed at solving the problems identified in the POE process and determining what should be accomplished. Teacher and student participation in planning for the future of the MCAE allowed their recommendations to directly influence the development of the campus master plan.

A POE conducted on Day 1 included an on-site data collection process aimed at identifying the major failures and successes of the building's performance. This required organizing all parties to be involved in the POE and the development of a research plan. Prior to the site visit, drawings of the campus plan were obtained, as well as complete documentation of the curriculum goals and factors affecting the demand for new and improved facilities. Data-recording sheets used in the assessment included such information as locational requirements, functional requirements, a floor plan, and the area of each existing space.

Two teams of two designers each had specific assignments regarding the parts of the campus they would assess. A schedule developed for the on-site data collection process allowed each team to meet with staff, faculty, and students in their respective workplaces to discuss and assess spatial adequacy. The walk-through assessment process required $4\frac{1}{2}$ hours on Day 1 to complete a review of all campus buildings.

A space planning exercise involving 200 students and 40 faculty members who worked collaboratively on a vision for their new campus was the agenda for Day 2. All participants assembled in the present performing arts area, where they received instructions about the planning process and the procedures to be followed in this exercise. A site plan, locating all existing buildings, and a floor plan of each building were prepared in advance by the architects. Lists of required areas developed from the interviews and walk-through evaluations provided additional information for the participants. Working in groups of five to eight people, student-faculty teams developed 39 proposals for their new facility, using sets of graphic symbols corresponding to the activity areas (Figure 3.14). These graphic props allowed participants to reconfigure the existing spaces in units of 100 square feet. Team members were responsible for analyzing the uses of existing buildings and proposing new functions if deemed appropriate. Not surprisingly, teams voluntarily formed according to their respective disciplines. Music students tended to group together, as did visual arts and performing arts students. Consequently, each group's bias was apparent in its solutions, as they had all experienced some

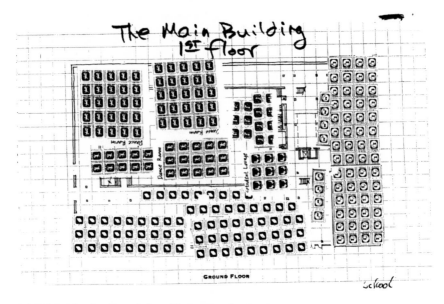

FIGURE 3.14 Graphic symbols used in the space planning process.

difficulties and inadequacies with their present working environments. The task required all groups to devote three hours to complete this phase of the planning process (Figure 3.15). The development of design alternatives constituted the activities of Day 3, with a final presentation on that evening, concluding the three-day intensive participatory process.

The interviews and walk-through assessment revealed a number of problems:

- There is overcrowding in the main building and the general computer lab.
- Classes are currently held in the cafeteria and in administrative conference rooms.
- Current music space has no rehearsal area, an inadequate number of practice rooms, a shortage of instructional space, and no acoustical treatment.
- Currently, painting and construction occurs within the theater itself; the dust and debris cause damage to lighting and sound equipment.
- Currently, performing students must use obsolete locker rooms that are poorly ventilated.
- The existing gallery area is often used by students as a spillover lounge and eating space, which jeopardizes the integrity of the artwork that is exhibited.
- A general lack of meeting space has compromised the outreach efforts, causing additional expense for locating programs off campus.

The space and site planning exercise allowed participants to consider the redistribution of all existing functions and to propose appropriate locations for

FIGURE 3.15 Work groups engaged in spatial planning. *(Photo: Henry Sanoff.)*

new uses. Considering that future space needs are double the available existing facilities, participants reconsidered the campus flow of movement in order to arrive at suitable locations for all functions.

The results of the space and site planning exercise revealed considerable insight, particularly about future campus development. A content analysis of the site drawings prepared by the 39 teams that participated in the exercise indicated that 38 percent of the teams proposed an expansion of the existing administration/classroom building, and several solutions proposed wrapping the existing building with new additions. Expansion of the area covered by Alpha and Beta dormitories represented the most substantial agreement. A majority (72 percent) of all teams noted the vicinity of the dorms as the most viable area for future expansion. Proposals for the reuse or expansion of that location included additional classrooms and dance, media, and performance areas.

The existing two-story administration/classroom building has at its core the theater/dance studio. Although there were several competing uses proposed for this building, including classrooms, administration, library and dance studio, the major preference was for a visual arts area that included art studios and an adjacent gallery. Although theater and dance have similar performance requirements, it was evident from the responses that their present location was ill suited for both to function simultaneously. Similarly, an atrium with skylights was a recurring theme for the building core, especially at the second floor, overlooking a dance studio or visual arts area.

Music students voiced concern about being isolated from other arts activities and attempted to relocate themselves centrally rather than remain in the GAIA building. The resource staff, who are presently without an identifiable workspace, opted for the GAIA building, which presently houses the music program, to locate resource programs and teacher education. Although teacher education is a major community effort of the MCAE, a majority of the student responses indicated a lack of awareness of the Center's outreach function and spatial requirements, as the school administration tended to place outreach personnel in a variety of unsuitable campus locations.

An analysis of the spatial organization results led to the development of three conceptual design alternatives. Each of the alternatives embodied the ideas expressed in the student/faculty space planning exercise. All proposals included the removal of the Alpha dorm to allow for the expansion of the existing administration/classroom building. Scheme 1 located a new theater arts building to the west of the existing administration building. Scheme 2 located a new arts complex to the east of the administration building. Both schemes maintained the campus character of disconnected buildings. Scheme 3 wrapped the existing building with new functions to alter the building's image, using a classroom wing to connect the Beta dorm to the expansion of the main building, thus changing the overall character of the campus.

Plan drawings and models for each design alternative allowed the faculty to compare and evaluate the schemes. The previous day's experience of manipulating the building on the site prepared the participants to comprehend technical site drawings. Consequently, faculty quickly arrived at consensus about their preferred solution, Scheme 3 (Figure 3.16). Their agreement resulted from the ability to fund this scheme in several stages, as legislative appropriations favor staged development of projects. Because the final day of this intensive process was a Saturday, the students were not available for the presentation, having returned to their homes for the weekend. Students reviewed the plan drawings and models displayed in the school gallery when they returned on Monday. Responses as to their preferences for the three design schemes indicated complete agreement with the selection of the faculty, albeit for different reasons.

Key strategic goals of the MCAE include alleviating overcrowded conditions, increasing enrollments, expanding and improving class offerings in functionally appropriate spaces, accommodating students' informal social needs, preserving Center assets and resources, meeting the needs of teachers statewide, encouraging community access, and providing safe and secure buildings that comply with all applicable codes. This project addresses all of these goals with the following outcomes:

- Alleviation of overcrowding in the main building by moving mathematics classes currently held in the cafeteria and language and literary arts classes held in administrative conference rooms, into spaces designed for instructional purposes.

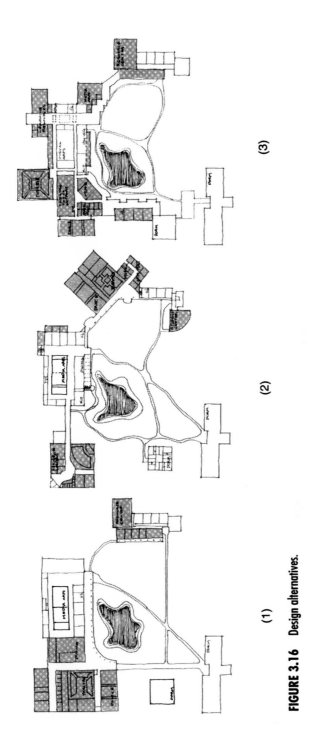

(1)   (2)   (3)

FIGURE 3.16   Design alternatives.

147

- Alleviation of overcrowding in the general computer lab in the main building by incorporating some computer capacity into the new classrooms.
- Provision of music and literary arts spaces that are more conducive to these art forms and allow for capacity enrollment and anticipated expansion.
- Provision of costume design, set construction, and storage space independent from the theater performance area.

The proposed master plan for the MCAE allows for expansion to occur in phases in order to achieve a cohesive campus plan and accommodate an increased student population of 300 to 400 students. The area necessary to meet the diverse space requirements is approximately two times the present area.

All new development is proposed to occur around the existing administration building, which will be expanded to include a new performing arts theater, dance studios, music rehearsal, and technical support area. This addition will also contain new science classrooms, laboratory areas, and classrooms for literary arts, social studies, and communications, to be located adjacent to the northwest corner of the existing facility.

A learning resource center and media arts complex are proposed for the opposite corner of the administration building. A new entry will connect these facilities with the existing classroom building, which will be expanded to include large group meeting areas and instructional studios for the teacher education center.

The final report summarizing the planning process included an evaluation of the existing facilities, a comprehensive architectural program, a phased capital budget plan, and probable construction costs. A separate document prepared for legislative review and subsequent funding for 1996 presented the participatory process and the justification for the capital requests at a legislative hearing in Minneapolis. Acknowledging this to be an exemplary, well-documented process, the legislature awarded $7 million to the MCAE for the first phase of construction, consisting of a new building, adjacent to the administration/classroom building, with space for music, literary arts, science, social studies, and communications. This new instructional resources facility allows the GAIA building to be vacated and available for use by resource programs for teacher education.

Design Phase

The Adams Group, along with several Minnesota architectural firms, was shortlisted for the design of the new facility. Based on the success of the participatory process employed during the first stage of this project, The Adams Group teamed up with the Minnesota architectural firm of Armstrong Torseth Skold and Rydeen and was awarded the contract to design the new performing arts building. To facilitate the decision-making process for implementing the first phase of construction, an advisory committee was established, consisting of faculty, staff, students, and parents. During the elapsed two years, the students participating in the first phase of the project had graduated and there was a new student body. Although it was expected that their full participation would be solicited for this phase of the project, it was equally important not to repeat the issues that were agreed upon during phase one. A second workshop was conducted with students, faculty, and staff to initiate the building design phase by proposing alternative design solutions according to criteria established by the newly formed building advisory committee. Criteria for evaluation were stated in the form of seven questions, whereby participants were required to select the most satisfactory design alternative:

- Which layout has the best location for the entrance?
- Which layout has the best circulation connecting the old and new buildings?
- Which layout provides the best security for people and property?
- Which layout creates the best informal gathering spaces for students and faculty?
- Which layout has the best arrangement for classrooms?
- Which layout has the best location for the music performance hall?
- Which layout do you like best?

Not surprisingly, more than 80 percent of the responses selected Scheme A, a design solution similar to the proposal selected during the first phase of the master planning process (Figure 3.17). With substantial agreement among students, staff, and parents, the process of designing the building began. Discussions between the architect and staff members continued as detailed space requirements

FIGURE 3.17   Alternative proposals evaluated by work groups.

FIGURE 3.18   Model of proposed facility. *(Model: Graham Adams.)*

were developed to meet the needs of the teaching staff. Computer simulations and three-dimensional models were developed to allow staff and students to visualize all elements of the building (Figure 3.18). Construction documents were prepared, reviewed, and approved by all participating agencies, and construction began in the summer of 1998.

Minnesota Academies for the Blind and the Deaf

Charrette Process   Participatory action research
Community action planning   Public forum
► Focus groups   ► Strategic planning
► Game simulation   Visioning
► Goal setting   ► Workshop
► Group interaction

In the winter of 1997, the Minnesota Academies for the Blind and the Deaf undertook a master planning process to examine the current and emerging needs of both campuses and to define the capital projects that would be required to ade-

quately address those needs. The architectural firm of the Adams Group in Charlotte, North Carolina, and design consultant Henry Sanoff were selected to lead the
process because of their significant experience in school design and the participatory predesign strategies they employ to obtain information used in developing
capital recommendations. The Academies campuses are located within a mile of
each other. For three days staff and students of the Minnesota State Academy of
the Blind (MSAB) and the Minnesota State Academy of the Deaf (MSAD) articulated deficiencies, needs, and desires and designed what they considered to be ideal
spaces for their respective campuses.

Academy for the Blind

The Minnesota State Academy for the Blind is presently located in a collection of
five buildings constructed during the past 60 years. Current changes in the campus
include the demolition of Dow Hall and its conversion to a memorial and additional parking space. The master planning process seeks to group functionally
related areas, to allow for the expansion of growth areas, and to improve pedestrian and vehicular access and movement around the campus.

The workshop began with a walk-through evaluation consisting of staff
interviews and assessments of major spaces of all campus buildings. A Spatial Data
Inventory Form was prepared to assess the adequacy of floor area and functional
requirements, using a floor plan of each building (Figure 3.19). On the following
day the school community was involved in identifying problems and prospects for
the campus. A group of 23 students met with a member of the design team. In an
open-ended discussion, describing their likes and dislikes, students commented
about their need for a place of their own to hold meetings and socialize. They
noted inadequate study places in the dorm and the poor arrangement of rooms
that did not allow for the needs of blind students. The lack of weather-protected
connections between buildings was also cited as a hardship for blind students.

Staff were given a site plan locating all existing buildings, a floor plan of the
main administration/classroom building (Lyson Learning Center), and scaled
cutouts of all needed spaces. Working in small groups of about 5 people, more
than 50 staff members developed ten proposals for improving the campus plan.
Many ideas were proposed for connecting the Lyson building with the activity
building (pool and gym) and creating a new entrance to the school.

An analysis of current and future activities at the Academy revealed the need for
improvement in three main areas: academic learning, vocational learning, and residential life. Through a series of six renovation and expansion projects, the campus will
have the needed improvements in all campus functions, including education, vocational training, physical fitness, residential life administration, and maintenance.

The administrative areas, health and physiotherapy rooms, and science classrooms will be combined to form a new building connecting the Lyson Learning
Center and the Gillan Activity Center. This new facility will allow for the expansion
of academic classrooms, a computer classroom, and a student activity room

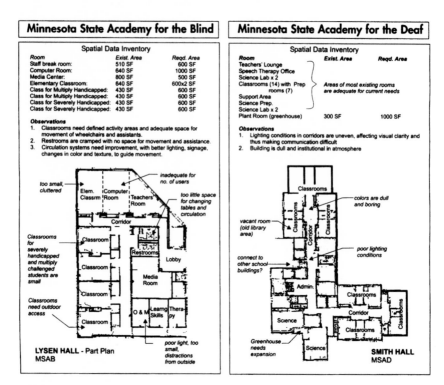

FIGURE 3.19 Spatial data inventory form.

(Gopher's Burrow) in the Lyson Learning Center. The new connector building will form a clearly visible entrance to the two main activity centers on the campus. Physical training and recreation programs will be augmented by the addition of a new wrestling area renovation of the shower and locker area. Residential improvements include new study halls and physical activity areas built between dormitory wings, and the construction of a new residential wing. West Cottage will be renovated to accommodate student needs for independent living. The industrial building will be renovated entirely for vocational training, with workshops for woodworking, metalwork, graphics, and science. Overall site improvements will include modifications to existing driveways to improve vehicular movement, new parking areas, new drop-off areas adjacent to academic areas, and improvements in safety crossings.

Academy for the Deaf

The Minnesota State Academy for the Deaf is presently located in several historically significant buildings constructed around an open landscaped area. In response to current and future needs at the Academy, the master planning process focused on improving residential life and vocational training at the campus. The workshop began with a walk-through evaluation consisting of staff interviews and assessments of major spaces of all campus buildings. A Spatial Data Inventory Form was prepared to assess the adequacy of floor area and functional requirements, using a floor plan of each building. On the following day, the school community was involved in identifying problems and prospects for the campus. A group of 30 students met with a member of the design team. In an open-ended discussion, students commented about the small dormitory rooms that lack privacy, the lack of vocational programs tailored to their needs, and the need for a recreational center (Figure 3.20). They view the inadequate gymnasium and lack of a swimming pool as limitations to their personal skill development and fitness. Students also commented that the present auditorium was not suitable for communicating through sign language because the floor is not sloped.

Staff were also organized into discussion groups of 30 people each. Using the nominal group technique (NGT), each participant was asked to identify and defend his or her two most important concerns for the future of the campus. Results from the staff discussion groups revealed that an important need was for an industrial life skills learning center to provide students with a wider range of careers once they leave the school. Staff also agreed that an upgrade of Frechette Hall, the boys' dormitory, was long overdue. Cramped conditions lead to inappropriate behaviors, conflict, and disagreements between students that create discipline concerns. The limited gymnasium facilities allow for only one team sport at a time. Consequently, many students have no team sports available, and special needs students never get gym time. A swimming pool was identified as a require-

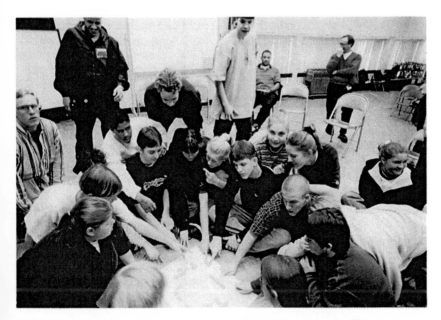

FIGURE 3.20   Students reviewing plans of existing buildings. *(Photo: Henry Sanoff.)*

ment for deaf students to receive swimming instructions in sign language, as well as to allow for intramural competition, exercise, and recreation.

The renovation of the overcrowded Frechette dormitory will allow for a reduction in the number of students in each room. It will require reworking the bathroom facilities and attaching additional activity rooms for skill development and group games. Tate Hall requires a reorganization of the Living Skills Training Center and shower facilities. Expanded training in independent living will be provided by renovating areas in Pollard and Tate Halls to create apartments for groups of three to four students each. An analysis of campus facilities also suggests the need for a recreational center adjacent to the present gymnasium. This new facility will include a fitness center, weight training, practice courts, and swimming pool. This will vastly expand the opportunities for recreation and physical fitness training at the campus.

Updating technology and introducing contemporary programs in photography, printing, and auto maintenance will expand opportunities for vocational training at the Academy. The industrial building, Mott Hall, will undergo significant renovations to meet these new requirements. Overall site improvements will include new parking areas, new drop-off areas adjacent to academic and residential areas, and improvements in safety crossings.

Eleven projects were identified and prioritized for the two campuses and the process was organized into a series of two-year increments and submitted to the Minnesota State Department of Finance for review (Figure 3.21). The Department of Finance in conjunction with the Department of Administration in the Division of State Building Construction reviews and prioritizes all applications before sending them on to the governor's office, where they become the recommended Capital Bonding Bill. The Minnesota Academies received a legislative appropriation of $9 million for academic expansion and campus improvement projects.

Montagnard Cultural Center

Charrette Process
Community action planning
▶ Focus groups
▶ Game simulation
▶ Goal setting
▶ Group interaction

Participatory action research
Public forum
Strategic planning
Visioning
▶ Workshop

A number of recent refugees from Vietnam formed an organization and proposed to construct a cultural center to preserve and document their way of life and to educate the surrounding community to their cultural uniqueness.

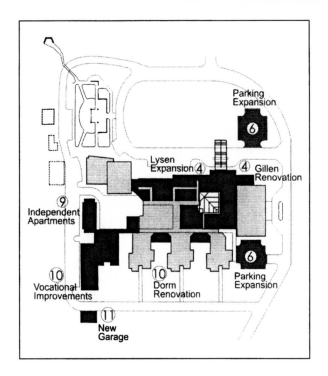

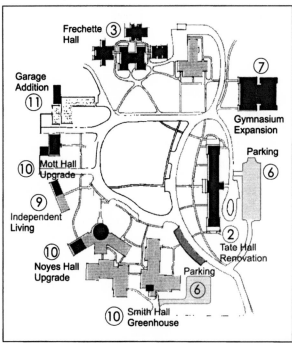

FIGURE 3.21 Proposed master plans for the Academy of the Blind *(top)* and the Academy of the Deaf *(bottom)*.

The highlands of Vietnam have been the setting for the Montagnard tribes, who claim they were the first inhabitants of that area. Ethnologists maintain that their Polynesian heritage is distinctly different from that of the Vietnamese residing in the low-lying areas of the county. The ravages of the Vietnamese conflict, however, led many of the Montagnards to their exodus from the highlands to North Carolina, where there are approximately 1,200 refugees who meet annually to renew friendships and share memories and visions for the future.

A major distinction between refugees and immigrants lies in their ability to prepare for and accept the difficulties in relocation. Immigrants often make extensive plans before their move to a new nation. Refugees' exodus is a traumatic experience. They have very little chance to plan for their new life. For example, more than half of the first wave of Vietnamese refugees to arrive in the United States had less than 24 hours to prepare (Gold, 1992). Refugees often encounter special problems in constructing new meanings for their lives. They have the potential to merge with the dominant culture, to create their own ethnic communities, or to engage in some combination of both activities. They must recreate their relations of kinship and community—frequently out of fragmented pieces—and attempt to maintain those ties even as their children rapidly accommodate to American culture (Haines, 1996). In the attempt to rebuild meaning, "many assert themselves by retaining and passing on traditions" (Gold, 1992, p. 200).

The Montagnard leaders in North Carolina and their design consultant, Holly Grubb (1997) of the Community Development Group, believe that a cultural-educational center can serve as a vehicle for cultural retention and learning. Recent studies attest to numerous benefits, such as social support, clearly defined roles and values, cultural preservation, and the economic and information resources that ethnic communities offer (Gold, 1992). Gold further describes the principle of "ethnic mobilization," a process whereby groups organize around some feature of ethnic identity in pursuit of collective ends. The idea of cultural memory, which requires an interactive process, rises to importance as a culture becomes more diffuse. Montagnard refugees tend to associate within small, intimate networks of family and friends. These groups reinforce social and economic ties between their members and build shared, situational interpretations of ethnic identity that reflect their common experience and concerns.

The Montagnard culture is composed of many different tribes, each with its own specific type of longhouse, where extended families co-exist under a single roof. Traditionally, tribal cultures display a continuity of building forms that express their beliefs and worldviews. A Montagnard cultural center can be a setting where people come together to share, which can be particularly important for this cultural group that is marked by diversity of region, immigration experience, religious outlook, ideology, and background. Such a facility will allow refugees to strengthen ties to the traditional culture as they cope with the pressures to assimilate in their new surroundings.

The goal of the project is to utilize the knowledge and involvement of the relocated mountain people as an integral component of the development of the center. An open discussion of the scope of the project, led by Holly Grubb, used focus groups to generate four primary purposes:

- To provide for the children
- To teach Americans
- To bring different tribes together
- To have a place for everyone

Although there are tribal differences, there is a common understanding for the need to create a special place that will symbolically represent the future and reflect on the past. To clarify value differences between tribes, a survey of 50 respondents conducted at an annual Montagnard gathering revealed broad consensus for a cultural resource center and preferences for the activities to be included. From a list of cultural objectives generated by focus groups, 32 participants identified those most important and linked them to activities that could occur in the cultural center.

Unique to the Montagnard culture is the collective house that represents the communal life of the tribes. This is in contrast to the village with its family dwellings, public edifices, chief's house, and the like. The Montagnard longhouse is connected to the symbolic aspects of the dwelling and to the coexistence of extended families under a single roof.

In a subsequent workshop, 21 participants made drawings of buildings reflecting their culture and developed floor plans identifying and locating the most important activities. The majority of the drawings were three-dimensional views reflecting the traditional tribal building form, the longhouse, with a 45-degree roof pitch (Figure 3.22). The floor plans were all arranged along a north-south axis, with a large social gathering space located at the main entrance. Smaller private spaces were aligned on one wall, arranged repetitively along the length of the building adjacent to a long hallway.

The key activity spaces designated by participants at the annual gathering were as follows:

- Large gathering space
- Teaching gallery
- Remembrance area
- Cultural exploration area
- Cultural discovery area
- Vocational activity area

In addition to the key areas, service and production spaces were also identified. Focus groups were instrumental in developing a flow analysis of preferred relationships between spaces, as well as the design requirements for each space. The same Montagnard focus groups responded to a visual preference survey depicting six variations of longhouse buildings (Figure 3.23), in which they ranked each according to their preference. Although this exercise elicited opinions, it also

DESIGN ELEMENTS

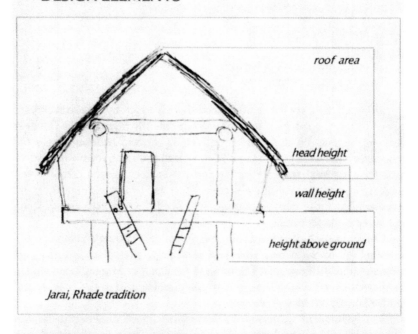

Jarai, Rhade tradition

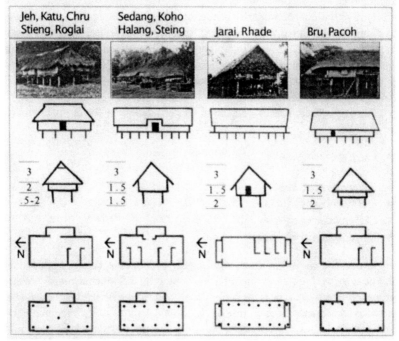

FIGURE 3.22 Typical participants' drawing of a tribal house.

Please respond on the sheet provided:
Indicate which image you prefer. Also, please commented on the features that
are seen as noteworthy.

FIGURE 3.23 Variations of longhouse buildings.

raised the participants' sensitivity to issues related to a building's image. The most preferred image corresponded to picture "A" because of its roof shape and height off the ground. Picture "F" received positive responses to its openness and raised platform, and "B" was least preferred because it was not open enough.

Knowledge of the Montagnards' requirements generated from the workshops provided the basis for developing design alternatives for the cultural center that represented the spirit of the community. The key factor in considering the overall site design of the facility was the location of outdoor areas in conjunction with the teaching and cultural discovery functions. A structured assessment process involving the Montagnards helped the designer to arrive at an understanding of the ritual and flow of people through the site (Figure 3.24). The results of this assessment were instrumental in the development of the final design proposal, which was unanimously supported by the Montagnard community. Fundraising was begun, with the use of the project report and a three-dimensional model of the future facility to describe the intentions of the Montagnards.

CulturalOutreachCenter PREFERRED ARRANGEMENT

Please indicate which scheme you prefer with a check mark in the boxes provided.

1	2	3	
			Which scheme has the best location for the Large Gathering Area? Comments:
			Which scheme has the best location for the Teaching Gallery? Comments:
			Which scheme has the best location for the Vocational Activity Area? Comments:
			Which scheme has the best location for the Cultural Discovery Area? Comments:
			Which scheme has the best location for the Cultural Exploration Area? Comments:
			Which scheme has the best location for the Remembrance Area? Comments:
			Which scheme has the best arrangement for the Outdoor Areas? Comments:
			Which scheme lends itself best to be constructed in stages? Comments:
			Which scheme has the best arrangement overall? Comments:

FIGURE 3.24 Assessment schedule.

School Participatory Games

Relating Objectives for Learning to Education (ROLE)

This exercise helps to establish a dialogue between teachers, students, parents, administrators, and designers in the process of creating a new school or renovating an existing school. Participants are involved in exploring aspects of the school environment by considering alternative approaches to teaching and learning. Educational objectives and learning methods selected from the educational literature allow participants the possibility of discussing numerous options (Figure 3.25).

FIGURE 3.25 Educational objectives and learning methods. *(Reprinted, by permission, from Henry Sanoff, School Design, p. 189. Copyright 1994 by John Wiley & Sons, Inc.)*

They are introduced to stimulate a discussion about the purpose of learning and the types of physical settings that can enhance student learning. In planning for efficient and effective achievement of educational objectives, it is necessary to consider the following:

- *Learning methods* to be used to accomplish the objectives.
- *Role relationships* between student and teacher, whether student or teacher directed. The difference is primarily who makes the decision about the learning activity.
- *Settings* or *environments* in which learning methods will be accomplished.

The game is to be played by groups of three to five people. There is no limit to the number of possible groups in this exercise. To begin, each player individually selects, from the list provided, no more than four objectives that seem to be the most important. Brief notes should be made justifying each choice. After each player has made his or her choices, the individual lists are pooled. Through discussion, the group chooses from the aggregated list, no more than four objectives that are agreeable to all participants. Group members are urged to forcefully support their individual choices, even if other members did not make the same choices, until they convinced or are convinced by others that an objective should or should not be included in the final list. When consensus is reached, the group records its choices.

The game record sheet (Figure 3.26) is used to report the final decisions. Next, each objective should be examined to identify the appropriate learning methods necessary to accomplish it. Three learning methods should be selected for each objective. Individual choices are then pooled for a group discussion and consensus about four learning methods for each objective. Each learning method should be qualified as to whether it is teacher directed (TD) or child directed (CD). (*Note:* This approach has also been used in many non-English-speaking countries). Combining these two components—objectives and learning methods—the best setting (Figure 3.27) should be identified to fulfill the requirements established by the group. All decisions are to be noted on the game record sheet. A final discussion of all groups may consist of representatives from each group reporting their collective decisions, with a total group summation of all decisions.

Learning Environments for Children

Planning a children's center or playroom is a task requiring the specialized knowledge of the architect, as well as that of the early childhood teacher. The problem is similar to a child's puzzle. There are a number of pieces that must fit together in some logical manner. Unlike a puzzle, however, there is not only one correct solution or best fit of the puzzle pieces. The differences may stem from a variety of values, goals, and needs of teachers, parents, and communities. Yet the aspect common to all groups is the nature of the activities in which children of all ages engage, what they enjoy doing, and how they learn.

FIGURE 3.26 Record sheet. *(Reprinted, by permission, from Henry Sanoff, School Design, p. 189. Copyright 1994 by John Wiley & Sons, Inc.)*

Whereas goals are generalized statements about the overall purpose of an educational program, such as "To advance and develop the child's functioning knowledge of his or her environment," learning objectives are statements that describe the desired characteristics to be achieved by each child. From the goal statement, the following learning objectives might be generated:

Positive self image

Language development

FIGURE 3.27   Photographs of educational settings matched to learning methods.   *(Reprinted, by permission, from Henry Sanoff, School Design, pp. 190–191. Copyright 1994 by John Wiley & Sons, Inc.)*

FIGURE 3.27 (*Continued*)

An activity area or learning center is a place within the children's playroom, described by materials and boundaries, where particular learning experiences occur. The basic arrangement of the playroom is a function of the appropriate learning objectives and the organization of activity centers.

Planning appropriate environments for young children is a strategy for effectively accomplishing learning objectives. This interaction game process consists of three stages:

- Stating learning objectives
- Identifying and matching appropriate children's activity centers
- Planning the playroom or center

This structured experience can be used by groups of three to five people, although many groups can participate simultaneously. To begin, each person selects, from the list provided, no more than three objectives that seem to be most important for a particular age group, such as infants, toddlers, two-year-olds, and so on (Figure 3.28). The list of objectives has been culled from the early childhood literature. Through collaboration, the participants should agree to three statements that can be incorporated into a unified program for their age group. Then, two activity centers are identified where each objective can be accomplished. All decisions can be noted on the record sheet, as in the preceding exercise.

A series of learning objectives are listed on the right whose fulfillment will have a direct impact on the organization of the playroom. From the list select the three most important statements by placing a check mark adjacent to your choice.

This activity is best conducted by groups of between three and five people, where individual choices are made, defended, and where collective decisions are made as they pertain to specific age groups. The group decision making process allows participants to learn from each and strive to seek consensus as relevant options are explored.

For each of the agreed upon objectives, three learning centers should be selected, from the list on the right, for each objective.

LEARNING OBJECTIVES

__To develop a positive self-image
__To develop problem solving skills
__To develop sensory awareness
__To develop self-expression
__To develop eye/hand coordination
__To develop large/small muscles
__To develop oral language
__To develop communication skills
__To develop a sense of confidence
__To develop social skills
__To develop self-control
__To develop self-motivation
__To develop thinking ability
__To develop persistence toward a goal
__To develop a sense of responsibilty

LEARNING CENTERS

__Art
__Block play
__Construction
__Cooking
__Dramatic play
__Indoor active
__Listening
__Manipulative
__Math
__Music & Movement
__Reading/Pre-writing
__Sand/Water
__Science

FIGURE 3.28 Learning objectives and learning centers.

To allow the effective participation of individuals not familiar with the purposes of activity centers, short scenarios are provided for each group (Figure 3.29). In addition to a description of the activity centers, there is a list of learning objectives that can be achieved in each center. It may be evident that the same objective may be achieved by more than one activity center.

The activity symbols represent what is common to all children's centers. How they go together, or what symbols are included, may vary between partici-

Reading

If a preschool child is to meet with later success in learning and enjoying reading, then becoming aquainted with books should occur as early as possible. At this age, children are involved with learning a language and are fascinated with words and sounds. Language is the externalization of thoughts, and words symbolize concepts. Words, as language symbols then become a medium for the exchange of thoughts. This center should provide opportunities and encouragement for reading and dictating experiences.

 ## Music

Activites in the music and movement center allow children to experiment with and enjoy rhythmic and musical skills. The basic elements of music are sound and soundmaking. Making music and responding to it can enhance and integrate all areas of development. Singing is an important aid to the growth of language and can be used to introduce and reinforce concepts. Songs, using instruments and exploratory movement activities teach children to understand themselves, to be aware of their social environment and to value cultural diversity.

 ## Block Play

Block play is an area where building structures from blocks allow children to express themselves. Children use their structures in a realistic and imaginative manner. When children explore their ideas structurally, they observe physical principles and form concepts of size, weight, shape, and fit. In the process of using blocks to build structures, children deal with the spatial and structural problems of balance and enclosure. Moreover, they must use their newly formed concepts in making decisions about what to build and how to proceed in building. Block play enables children to learn how to work and cooperate with their peers and achieve the following learning objectives.

 ## Indoor Active

Young children develop a concept about themselves when they are able to move their whole body through space confidently. Body movement also lays the foundation for the development of concepts. An indoor active center can provide children with a variety of activities for the development of fundamental motor patterns and large muscle development. Climbing, balancing, skipping, hopping and jumping are several types of play that can occur in this center.

 ## Art

The art work of children is a visual expression of their feelings. In order to express these feelings visually, children must think about themselves, and their physical and social environment. The feelings they choose to express can result from direct involvement in home or school activities or from vicarious experiences in listening to stories and reading. With paint, crayons, markers, playdough, paste, paper, scissors, boxes and string children can represent things they've done, seen and imagined. Their main interest is in the process of experimentation rather than in the product.

 ## Dramatic Play

Fascinated by the experiences of everyday life, children enjoy interpreting these experiences and re-enacting them. They learn what it is like to be a mother, father, police officer, and what their peers feel about people in such roles. The importance of dramatic play lies in children's development in understanding themselves and others and in their gaining confidence that they can be whatever they wish to be. They begin to achieve the following learning objectives:

FIGURE 3.29 Activity scenarios.

pating groups. This exercise, however, can provide the preliminary steps in planning for physical changes.

Each of the symbol diagrams represents an activity center in the playroom, as well as activity areas in the children's center (Figure 3.30). Through comparisons

FIGURE 3.30 Graphic symbols of learning centers. *(Reprinted, by permission, from Henry Sanoff, School Design, p. 194. Copyright 1994 by John Wiley & Sons, Inc.)*

between the activity symbols it is possible to decide which centers should be adjacent to one another and which require some separation. To facilitate the planning process, a grid should be prepared to correspond with the size of the activity symbols (Figure 3.31). The sizes of the activity symbols correspond to the areas necessary for the activity centers, which usually accommodate two to four children.

SPATIAL LAYOUT GRID

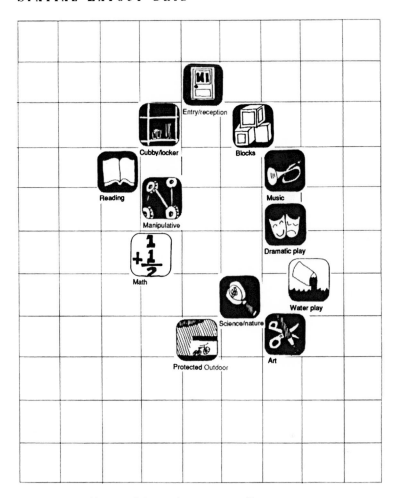

FIGURE 3.31 Spatial layout grid showing the organization of learning centers.

Therefore, the spaces between the symbols correspond to areas for movement and circulation. The rules for locating the symbols are as follows:

- Each activity symbol should be placed on a vacant grid.
- Symbols should not overlap or occupy more than one grid cell.
- Blank space between activity symbols should be provided for circulation.
- Activity centers should be located on the basis of their requirements for privacy, quiet, or accessibility to each other.

Although many of the activity centers appear to be related to each other, their placement will require a decision about which are the most important relationships. A final stage in the process explores the physical features of activity centers. Several drawings of different and unidentified centers are used to promote a discussion among participants about the appropriate character of the center and the image it evokes. Although the drawings are not intended to offer design solutions, they can be instrumental in increasing participants' awareness of the "silent messages" conveyed by the physical environment.

The shape and proportion of a playroom are important factors to be considered in planning the learning centers. There are several proposed playroom shapes that represent the range of possibilities (Figure 3.32). Each playroom con-

During this process you may need to modify your original decision for the location of the entrance to the playroom.

__Art
__Block play
__Cooking
__Construction
__Dramatic play
__Indoor active
__Listening
__Large group
__Manipulative
__Math
__Music & Movement
__Reading/Pre-writing
__Sand/Water
__Science

Finally, select the best shape for planning a flexible playroom by placing a check mark alongside the appropriate letter.

__A   __B   __C   __D

Please explain the reasons for your choice._____

Discuss your decisions with other members of your group and try to achieve consensus about your decision.

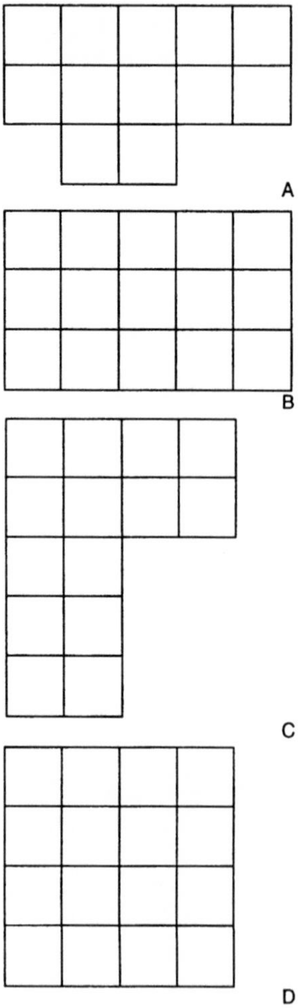

FIGURE 3.32 Classroom shapes.

tains the same floor area, with the floor grid divided into squares corresponding to 8 by 8 feet. One square approximates a learning center suitable for four children. From the list of learning centers, participants select six of the most appropriate and locate them in each playroom plan. When arranging the learning centers, they consider space for circulation between learning centers. Group members then discuss their conclusions about the most appropriate playroom shape. A similar exercise can be constructed for K-12 classrooms.

Classroom Environment Ratings

The physical assessment of classrooms can be accomplished by comparing user ratings of different settings employing the same descriptive statements, as well as by comparisons of the *actual* and the *ideal* classroom. The technique, identified as a Q-sort, consists of descriptive statements (which follow) printed on separate cards. Students sort the cards into piles according to the issue under consideration, such as "Most like my classroom" or "Most not like my classroom." This technique, which David (1982) describes as a Classroom Environment Q-sort, is most effective when it supplements other information-gathering approaches.

Classroom Environment Descriptive Statements

1. I have enough space to work without others crowding me.
2. My room has places where you can be by yourself if you want to.
3. I have a place of my own where I can keep my things.
4. In my room it's easy to concentrate on what you're doing.
5. I get to choose where I sit.
6. I can see everything that goes on in our room from where I sit.
7. I spend most of the day at my desk.
8. The furniture in my room is arranged to help us work together easily.
9. I feel as though I have a place here that belongs to me.
10. I can fix up my place the way I want it.
11. There are lots of good places to work in my room.
12. It's quiet enough for me in my room.
13. We often change the way my room is arranged.
14. My room is neatly arranged.
15. My room is clearly organized.
16. My room is just the right size for me—not too big and not too small.
17. My room is pleasant to look at.
18. My room is a special place for me.
19. There are lots of comfortable places in my room.
20. I get to help decide how our room will be arranged.
21. There are lots of interesting things to do in my room.
22. I get to help add things to my room to make it even better.
23. There are places for me to display my work.

Planning Outdoor Play

Planning for outdoor play is an integral part of the design process and a vital component of a child development center. Typically perceived as a staging area for large muscle development, the outdoor play area is not only important for the child's health but also contributes to the child's learning experiences (Threllfall, 1986). Outdoor play space offers opportunities for adventure, challenge, and wonder in the natural environment (Frost and Klein, 1983). The only substantial difference between indoor and outdoor activity is that one has a roof over it. Both, however, need architectural and landscape definition, and both must provide for the multiplicity of children's developmental needs. For example, a play yard with 12 tricycles, a rocking boat, a tumble tub, a jungle gym, a dirt area, and a sand table with water, has 17 separate play units but only four different kinds of things to do (Kritchevsky, Prescott, and Walling, 1974). Variety can be an important measure of interest. Moreover, complexity, or the number of subparts of a piece of equipment, such as a sandbox with play materials, water, climbing boards, and crates, can increase a child's interest.

The process of creating outdoor play spaces is age-group oriented and begins with developmental objectives that help to generate the activities in which children engage (Sanoff, 1994). The teaching staff and design team work together to establish linkages between objectives for outdoor play, the related children's activities, and the play settings required.

To complement the indoor environment, the outdoors provides play settings that stress muscle development as well as natural settings that provide experience in the life cycle of plants and animals. The props used to enable the teachers to make spatial decisions include drawings of different play settings as well as statements of objectives and lists of activities. The planning group moves through a series of collaborative stages in which all members should reach consensus. Finally, the activities and play settings are organized into play zones that range from passive to active play, and from private to group activities (Sanoff, 1994). This part of the planning process helps to generate discussions about the purpose of outdoor play, usually dispelling many of the myths about large muscle development as the primary purpose of children's outdoor activities.

Learning objectives for outdoor play are discussed in a similar way as those in the planning of playrooms. Objectives such as problem solving, concept development, and social development are key concerns of the teachers. Supporting activities like role playing, climbing, feeling and handling, balancing, sliding, and construction constitute the array of choices most frequently made. As a result of making these linkages, the subsequent choice of play equipment and play areas is based on a clear understanding of the developmental needs that the outdoor play area should serve. Other types of individual or quiet activities, group games, and opportunities for exercising imagination are also appropriate for outdoor use, but may not necessarily require the construction of special equipment.

An analysis of the building site and its topography can influence the location and options for various play settings. A site map should be used as the basis for planning areas where play settings can be clustered according to similarity of requirements. Play zones include areas for drama, nature, adventure, and large muscle development. Equipment and zone choices are then related to specific site requirements, such as solar orientation.

Planning outdoor play is a method of facilitating the design of children's outdoor play areas. Participants involved in the playroom exercise can continue planning for their age groups in an outdoor area contiguous to their playroom. Using the same list of educational objectives employed in playroom planning, participants may select three, using the same consensus decision-making process. Each objective is matched to three outdoor activities from the expanded list (Figure 3.33). The selected activities can then be used to identify the appropriate graphic symbols (Figure 3.34). When all the outdoor play symbols are selected, they can then be organized into play zones (Figure 3.35). The setting drawings, which range from active to passive play and private to group activities, are provided to aid in visualizing how the activities can be spatially organized according to the symbol diagram. Establishing zones is a planning strategy for enabling activities with similar requirements to be clustered together.

Role-Playing

Direct human involvement in decision making integrates thought and action. Yet with increasing participation comes the inevitability of conflict resulting from value differences between participants. An effective approach to solve a problem within a controlled set of circumstances can be achieved through role-playing, in which a plot or basic conflict situation is designed. Information is given to each participant in the form of a profile that describes a character and the factors influencing the player's behavior. A scenario describes the setting in which the role-playing activity will occur. In a free role play, as compared with a structured event with rules, participants begin interacting immediately after receiving the profiles and the scenario.

For example, a school building committee with broad-based representation from the administration, the teaching staff, parents and students, and the architect has the potential for conflict during many stages in the design process, particularly in the earliest stages of establishing educational goals. From the architect's point of view, one of the main objectives of a role-playing simulation is to prepare the design team for the unexpected conflicts that may occur during community meetings.

Typical profiles for the composition of a sample committee are shown in the following list. The scenario can identify the purpose of the meeting, with a playing time limited to one to two hours. An observer can lead a follow-up discussion with

ACTIVITIES (What children do outdoors)

Select three activities from the list that satisfies each objective. As a group, discuss the individual selections and record those reached by consensus.

OUTDOOR ACTIVITIES

__Swinging
__Role Playing
__Throwing and Catching
__Digging
__Balancing
__Climbing
__Pouring-Splashing
__Stretching
__Crawling
__Feeling and Handling
__Body Contact w/ Animals
__Painting
__Sliding
__Constructing
__Vehicular Motion
__Dressing Up
__Mixing
__Cooking
__Sitting

Objective A

Activity 1. _____
Activity 2. _____
Activity 3. _____

Objective B

Activity 1. _____
Activity 2. _____
Activity 3. _____

Objective C

Activity 1. _____
Activity 2. _____
Activity 3. _____

Objective D

Activity 1. _____
Activity 2. _____
Activity 3. _____

FIGURE 3.33 Outdoor activities matched to objectives.

the participants to ask several questions. What kinds of decisions were made? What influenced the decisions made? What did the participants learn? What did they feel they had done wrong? Were conflicts successfully resolved? How closely did the role-playing situation approximate a real one?

GRAPHIC SYMBOLS FOR OUTDOOR PLAY ▬▬▬▬▬

FIGURE 3.34   Graphic symbols for outdoor play.

Profiles of Committee Members for an Alternative School

Parent No. 1: You believe that the public schools do not understand your child. She does not get along with her teachers. They pick on her for things she does not do and accuse her wrongly. You think that with smaller classes and better teachers, your child will be better understood and do well.

Parent No. 2: You are seeking a school where your child can be with children of his own social level. The typical public school exposes your child to children you would not want him to become involved with—children not of his own kind.

Parent No. 3: You are seeking a school where your child would have better academic opportunities. You are interested in your child's being a high achiever, getting good grades so she can succeed in life.

Parent No. 4: You, the doctor, feel that academic achievement is of utmost importance. There should be an emphasis on learning facts and information, instead of all this freedom of the child's pursuing his or her own interests. Your child should learn and get good grades so he can get into a good university.

EXAMPLES OF GRAPHIC SYMBOLS ORGANIZED INTO PLAY ZONES

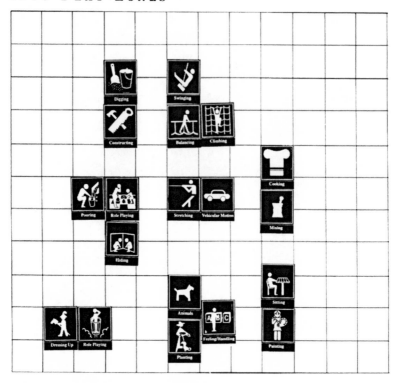

FIGURE 3.35 Graphic symbols organized into play zones.

Parent No. 5: You, as a builder, are concerned with building cost. To you, a good school means sound brick construction for a low price. You will support most ideas about education as long as they do not interfere with the creation of a sound building.

Student No. 1: You believe it is important to have personal control over your daily activities and to be involved in group projects.

Student No. 2: You believe that an athletic program is a basic need for a good educational program, because it builds healthy bodies and healthy minds.

Teacher No. 1: You believe in a strict schedule, whereby all children do all their activities together, are assigned tasks, and must fulfill their assignments.

Teacher No. 2: You believe that with appropriate materials and guidance in their use, children can proceed according to their own rates and interests.

They are free to question the teacher and ask for help when needed. Children can move about freely with the teacher's permission.

Architect: You are designing a school for this community. To successfully achieve this end, you must find out from this representative group what the educational objectives are. The objectives of the participants' ideas may conflict. Your role is to direct the group to reach some agreement about their goals.

Principal: You believe that education is self-directed. Each child pursues his or her interests at his or her own rate of development. Each child receives individual instruction as required.

In addition to the analytic component of a role-play simulation, there is an emotional, dramatic element as well. Participants openly express their beliefs and opinions, all of which are a reflection of their attitudes and values. The recognition of value differences that generate conflict early in the planning process enables designers to identify means for reconciliation of those differences. Conflicts can be resolved when dissenting participants are asked to restate ideas they oppose by identifying and stating the positive features of those ideas. This procedure attempts to maintain a positive discussion while enhancing individual listening skills.

Role-playing games can enable participants to analyze and practice solving specific problems that arise during the school design process. They simulate the communication of information and decisions in the actual situation in which they may be employed (Abt, 1970).

Photo Questionnaires

Buildings and spaces convey messages reflecting the inner life, activities, and social values of the users. Characteristics like shape, color, and arrangement enable people to make vivid mental images of the environment. These environmental cues have something to say about the people who occupy the buildings as well as about the people who created them. Similarly, people read these cues, make judgments, and act accordingly. These messages play an important role in people's comprehension of the environment. Specific environments can be evaluated as to the appropriateness of the messages conveyed. An effective method for eliciting responses to the environment is the use of visual prompts, such as drawings, photographs, and video recordings.

Photo questionnaires and interviews are also effective means to elicit evaluative comments about physical settings. People interpret the identity and meaning of their environment from the interaction of, and their interaction with, a wide variety of physical features. In the school environment there are a variety of inside and outside places that evoke either good or bad feelings (Figures 3.36a and 3.36b).

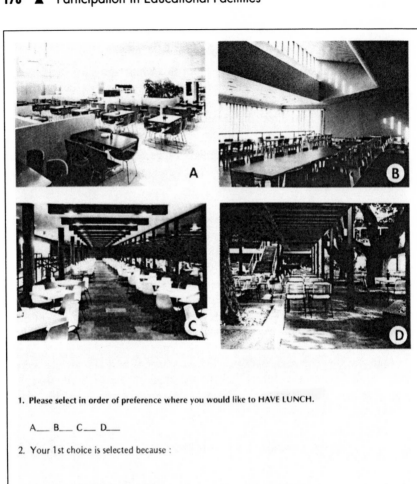

1. Please select in order of preference where you would like to HAVE LUNCH.

   A___ B___ C___ D___

2. Your 1st choice is selected because :

3. Your last choice is due to :

FIGURE 3.36a Photo questionnaire: Best location to have lunch. *(Reprinted, by permission, from Henry Sanoff, School Design, p. 203. Copyright 1994 by John Wiley & Sons, Inc.)*

Becoming aware of perceived environmental effects is a necessary first step in striking the delicate balance between familiarity and monotony and boredom, and between variety and confusion and disorientation. With understanding of how physical surroundings affect us psychologically, we can become more aware

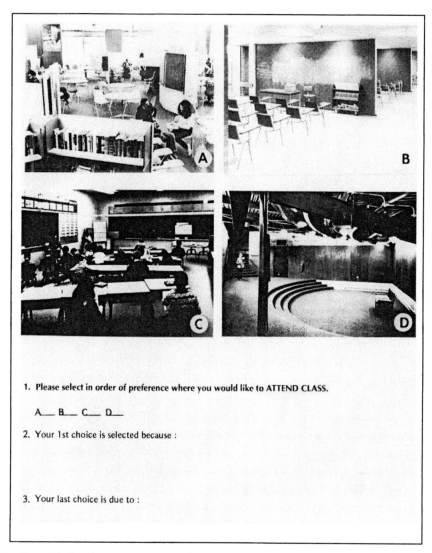

1. Please select in order of preference where you would like to ATTEND CLASS.

A____ B____ C____ D____

2. Your 1st choice is selected because :

3. Your last choice is due to :

FIGURE 3.36b Photo questionnaire: Best location to attend class. *(Reprinted, by permission, from Henry Sanoff, School Design, p. 201. Copyright 1994 by John Wiley & Sons, Inc.)*

of our effects on them, and on ourselves, when we allow them to be changed. We will then start to realize the importance of our concern for our surroundings and can eventually work toward the improvement of their quality.

CHAPTER

4

Participation in Housing

W ho decides what for whom is a central issue in housing and human settlement. John Turner, an advocate of self-determination, believes that when people are in control of decisions about the design, construction, and management of their housing, the process and product will enhance their social well-being. When people have no control over the housing process, the housing produced may instead become a barrier to achieving personal fulfillment and a burden on the economy.

People become invisible in the housing process to the extent that housing providers either do not see them at all or see them as stereotyped individuals. Yet this blindness is the result of a genuine desire to improve the living conditions of as many people as possible. Providers have a fixed idea of what is considered to be good housing and, consequently, discount the role of the dweller in the housing process. This contention is generally based on the assumption that public participation is inefficient and time-consuming, that people do not know what they want, or that people trained in housing know better about user needs than the users do. On the basis of these beliefs the housing needs of many people in the world have been reduced to specifications of codes and standards, however well intentioned they may be.

Housing is a complex world of cultural action and material practices, not merely an artifact. The symbolic meaning and use of the house varies greatly, not only between different cultures but also between different groups within a society (Duncan, 1985). Customs, habits, and classification of categories of the residents order its form and design. Moreover, its rooms or other kinds of spaces are usually classified, named, and used according to cultural and social conventions (Lawrence, 1989).

In most housing production systems, individual houses are often designed to be standard. Thus, families who differ greatly in their sociocultural needs live in houses designed for average family needs. These houses are built with the same walls, the same windows, the same-shaped bedrooms, and the same-shaped kitchens and bathrooms (Alexander, 1985). In recent years studies that discussed the importance of sociocultural factors in housing design and the failure of present housing policy to meet users' sociocultural needs have concluded the following:

- A house is not a thing that can be designed or built. It is the result of a housing process. The important act in this process is that of the user who lives there. The act of living there is the only act that makes a house something special. If the house is not a thing but an act, the act (user) becomes important (Habraken, 1986).
- Users are far more accepting of what they have designed and built than that which has been built by someone else (Hardie, 1988).
- In most societies a house is more than a physical structure. It has a social and cultural value, whose shape is often determined by cultural tradition. So, housing options have to be socially, economically, and culturally more appropriate than those generated by theories of housing development tied to fixed notions, static formulas, and ideological commitments rooted in Western industrial society (Sanoff, 1988).
- Because housing providers place an emphasis on producing "units" to meet housing demands, there is an argument for the redefinition of housing problems as functions of mismatches between people's socioeconomic and cultural situations and their housing processes and products (Turner, 1977).

In opposition to institutional methods of housing delivery and the inability of public housing programs to meet housing demands, an informal housing system has emerged in many parts of the world. Informal housing varies from country to country and can include everything from well-constructed middle-income housing to cardboard shacks built in swamps, to multifamily housing, to occupied condemned and dilapidated buildings. Informal settlements are defined as spontaneous settlements, in reference to the absence of governmental aid and control; uncontrolled settlements, in reference to their lack of regulation; and shantytowns, in recognition of the fact that they are inhabited by low-income people. The appearance of informal settlements varies according to the availability of building materials, the finances of the squatters, and the prospects for continued possession.

The remarkable fact is that much of the world's housing is being produced and finished outside the institutional framework of the official, or subsidized, housing sector, often resulting in solutions that are both socially and economically more viable than much of the lowest-cost housing provided by public subsidy. The informal sector is able to build and does build houses suited to its needs and within income capacity. This housing is built by the owners themselves, often with the assistance of family and friends and with various amounts of hired help (Hamdi, 1991).

A more well-organized approach to housing the poor is referred to as self-help, which leads to a gradual improvement in housing on the basis of realistic standards and overall costs, as well as to generating income and employment within the physical and social infrastructure (Habitat, 1987). Habitat for Humanity employs the concept of mutual help, whereby people join together to achieve a common economic end through the formation of a democratically controlled business organization, making equitable contributions to the capital required and accepting a fair share of the risks and benefits of the undertaking (Habitat, 1987). People participate by providing the labor for the construction of their dwelling but are rarely involved in the planning and design stages. A basic assumption in human settlement planning is that because it is for the people, the people should participate in the planning and management of their housing. Opinions on who should participate, in what, and how, vary widely between and among project agencies, politicians, and residents.

Most of the U.S. government's housing programs have stipulated little or no role for citizens other than as users. Yet although residents have not had a mandated role in federal housing programs, they have not been passive bystanders. Dissatisfaction with federal housing programs, high housing costs, low vacancy rates, and inadequate supply have stimulated resident activism to improve living conditions. Today there are a variety of citizen-initiated programs that represent alternatives to the traditional methods of supplying housing. The following are types of citizen-initiated programs that have been used as models for nationally oriented programs (Bratt, 1987):

- Neighborhood services program
- Small-scale home ownership programs
- Tenant management of public housing
- Alternative management/ownership of private rental housing

Citizen-initiated housing programs have generally cycled through the stages of problem definition, program development, and implementation. A model of how bottom-up, citizen-initiated programs operate is as follows (Bratt, 1987):

- Identification of serious housing need.
- Action plan developed by community group.
- Community group receives financial and technical support from public and private sectors.
- Funding support maintained after program is initiated.
- Resident control and participation are maintained throughout the program.

- Consumer safeguards are incorporated into the program.

Bottom-up citizen participation processes reflect the actual needs and aspirations of the community and depend on continued citizen participation. Langton (1978) makes the distinction between this and top-down participation, which is government-initiated participation. Commonly referred to as citizen involvement, government initiates and controls participation through such activities as public hearings, consultation and attitudinal surveys, some of which citizens are obligated by law to participate. Langton suggests that those who are strongly committed to one viewpoint are often suspicious of the motives of those committed to another. Bratt suggests that the federal government should seek to develop top-down programs that are based on successful bottom-up programs.

Weller Street Housing Co-Op

A housing co-op, organized by eight young homemakers, allowed Liverpool's Weller Street residents to leave their deteriorated housing yet maintain the social networks established over several generations (McDonald, 1986). They were determined not to put up with the kind of life that went on in some of the outlying housing estates. This initial action group expanded its numbers to 62 households before it received legal recognition as a cooperative. The group included pensioners as well as families with children.

Realizing that there were technical and legal requirements it had to digest, the group formed several subcommittees, or working parties, that assumed responsibility for site and space planning, education and information, and fund-raising. The working parties quickly learned the language of the experts they consulted and persuaded the experts to express themselves more simply. Although co-op members had all had previous experience of dealing with officials, they believed their future dealings would be more effective as representatives of an organization. They also wanted to ensure that they were not merely informed but actually able to take part in all the key negotiations with the different departments of the city council, with the Housing Corporation, and with the Department of the Environment. Early on the co-op negotiated a development agreement with Co-operative Development Services to have complete control, to be informed at every step in the planning and design process, and to have the decisive word. The same applied to the choice of architects. The architectural firm was given a working brief that made it clear that at every stage its expert was to be "on tap but not on top."

There were delays in selecting an appropriate housing site, but when it was chosen the co-op held a carnival on the site. Members brought picks, shovels, and a pneumatic drill to open the site by digging out stone cobbles, later used to landscape the courtyards on the completed estate. During the construction phase co-op members frequently visited the site of their new homes and found the construction workers more committed to the project because they knew each family they were working for.

To produce a culturally responsive environment and to ensure acceptance as well as affordability of the end product, it is necessary for the community to be involved in the formulation and assessment of objectives. It is only through direct involvement that it is possible to obtain the views of the local community/end users when preparing project proposals.

Communal Housing

Participation is not an idea that originated in the twentieth century. The beginning settlements humans formed during their evolution were the result of community participation. Individuals grouped together in tribes to secure their basic needs—namely, food, clothes, shelter, and social contact. The life-style of living together in tribes lasted until the large-scale division of tasks and responsibilities emerged with the formation of agricultural societies. There are some groups that have continued as communal settlements over the years, but because of their remote locations they have no contact with modern society.

The art of communal living has, for the most part, become extinct. Any commune started today is an experiment, yet its residents continue to emphasize individual ingenuity. A review of the various types of communal settlements can illustrate architectural achievements often ignored.

Experiments in communal living have sprung up throughout Europe and the United States. These experiments are usually in the tradition of free and voluntary associations of people living by principles of cooperation, mutual aid, spontaneity of relationship, and organic growth. In its extreme form this tradition may be seen as a reaction against the prevailing social system, whose intentions do not provide adequately for the communal aspiration (Broido, 1971).

A movement that gained impetus in the 1970s, loosely described as the human potential movement, concerned itself with the deliberate creation of conditions that existed naturally at earlier times when the "community" was a living social entity. One method of recreating such conditions is voluntarily to live with others and share one's life and abilities with them to a greater or lesser extent. This may be seen as an attempt to revive the old kinship system with persons who are not blood relations. Such a communal ideal goes not against the family but beyond it; it places the family in a natural setting in contrast to the isolation that is often the condition of the contemporary nuclear family (Faraday, 1970).

A successful communal atmosphere can foster the human qualities of sympathy, perceptiveness, and understanding that are essential for individuals to realize themselves fully. Communal living makes it easier for people to maintain a full, natural social life when they want it. In such a group situation there is a continuous ebb and flow of people wherein each individual or couple has at least their own place, as well as specifically designated communal places. The living arrangements allow a continuous gradation between privacy and community according to individuals' needs of the moment. Conventional self-contained single-family housing units do not allow this. When two people live together, their mutual dependence and isolation from others is often such that they cannot express any negative feelings without fearing a catastrophe. Psychologists believe that the ability to express both positive and negative feelings toward the same person is characteristic of emotional maturity; people may not be able to achieve this sort of maturity in isolated pairs. Group living can create better opportunities for an honest, liberating expression of feeling without catastrophe and reduce the tendency for people to withdraw into sullen resentment.

These conclusions are based on the experience of people living in communes. The possible practical benefits in such matters as buying and cooking food, sharing expensive consumer durables (washing machines, etc.) and other tools and equipment, are more obvious. A significant practical advantage of communal living is probably in the sharing of certain jobs: baby-sitting, driving, nursing, and housework.

The provision of preschool education in play groups has practical child rearing advantages, such as the interaction by children of different ages and the subsequent independence developed in children by each other.

Participation in the Kibbutz

A unique practice of child rearing occurred in the early kibbutz, which functioned like a large family of 20 boys and girls, that developed in Israel as a result of the increase in the amount of land under cultivation and the rise in population. An examination of Israeli kibbutzim provides a good example of levels of participation and how they change over time. The early stages of a kibbutz, the *Gariin*, consists of a group of young people (much like a scouting troop) committed to the egalitarian goals of kibbutz life. They are basically lacking in structure, but with some adult link to a host kibbutz. All participate in whatever they so chose, as all is informal (Sharon, 1976).

The second stage of development, the *Hachshara*, also has little structured organization. This step occurs when members of the *Gariin* mature enough to be committed to facilitating the reality of the kibbutz existence. The leader from the *Gariin* becomes the leader who provides guidance to the group throughout kibbutz life. The *Hachshara* becomes a part of the jurisdiction of the host kibbutz, living on the host's property and becoming a part of its work force, with no group or individual power within the kibbutz. As yet, there is no real power structure. The only committee that exists is that for social activities. All members discuss decisions in a voluntary, uncontrolled way; the group is young enough that its realization envelops all personal thought and interaction. The singularity of goals (realization of the kibbutz) is enough to prevent disparity and, therefore, to preclude the need for structure.

When the *Hachshara* moves away from the host kibbutz and gains independence, the need for some organizational structure arises. Kibbutzim are societies within themselves, encompassing production (agricultural), consumption and repair of finished products (clothing and food delegation, tailors and shoe repair services, etc.), social activities, educational activities, and jobs. The goals of the kibbutzim are to be autonomous and relatively self-sufficient, to equitably distribute work, responsibilities, and benefits, and to democratically make decisions that, by definition, affect all. Every member of the kibbutz is a member of the general assembly that has final power in almost all decisions. This is the place where all people meet in their various roles and relations and try to develop a consensus. In the early stages of a kibbutz this is usually an easy accomplishment, as all are committed to and enveloped by the ideals of kibbutz. There is still, however, a need for power differentiation. The kibbutz must deal with the external realities that affect them, such as obtaining loans and selling products. It is necessary to delegate authority and responsibility to individuals and groups smaller than the general assembly in order for the daily routines to be accomplished. Roles frequently change, and elected positions are subject to swift turnover if so desired by the members of the kibbutz.

Through role and power differentiation, while the ideals of kibbutz life are burning strong, consensus remains and all are part of the decision making. As the kibbutz matures, it grows in population and heterogeneity and daily operations require increasingly complex management. Members have different physical limitations that must be considered, at times producing conflicts between individual needs and general kibbutz goals. When there is overwhelming consensus among members (in early stages), this does not present much of a problem as the individual, voluntarily or through peer pressure, gives in to the general welfare. But in older kibbutzim, where heterogeneity and size give way to divisions and a lack of primary commitment to the kibbutz, such conflicts become more problematic. Without ideological commitments to induce compliance, and without general awareness and pressure to conform, organizational authority becomes an imposing force. Apathy is still considered to be deviant behavior, but a lower level of commitment is expected. People are less aware of all that is going on (particularly because there is so much going on as a result of the community's size). Occasionally kibbutzim run campaigns to increase participation, but these rarely have lasting effects. This atmosphere has given rise to the development of discipline committees and "field courts."

The self-governance and management in all aspects of life that was (and still is) the initial goal of kibbutzim is subjected to severe compromise over time. Growth and change, largely because of early success, necessitate stratification of functions, differentiation of power, and the exclusion of many from the decision-making processes.

As in business corporations, there is a level of participation that is appropriate for individual situations. The kibbutz, its functions, needs, and problems vary over time. To succeed, members must adapt power differentials and levels of participation to fit the current situation. The experiences of the kibbutzim exhibit the need for greater authority and less participation as an organization becomes more complex. Complete self-management is not optimal when the complexity of the organization requires experts. In addition, people do not always want to participate, requiring others to accept responsibility and have the power to do so.

These economic, social, and ideological developments affected the physical layout and building character of the kibbutz. Although there are several other types of villages in Israel, none could serve as a model for kibbutz community based on collective life, work, and land. The early kibbutz of the 1920s, built as a rectangular courtyard with dwelling quarters on one side, farm buildings on the other side, and a dining hall, later added children's houses in a central position. This compact layout enabled the farmers to see all that was going on in the various parts of the settlement and shortened the walks from living quarters to stables and orchards. As the population increased and the economy burgeoned, the new farm buildings began to move beyond the courtyard and an urgent need for functional planning arose. By the 1940s and 1950s many of the older kibbutzim extended their agricultural branches, added workshops and factories, and increased in numbers. Many of them reached or exceeded a population of 800 to 1,000, including children, new immigrants, and students. This population is regarded as an efficient number for a productive economy and a social optimum for a culturally and socially flourishing collective ambiance. The settlement plans based on those population data conceived of functional building zones separated by garden strips, each of them able to expand organically.

Today the residential zone consists of single- or two-story buildings containing several small apartments, with every building surrounded by trees and gardens (Figure 4.1). The kibbutz tries to create for each couple an environment of

FIGURE 4.1 Kibbutz dwelling. *(Photo: Geoff Sifrin.)*

privacy and serenity. The children's area, located in the residential zone, consists of different houses designed according to age groups: the babies are in the infant houses, the toddlers in a second group, and older children in a kindergarten. At the age of six they enter the first class of elementary school, and at twelve, the adolescents' society. The various children's houses form closed units for each age group and consist of dormitories, playroom, and classrooms, with an adjoining courtyard for the children's outdoor activities. The adolescents' society is one in which 200 to 300 youngsters aged twelve to eighteen, learn, study, live, and work together. This society may be an organic part of one large kibbutz, or may serve three or four smaller kibbutzim. It is organized as a small educational and social entity, and general subjects are taught as in any school, except that agricultural subjects are stressed. The youngsters run their own lives according to the kibbutz pattern, through general meetings and committees. Teachers participate and guide but do not dictate or interfere directly.

The layout of the buildings needed for adolescents generally resembles that of the kibbutz itself (Figure 4.2). There are several housing units, for 30 boys and girls, each one containing bedrooms and a classroom, where they study and work. The central kibbutz building is the dining hall, in which the members meet at least

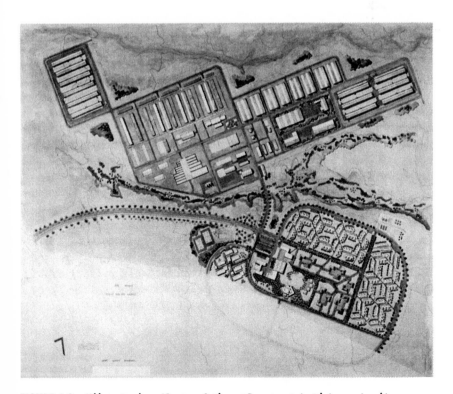

FIGURE 4.2 Kibbutz site plan. *(Courtesy: Settlement Department, Jewish Agency, Israel.)*

three times a day for their main meals. In the evenings, lectures, election meetings, discussions, social events, and festivities take place. The dining hall usually opens onto a central lawn, surrounded by other public buildings: the secretariat, the library and reading room, a service buffet, club rooms, and lecture rooms. The lawn itself serves the whole kibbutz population, including the children, as a rest and play area. In summer members use the lawn for open-air cinema performances or lectures. The kibbutz has its roots in economic viability, unlike the communes of the 1960s and 1970s that proposed alternative life-styles.

Dome Cultures

The use of domes as social pivots, and their symbolic newness and geometric simplicity, were more important to their builders than their advantages as mass-produced, lightweight modular components or efficient hi-tech commodities, as expressed by Buckminster Fuller. Because it is a mathematical form, the emphasis in building a dome is on individuals working together, rather than on the more personal modes of building where there is a need for mutual agreement on style.

The Red Rockers (1973) a group of eleven men and women wanted to create a structure that was free of traditional symbols—a new kind of space in which to create new selves. They also required a space that was large enough to house the original 11 men and women, as well as a space voluminous enough to assume different shapes as their needs changed. A 60-foot dome was created, followed by a celebration attended by 180 people holding hands in the predinner circle (Figure 4.3). The circular form is a symbolic shape supporting egalitarianism.

During the first winter the inhabitants all slept in a circle along the walls of the dome. By the second winter, new additions included a child's room and a mezzanine sleeping platform that extended three-quarters of the way around the dome's circumference. The platform improved the lives of the residents, because it was considerably warmer in the wintertime and most of the beds had a splendid view through the windows that served to heat the dome on sunny winter days.

During the summertime most of the Red Rockers moved out of the dome into tipis or temporary shelters. Subsequently, many people built small houses—sleeping spaces designed for one, two, or three people and without kitchen facilities. After three years of living in a "heap," most of the dome residents decided that in order to keep becoming new people, to keep growing and changing, they needed more privacy. They still continued to be a communal family, but they needed a new kind of shelter to encourage personal growth. The dome continued to be a center, and the mezzanine platform was converted into a crafts area.

Christiania

The Christiania movement had its counterparts in many parts of the world, but none was as notable as that in Denmark in the free town of Christiania, an area of 22 hectares less than one kilometer from the center of Copenhagen. At the southwest

FIGURE 4.3   Dome dwelling.

end of the town stand solidly built four- to six-story military barracks and factories, and toward the northwest the settlement becomes increasingly rural, with small clusters of farmlike buildings surrounded by trees. A reed-lined river, crossed only by a wooden footbridge, traverses the site. The military used the place as a camp and munitions factory from the middle of the nineteenth century until 1970, when it moved elsewhere and boarded up the site. It was to become the property of the Ministry of Culture for educational and cultural institutions, but, being a prime site, its land value was high and the city authorities wanted it for housing, new roads, sports facilities, and more lucrative uses. While the authorities procrastinated, a few hundred people invaded the area in 1971 and took over the vacant buildings. The free town of Christiania was declared.

In the ensuing years the population has grown to almost 800, with many more during the summer months. It is the largest squatter settlement in Europe. Many different types of life-styles can be found in Christiania, ranging from people living in self-built huts, families living in small wooden houses (Figures 4.4a and 4.4b) to collective communal living in converted factories and munitions storage buildings (Wates, 1978).

Most people are in their thirties and forties, but there is a scattering of older people and some children, many of whom were born there. These people, who come from a variety of social backgrounds, include professionals as well as some who would normally be described as deviants: alcoholics, drug addicts, runaway children, and so on. Many of them might otherwise be in social institutions, but in Christiania they are tolerated.

People come to Christiania because they are not willing or able to adapt to the ordinary demands imposed by society and find there a refuge where they can be accepted and function in a "noninstitutional fellowship," as some call it. Although some of the inhabitants have moved from a hopeless or distressing personal situation, others come because of a positive desire to develop alternative ways of living. Instead of a community based on institutional rules, orders, and control, they want to create a society based on the acceptance of everyone without asking about the past, on nonintervention, low standards of material consumption, reuse of materials, biodynamic food, and so on. Although some people have full-time employment outside, the majority have created jobs for themselves inside the community.

A variety of enterprises have grown up: restaurants, bars, bakeries, and workshops making everything from boots to bicycles. The town has its own art gallery, radio station, kindergarten, and a health clinic that is devoted mainly to herbal and homeopathic medicine.

Christiania has a decentralized structure with 11 districts, each of which settles problems and conflicts at biweekly meetings. Open meetings of the whole community are also held regularly, or more frequently in times of crisis. There are various working groups to deal with particular aspects of community life, such as information, publicity, external negotiations, cleaning up, tree planting, health and fire protection, and festival organization.

FIGURE 4.4a   Christiania new housing. *(Photo: Henry Sanoff.)*

FIGURE 4.4b   Christiania entrance. *(Photo: Henry Sanoff.)*

From a physical planning point of view, Christiania appears to be spontaneous and totally based on the practice and ingenuity of the users. Because the normal building restraints have been removed, individuals and groups are free to shape their spaces, buildings, and furniture to suit their own needs. Every house, room, table, and stove is different because of the different requirements of its users and makers. The factories and munitions depots have been modified and decorated by their new inhabitants. Balconies, rooftop platforms, and greenhouses have been added with the use of timber from demolition sites. Some people have built complete houses from scratch.

Different areas of Christiania have developed different characteristics and different atmospheres. There is a downtown where a conglomeration of bars and small stalls give the place the appearance of a Wild West town.

Inevitably, the authorities have tried to crush Christiania because it is seen as a threat to the established order and traditional values. When the initial occupation occurred in 1971, the government considered it impracticable to evict the inhabitants immediately, as there were no ready plans for the site. Three years later it was agreed to allow the situation to continue as a "social experiment" for three years; however, the city authorities required that building conditions be brought up to legal standards. When the Ministry of Defense, the legal owner, calculated that this would cost $3 million that was not forthcoming, it cut off water and electricity and began demolition of the worst buildings. Both moves were defeated by legal action.

When the agreement came to an end in 1976, the authorities decided to terminate Christiania but were met with opposition from the residents and from a wide section of the public who were in favor of continuing Christiania as a social experiment. Today Christiania thrives with well-constructed new housing, a radio station, art galleries, restaurants, and frequent weekend visitors.

Cohousing

Other new forms of group living developed in Denmark, Holland, and Sweden have been inspired by practical rather than religious or ideological concerns. Cohousing began as a grass-roots movement that grew out of people's dissatisfaction with existing housing choices. Its initiators were influenced by the popularity of shared households, in which unrelated people share a traditional house, and generally by the cooperative movement. A cohousing community is distinct in that it consists of individual households with private dwellings and shared common facilities (McCamant and Durrett, 1989). Cohousing communities are unique in their extensive common facilities and, more important, that the residents themselves are responsible for organizing, planning, and managing.

A group of families who wanted a greater sense of community than was available in suburban subdivisions or apartment complexes built the first cohousing community in 1972 in Denmark. Architect Jan Gudmund-Hoyer and many families met to discuss the advantages of living together. This resulted in a small number of them attempting to buy a site suited to their goal of collective develop-ment. All agreed that the development should be designed to be open for com-munity activities. After many difficulties in locating a site and obtaining loans, they succeeded in constructing 33 individually owned houses and a community center situated near Copenhagen in an area named Skraplanet (Figure 4.5). The houses were built close to each other on the south slope of the site so all had an open view to the south. For this reason, all of the houses had flat roofs. The basic housing units were all alike, both for economic reasons and to conform to the desire for similar conditions within the collective. There was direct access to each house from the common areas, paths, and open squares. In each house the living room had a window to the communal area outside, so that visual contact would encour-age spontaneous visits.

This was the first in the world of the communal housing projects that enjoyed continued existence in spite of divorces, children growing up and leaving, and inflation (Figure 4.6). In all of the cooperative housing developments in Den-mark, France, Germany, Sweden, and the United States the social experiment of households living together and sharing facilities has been seen as beneficial (Fromm, 1991). Communal dining, households having meals together, is available almost every evening when families rotate cooking responsibilities. In most Euro-pean communes, young professionals with one or two children have been the pio-neers of communal housing, primarily because they have the income to experiment.

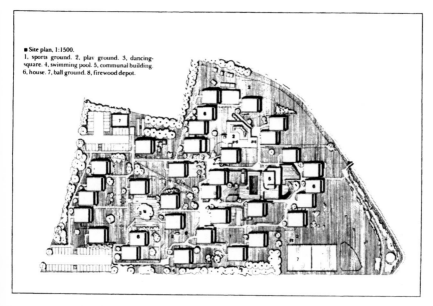

■ Site plan, 1:1500.
1, sports ground. 2, play ground. 3, dancing-square. 4, swimming pool. 5, communal building. 6, house. 7, ball ground. 8, firewood depot.

FIGURE 4.5 Plan of Skraplanet.

FIGURE 4.6 Skraplanet housing. *(Photo: Jan Gudmund-Hoyer.)*

The development has a community center containing a nursery school, a hobby workshop, a bar, a meeting room, and an arrangement by which parents with school-age children look after each other's children after school. The residents eat together in the community house four times a week. The idea of designing the development in an open way, with the houses strongly integrated into the community, has provided, in practice, the expected high level of activity among the residents. Both large and small cooperative groups have been established, and there are club activities, regular community meals, and other joint functions of many kinds.

The first American cohousing development, located in Davis, California, opened in 1991. This development includes all the elements of European cohousing, such as resident participation in the development process and pragmatic social objectives. Most American cohousing developments look and function similarly to Danish cohousing, with low-rise attached housing clustered on the site, a centrally located separate common house, and parking at the periphery of the site. American cohousing often differs from the European in financing, tenure, and overall dimensions, but does not differ as to the intentions of the residents to create a supportive living environment and a sense of community.

Sustainable living has been a goal of American cohousing groups because it provides an organizational framework for buying and maintaining alternative technologies and systems. Cohousing participants realize that sustainable design has a great deal to do with location near services, not necessarily building on farmland, but rather in existing metropolitan areas and in higher densities. Cohousing appears to be one method of revitalizing urban neighborhoods, bringing in home ownership and stability, plus providing a built-in sense of security for the cohousing residents.

Several studies conducted on North American cohousing communities revealed that these developments have a diverse mix of ages, incomes, religions, family makeup and sexual orientations. There is not much racial or cultural diversity (Pais, 1995). Residents' satisfaction with the development process in the first wave of cohousing communities is understandably low, as a timely delivery process is yet unresolved due to financial and construction limitations.

In a postoccupancy evaluation survey a majority of respondents used the word "community" or words associated with the feeling of community such as "a sense of family" and "support" in describing the advantages of cohousing. American cohousing provides a strong sense of community. That this community is much harder to develop than was envisioned, that it requires large amounts of time to maintain, that making decisions as a group is not as smooth as anticipated, and that often a sense of privacy is decreased—these are the costs. And that there are Americans willing to pay the costs demonstrates the value of community to them, and of the cohousing concept as an alternative to the American Dream.

Farm Worker Housing

Charrette Process	Participatory action research
Community action planning	Public forum
▶ Focus groups	Strategic planning
▶ Game simulation	Visioning
Goal setting	▶ Workshop
▶ Group interaction	

In North Carolina, where agriculture provides a large portion of the state's income, farm workers contribute significantly to its economic development. The 70,000 migrant laborers who come to improve their own economic situation contribute to the state's economic prosperity as well.

The primary reason for improving the conditions in which farm workers live is that they, just like anyone else, deserve a safe and appropriate dwelling. Justifications such as "This is better than where they live at home" are unfounded and inappropriate for a variety of reasons. The only opportunity for workers to voice concerns is when housing conditions are so bad that they do not meet the Department of Labor regulations.

Studies have noted the current abundance of agricultural laborers as one reason that farm labor contractors are unwilling to provide housing, or the appropriate level of housing, for workers. As labor camps age and maintenance costs to meet the standards of the Occupational Safety and Health Administration (OSHA) increase, employers often close camps, raze the buildings, or sell a camp to a third party to manage rather than invest in needed repairs. "From the perspective of the grower who needs apple pickers, a shelter need not offer much for two weeks; from the point of view of the migrant, living in barns and using privies can be a way of life week after week, month after month" (U.S. Department of Agriculture, *National Farmworker Housing Survey*, 1980).

The public is generally unaware of farm worker housing needs. The press rarely covers issues of substandard farm worker living conditions. Housing problems are frequently balanced with arguments about "increased prices for a head of lettuce" or "growers' responsibilities for housing." The first comment implies that if people were willing to pay more for fruits and vegetables, then farm workers could be paid enough to afford decent housing. The second ignores the importance of seasonal labor to the overall economy of the state, not solely for the well being of growers who are responsible for providing farm worker housing.

According to the *National Farmworker Housing Survey*, health status indicators show that migrant workers' health is worse than that of the general population—25 percent higher infant mortality, with nine times as many births occurring outside hospitals; 20 percent higher death rates from influenza and pneumonia; 2.5 times more deaths from tuberculosis. These factors are important indications that housing conditions reflect many opposing forces and highlight the need to improve conditions so that housing supports the needs of farm workers.

The effort to produce new housing units in North Carolina is being accelerated by the scouting program initiated by the Department of Labor in 1996. Inspectors are actively searching for occupied but unregistered migrant housing units throughout the state. The locations of all camps are being precisely recorded with the use of global positioning technology. This system will help to identify and eliminate unregulated and inappropriate migrant housing.

The *National Farmworker Housing Survey* (U.S. Department of Agriculture, 1980) estimated that of the 500 camps inspected in its survey, only 3 percent are public owned and 92 percent are privately owned. Another 5 percent are owned by employer-related cooperatives. The survey indicated that dormitory-style arrangements were found to be most prevalent in the Carolinas. At that time more than 60 percent of the buildings inspected in the Carolinas were found to expose the occupants to the elements, and buildings in that region were consistently in the poorest condition. The Carolinas offered fewer facilities per occupant than any other area of the country. Family composition also affects housing adequacy; three or four individual workers can share housing designed for families, but housing designed for individuals—typically barracks and dormitories—lack the space and privacy necessary for families (*National Farmworker Housing Survey*, 1980).

Crowding is an important concern in farm worker housing, inasmuch as the suggested square footage per person is extremely limited. Small, restricted spaces, considered to be "cramped," can result in disruptive behavior, heightened stress, confrontations, or violations of personal space. Crowding stress is a consequence of a person's having to interact with too many other people. Research findings suggest that architectural solutions that fail to provide suitable space easily converted to semiprivate, defensible space, have unpleasant and stressful consequences for residents (Baum and Valins, 1977).

The health implications of the inadequate supply and quality of farm worker housing are alarming. Housing conditions that directly relate to disease include cold, damp interiors, where there is an increased incidence of ear and respiratory infections in farm workers as compared with the general population. The presence of a toilet within a sleeping area is associated with an increased incidence of gastrointestinal distress, anorexia, and gastroenteritis. Substandard and unheated rooms are associated with an increased incidence of measles and upper respiratory infections. Single-bed usage by families is associated with an increased incidence of impetigo and emotional distress. Multiuse sleeping rooms are associated with an increased incidence of bronchiectasis, disseminated tuberculosis, influenza, and tonsillitis. The lack of laundry and hygienic facilities leads to bathing and laundering in the kitchen sinks, exposing food preparation surfaces to the pesticides and fertilizers that workers may contact in the fields.

Department of Defense housing requirements for enlisted soldiers, for example, was examined because they provide a basis for minimal housing requirements in regard to health. Old standards that called for a minimum of 72 square feet per person of living/sleeping space (excluding bath, lavatory, entry foyer, and other shared amenities) are currently being converted to newly adopted standards requiring an absolute minimum of 85 square feet of living/sleeping space per person. Under the old standards, two people shared a room, and two rooms shared a bathroom, with each room having its own sink. People had their own wardrobes for storage. The new standards suggest that each person have his or her own room and share a bathroom and living areas. In converting buildings to these new requirements, if this preferred arrangement cannot be achieved, it is stated that under no circumstances shall more than four persons share a room.

Field Visits

Several visits to farm labor camps of various sizes revealed a number of undesirable conditions. A poor physical and social environment characterizes most of the sleeping areas. These areas were often overcrowded, with very little concern for privacy and territoriality needs. Bathrooms showed a lack of consideration for privacy and hygiene needs. Showers and toilets were located in the same space, with too few facilities for the number of people. Dining areas lacked security and maintained low hygiene standards. Individual privacy was lacking, and there was no access to the kitchen facilities. From the siting of housing units it was apparent that no consideration was given to the orientation, arrangement, or accessibility of the buildings. Workers had to travel long distances between sleeping areas and communal buildings, and family housing units were often integrated with single men's housing. There was an obvious lack of adequate space for social activity, for any consideration of children's needs, or space or provisions for outdoor sports in all facilities visited.

Design Game Workshop

A series of workshops were held with groups of farm workers in different locations to substantiate the results of field observations and to identify housing priorities. The workshops were conducted with the aid of a translator so that the workers could express themselves in their native language. The farm workers played a spatial layout game to discern their preferences for individual and communal living conditions. Wood blocks representing single men's housing units, family housing units, bathroom units, kitchen units, and a dining facility allowed participants to arrange an ideal farm worker housing community (Figure 4.7). The rules of the game required that they play in groups of five people and reach a consensus about their preferences. The environments created by the teams demonstrated the following patterns:

- Communal facilities, such as the dining hall, were located at the center of the site.

FIGURE 4.7 Farm workers engaged in the planning process. *(Photo: Holly Grubb.)*

- Small social spaces were created through the arrangement of the dwelling units.
- Family housing was separated from single men's housing.
- Family houses were always allocated their own kitchen and bath facilities.
- Single men were usually allocated their own bathrooms, but rarely their own kitchen facilities.
- Single men viewed the dining hall as the social facility.
- Families viewed the child care facility as the social center.
- Trees were used to create separation and privacy.

From the results of this game, specific design guidelines were developed:

- Ventilate all livable areas for good hygiene.
- Separate showers and toilets for privacy and hygiene.
- Provide secure storage space in the rooms.
- Privacy should be attainable in the sleeping area.
- Provide and maintain sufficient levels of security.
- Provide access to electrical outlets for each occupant.
- Provide access to the kitchen facilities.
- Provide and maintain both indoor and outdoor recreation areas.
- Provide children's outdoor play areas.
- Orient buildings to take advantage of the natural resources for pleasant views and control of temperature.
- Provide easy access to community buildings.
- Provide separation between family and female housing units from those of the single men.

A second series of participatory workshops conducted had two purposes:

1. To identify the needs of the farm workers
2. To familiarize farm workers with the design process

First in this series was an opportunity for the participants to get to know each other. Two exercises were performed in a group setting: "My favorite place . . ." and "I wish my home . . .", in which participants were asked to complete each of the phrases.

The participants' responses in this exercise indicated a fondness for the outdoors and a desire for more accessible natural spaces in which to rest and relax. This desire is highly understandable, given the limited amount of space in which most farm workers live. Rarely is space provided for activities other than sleeping, eating, and washing. By necessity, farm workers may spend a great deal of their leisure time outdoors. Several responses also indicated that the workers desired a space that they would be able to personalize. The person whose favorite place was his car liked it because it was his and liked the feeling of being in control that being there gave to him. Moreover, it was a place where he enjoyed being alone. Because of the hardships posed by a migratory life-style, the participants desired spaces that had the appearance and feeling of permanence, security, and accessibility.

The second exercise, "I wish my home . . . ," was an opportunity for workers to specifically express their housing preferences, particularly significant because the migrant work force is made up of individuals from different countries and regions who may not have shared experiences. It cannot be assumed that housing preferences of one group of migrants will be appropriate for all. However, it was observed that the desires of the workers were limited to basic necessities and none exceeded what should be present in any housing environment.

Most of the workers' wishes should be met by the existing state regulations. The one condition expressed in "I wish my home . . ." that the regulations cannot address is that of ownership. However, this wish can be interpreted as the workers' desire for some control over their environment and a sense of belonging, as it was personalized to reflect the desires of the inhabitants.

The second workshop sought worker responses to what trade-offs they would make to obtain privacy. Attitudes toward bedroom and bathroom spaces were investigated. Participants were given work sheets showing alternative floor plans and asked to select the preferred locations for specific activities and to give their reasons (Figure 4.8a). They were encouraged to make suggestions for changes by marking the plans to indicate a preferred arrangement. Farm worker responses indicated a strong desire for privacy in both the bedroom and the bathroom (Figure 4.8b).

Loft spaces were the preferred option for the bedrooms because they afforded the most privacy. In the bathroom, people accepted fewer fixtures in order to have more privacy. This indicates the willingness of people to prefer the opportunity to get clean quickly over the opportunity to get clean privately.

Bedroom Schemes. Workers preferred Scheme 3 as it provided the most privacy because the loft divided the sleeping area. Scheme 2, with sleeping areas separated by storage units, was also acceptable. Scheme 1 was the least preferred because of the lack of physical separation. Results from these activities emphasize the importance of privacy for farm workers, a concern not usually recognized by housing providers.

Bathroom Schemes. Scheme 3 was the preferred arrangement because it provided the most privacy in the shower area and the most enclosed locker area. Schemes 1 and 2 provided a greater number of showers, but were less preferred. Scheme 2 was always rejected because it provided no privacy in the shower. Conditions in the bathroom should ensure privacy so that workers can clean themselves of pesticides when returning from fields.

Results derived from comparisons between the housing schemes generated a number of housing and related user needs, described as follows:

Housing Needs. "Personal space," a place to claim as your own, to which other people do not have access unless invited, is a space that does not require sharing. A lack of physical barriers may cause people to put up psychological

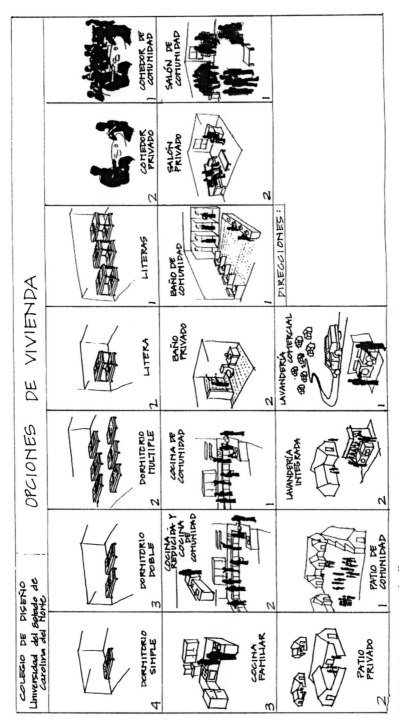

FIGURE 4.8a Housing trade-offs.

203

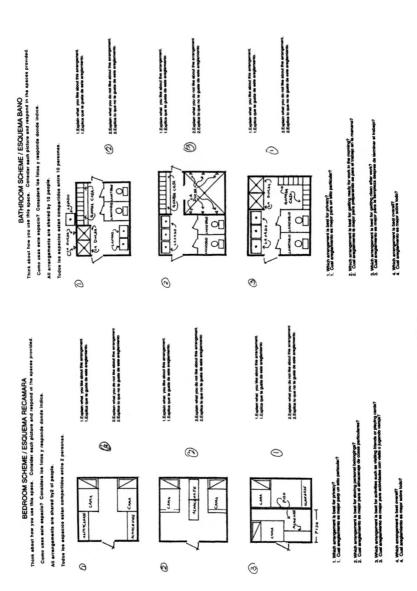

FIGURE 4.8b Alternative floor plans for bedroom and bathroom.

barriers. "Privacy," another basic need, is the ability to control the access of others to your activities or to your interaction with other people. Having only a bedroom to retreat to may make a person feel isolated, when all that is desired is a place for quiet activity. Dormitory-style rooms can turn into passageways, disrupting the lives of occupants of the space. "Personalization" lets people make a space feel as though it belongs to them, such as by displaying personal articles or deciding about the arrangement of items in the space.

Bathroom Needs. The ability to address health concerns is an important issue in a shared bathroom. An essential aspect is the location of the shower in relation to personal storage facilities. A person should be able to enter the shower area, retrieve toiletries, and get clean before entering the living or dining area. This is of particular concern for farm workers, who need to remove pesticides upon coming home from the fields. Having an entrance to the bathroom directly from the outside allows workers to enter the bathroom without having to contaminate their living spaces with dirt and pesticides. In a single-family home, soap, shampoo, and towels are kept in the bathroom and do not have to be carried to and from the bedroom at each use. Having ample and secure storage in the bathroom area makes the functioning of the facility more homelike. Everyone who uses a particular bathroom should have a place there to store personal items. This will help to establish regular users of each bathroom. It will be easier to have workers participate in the upkeep of the space if they feel some connection with the space. Unpleasant smells can make a place seem crowded. Spaces that are always damp can grow mold and bacteria.

Sleeping Needs. A feeling of privacy will enhance occupants' sense of ownership of the space. A buffer zone between public and private areas helps to define the boundaries of a person's territory. For example, giving each occupant an individual entry clearly distinguishes that person's space from those belonging to the community. People should be able to secure personal belongings and display items to create a more homelike setting. Family pictures and mementos are an important part of a person's ability to connect with those who are far away. Personalization of a space will help inhabitants to care more about where they are living and will encourage them to participate in maintaining the space.

From the workshop it was clear that farm workers preferred housing that was homelike. Although the length of stay at one particular location may be short, farm workers live in temporary housing more or less permanently or for an extended length of time—the situation can be considered permanent, but the location itself is temporary. Therefore, provisions for appropriate housing are necessary for any worker, irrespective of the amount of time a particular worker remains in one location. Similarly, a comparable level of housing should be provided in all locations as that worker moves from farm to farm.

To this end, a series of design guidelines (Figure 4.9) and floor plans for single farm workers (Figure 4.10) were developed in order to ameliorate the present intolerable situation. The Agricultural Safety and Health Council of the State of

GUIDELINES

Bathrooms

Department of Labor standards requiring one shower for 10 people is not adequate to meet the serious need of farm workers to thoroughly remove pesticides.

Department of Labor standards requiring one toilet for 15 people is not adequate to meet the needs of farm workers.

Suggested Guidelines:
6 People per shower

Suggested Guidelines:
6 People per toilet

FARM WORKER HOUSING

Bathrooms

•Allow farm workers access to clean and private bathrooms to encourage the removal of pesticides and soil quickly upon arrival from the fields.

•Include outside sinks and showers so that rinsing may occur before workers enter the building. This will help ease crowding of the facilities during peak use times.

•Provide a prominent entrance directly into the bathroom from outside, so that workers do not pass through living spaces and contaminate or dirty them while passing through to the bathroom.

•Subdivide the room into different areas: a place for showering and storage of personal items, a place for washing hands, and a place for private toilets.

•Make the rooms big enough for several people to have access at the same time, or divide the rooms into private facilities.

•Arrange the spaces so that more than one person can use the different areas while others are occupied.

•Keep the bathrooms small and private, since too many people sharing a space may lead to its becoming uncared for, thus posing a health problem.

•Provide shower curtains that are opaque enough to provide privacy when being backlit.

•Provide a source of light in the shower to eliminate the growth of mold and bacteria.

•Place numerous operable windows up high so that there is ventilation without exposing the people inside to public view. High windows are a good source of light in the shower area.

•Use two openings if possible, locating them in adjacent or opposite walls to provide cross-ventilation.

•Provide shelves near sinks so that it is convenient to position personal items for use. Think about places to set soap, toothbrushes, razors, etc.

•Provide direct access to the bathroom from other living spaces so that the facility is more homelike.

FIGURE 4.9 Housing design guidelines.

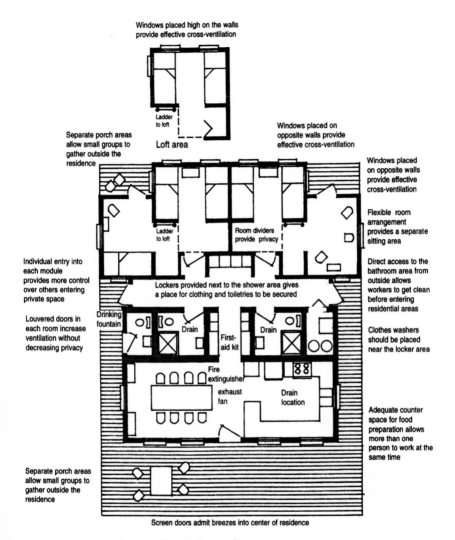

Windows placed high on the walls provide effective cross-ventilation

Ladder to loft

Separate porch areas allow small groups to gather outside the residence

Loft area

Windows placed on opposite walls provide effective cross-ventilation

Windows placed on opposite walls provide effective cross-ventilation

Flexible room arrangement provides a separate sitting area

Individual entry into each module provides more control over others entering private space

Ladder to loft

Room dividers provide privacy

Direct access to the bathroom area from outside allows workers to get clean before entering residential areas

Louvered doors in each room increase ventilation without decreasing privacy

Drinking fountain

Lockers provided next to the shower area gives a place for clothing and toiletries to be secured

Drain

First-aid kit

Drain

Clothes washers should be placed near the locker area

Fire extinguisher

exhaust fan

Drain location

Adequate counter space for food preparation allows more than one person to work at the same time

Separate porch areas allow small groups to gather outside the residence

Screen doors admit breezes into center of residence

FIGURE 4.10   Floor plan for eight single farm workers.

North Carolina Department of Labor endorsed these efforts in order to raise awareness to the significance of housing design for farm workers. These guidelines were published in the 1998 document *Introduction to Migrant Housing Inspections in North Carolina* (North Carolina Department of Labor, 1998).

Assisted Living Housing

Charrette Process

Community action planning

Focus groups

▶ Game simulation

▶ Goal setting

▶ Group interaction

Participatory action research

Public forum

▶ Strategic planning

Visioning

▶ Workshop

Assisted living represents a significant movement in large-scale elderly housing and health care. It provides individualized care to vulnerable frail older people in a residential environment. Regnier (1994) views it as "combining the residential qualities and the friendly scale of board and care housing with the professionalism and sophistication of a typical personal care setting targeted towards residents who in the past would have normally resided in intermediate and skilled nursing facilities." A composite list of environment-behavior principles, adapted from Regnier and Pynoos (1987) and translated into qualities of assisted living facilities, include the following:

- Appear residential in character
- Support informal social interaction
- Provide residential privacy
- Promote orientation to assist wayfinding
- Promote individuality and choice
- Provide a challenging and stimulating environment
- Provide opportunities for personalization

Although there is a growing body of environment-behavior literature describing the desired characteristics of assisted living housing, the elderly, a rich resource of knowledge and experience, have often been excluded from the design process. Older people should not be viewed as a homogenous group with the same needs and desires, but as unique individuals with a common goal—living life with dignity.

In December 1993, the Moore County Department of Aging requested assistance from the Community Development Group in designing assisted living housing and a senior enrichment center for Moore County, North Carolina. The design team's work included assessing Moore County's existing services and facilities for the elderly community, planning and conducting participatory workshops, and proposing alternatives for the enrichment facility. The workshops were especially helpful in educating the Moore County Department of Aging (MCDOA) on how best to address the variety of community concerns while getting the most from the county's resources. In the process, the Moore County Department of Aging developed an understanding of the relationship between social issues that are significant to older adults and the ways in which the built environment can facilitate those specific issues.

Moore County, nationally known for its golfing resorts and retirement communities, is located in the central portion of North Carolina. The resort industry in the southern part of the county, concentrated around Pinehurst and Southern Pines, contrasts with the predominantly rural agricultural regions of the county. Moore County supports one of the largest concentrations of older adults on the East Coast of the United States, many of whom relocate to the area specifically for retirement in the county's upscale communities. On the other hand, there is also a significant segment of the elderly population living below the poverty level, mainly in the northern part of the county. Presently, 27 percent of Moore County's population is 60 years old or older. By the year 2010 the percentage of older people is expected to increase by 70 percent. A resource map displays the concentration of services in the southern part of the county, noting existing medical, housing, social services, and cultural facilities. An assessment of the social and physical conditions of the county's elderly population revealed the need for increased housing options to include provisions for those who are independent, who require some assistance, and who require substantial assistance. From the geriatric literature it was gleaned that concerns for security, social interaction, and accessibility are important considerations in designing for the elderly.

A community development approach that included planning and conducting participatory workshops was especially relevant for MCDOA's plans because it allowed for the integration of a variety of community concerns that would maximize the use of the county's resources. Any effective program for older people requires their insight and participation. To this end, workshops engaged senior citizens of the county, the Board of Aging, and Department of Aging administrators.

An important factor in the development of participatory workshops is the readability of materials for participants not trained in design or planning. Consequently, color used to differentiate various areas enabled the readability of drawings and three-dimensional models. Another requirement is the opportunity for all participants in the workshop to be heard. To this end, all workshops evolved in three stages. First, participants usually worked in small groups of three to five people. Next, participants made individual decisions, discussed their decisions in their respective groups, and tried to reach consensus. Finally, each group's decisions were publicly presented to all participants in the workshop.

An initial community workshop focused on site alternatives that proposed several housing arrangements. Thirty participants, including citizens and members of the Board of Aging, rated each proposal on the basis of a number of criteria:

- Which proposal provides the best connection between the senior center and the housing types?
- Which offers the best opportunities for social interaction?
- Which has the most suitable relationship between housing types?
- Which provides the best sense of security?
- If you were to live here, which plan would you choose?

Workshop results indicated that most of the participants preferred privacy, or the scattered site development (Figure 4.11). A second workshop with the county's elderly focused on alternatives for congregate housing. A predominantly rural elderly population participated in this workshop, many of whom could not read, as a result of illiteracy or poor vision. The intention was to expand the participants' awareness of housing options, given that their experience was primarily with traditional retirement housing. Most participants associated any form of retirement housing with a "nursing home." Four plan arrangements allowed participants to examine differences between group homes, and between cluster and conventional housing. Criteria for evaluating alternatives included security, social interaction, privacy, circulation, and orientation. They unanimously rejected any housing arrangement that appeared "institutional." Their primary concerns were with privacy and maintaining independence. They preferred a housing arrangement that allowed for, yet did not force, social interaction.

The third workshop presented alternative conceptual plans to introduce participants to key social issues requiring consideration in planning their senior center. The most preferred plan received the highest ratings for "social interaction." Plan alternatives were rank ordered according to their successfully accommodating the following criteria:

- Circulation
- Security
- Social interaction
- Wayfinding
- Stimulation
- Overall preference

The final workshop allowed participants to identify the activity spaces they desired in their senior center. Beginning with goal setting, small groups of elderly participants selected and matched goals with key activity spaces. A layout sheet divided into grids allowed them to develop a conceptual floor plan, using graphic symbols corresponding to the activities. Workshop results suggested that the goals of physical fitness and proper nutrition received the highest priorities. Improving the public image of the elderly and making new friends were also important goals. This workshop had the distinct advantage of both giving and receiving information. Workshop materials allowed participants to manipulate activities on a game board and to generate building concepts, such as the clustering of social activities around a lounge (Figure 4.12).

Involving the elderly in the design decisions to promote a healing environment informed the Moore County Department of Aging staff of a number of unmet needs. This knowledge was instrumental in shaping the Department's recommendations to the county commissioners for future housing and senior center facilities.

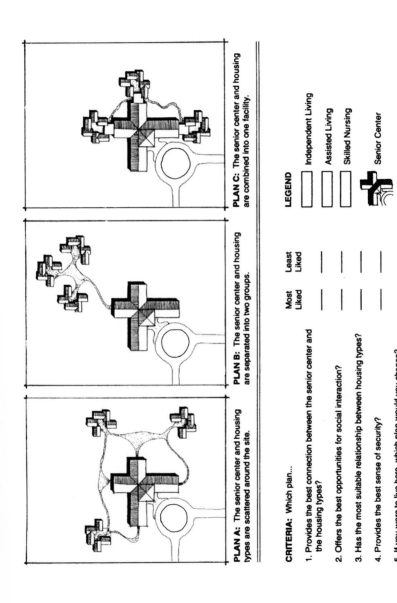

PLAN A: The senior center and housing types are scattered around the site.

PLAN B: The senior center and housing are separated into two groups.

PLAN C: The senior center and housing are combined into one facility.

LEGEND

Independent Living

Assisted Living

Skilled Nursing

Senior Center

CRITERIA: Which plan...

	Most Liked	Least Liked
1. Provides the best connection between the senior center and the housing types?	—	—
2. Offers the best opportunities for social interaction?	—	—
3. Has the most suitable relationship between housing types?	—	—
4. Provides the best sense of security?	—	—
5. If you were to live here, which plan would you choose?	—	—

FIGURE 4.11 Housing and senior center site alternatives.

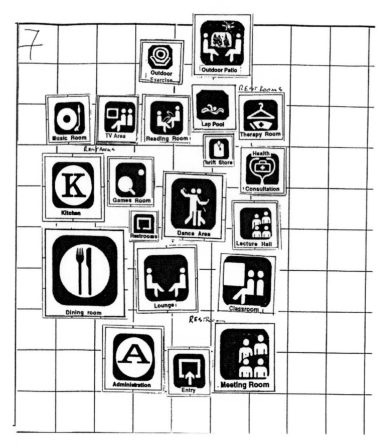

FIGURE 4.12 Senior center game board.

Housing Games

Housing Trade-Offs

The concept of trade-off, which is integral to the participatory process, compares competing alternatives, particularly according to the types of amenities offered. Trade-offs imply compromises, exchanges, or substitutability between multiple—often mutually exclusive—goals; they reflect the need to give up or sacrifice something in order to gain something else. Community groups are often confronted with choices that must be weighed for their appropriateness, as there are often constraints that limit the range of viable choices. People involved in making trade-offs evaluate the costs and benefits of available options.

Most housing trade-off games confront players with a number of environmental features, each with several possible quality levels. Typically, each quality level has an associated cost, defined in terms of dollars, or points. Game participants are allocated a budget and allowed to "purchase" the quality levels they desire. However, by making the total budget insufficient to permit purchase of the highest level of all qualities, the players are forced to make trade-offs (Robinson, 1987).

This technique was successfully used in a habitat owner-built housing process. A neighborhood housing service agency identified ten families, with relatively low incomes, who agreed to utilize personal labor as a form of equity in reducing labor cost in building a house. Construction cost was the major constraint, within which future home owners would be required to make spatial choices. Although construction cost is always an important consideration, there are also certain family life-styles that are influential in making planning decisions. People who are confronting a purchase decision often look to market availability for a suitable selection, rather than examining their work-flow and living patterns. Concepts such as family solidarity, use of leisure time, and child rearing practices may influence living patterns and residential preferences in different ways. The opportunity to confront the complexities of privacy needs, spatial interaction, and conflicting goals between members of a family prior to purchase can have a dramatic effect on the selection of a suitable choice.

To make the decision process "transparent'" in reflecting the value differences between the families, workshops were organized in which decisions about the house were divided into categories of activities, house image, and site arrangements. Faced with budget limitations that influenced the size of the dwelling and level of amenities, families were able to use the housing trade-off exercise as a preliminary step in discovering their particular residential needs.

The first planning workshop introduced the trade-off concept by subdividing the dwelling into activity components such as living-dining and kitchen, or living, dining, and kitchen. Three options were provided for the living-dining component of the dwelling, each requiring a different amount of area, signified by the number in the left lower corner of the picture (Figure 4.13). Similar components were developed for the adults' and children's sleeping areas. Each family was allotted 45 points, which corresponded to their budgets and reflected the total area of the dwelling. All family members worked through the process in family groups, making trade-offs between spatial alternatives that provided more or less space for personal or family activities.

The Housing Image Exercise considered a series of dwelling photographs that described subtle and profound character differences (Figure 4.14). This exercise is important in suggesting how buildings convey clues about the values of the people who own and occupy them (Becker, 1977). Future home owners were to consciously recognize this environmental message reflecting the inner life, actions, and social conceptions of the occupants of a home. In the Housing Image Exercise individuals in small groups made personal choices and discussed their decisions within the group. The process allowed families to learn about each other's values and become aware of the meaning conveyed by different buildings.

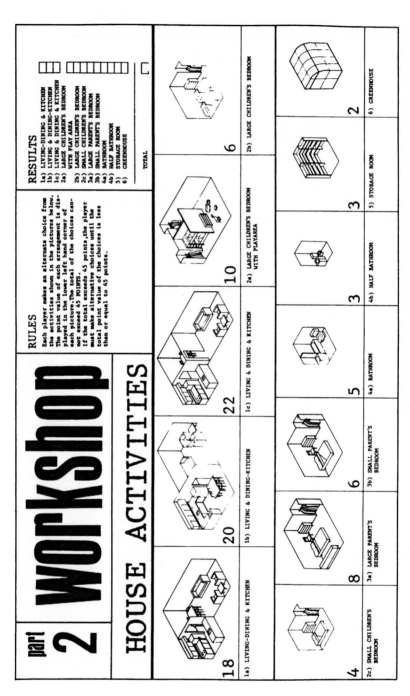

FIGURE 4.13 House activities trade-off game.

214

part 3

workshop

HOUSE IMAGES

RULES

Each player selects the picture that he likes the most and the one he dislikes the most. Then he describes the particular characteristics of the first as well as of the last choice.

After each player has completed this step in the process—his individual selections are recorded. Through negotiation the group must agree on the pictures they like and dislike the most.

PERSONAL RESULTS

like the most: _____

dislike the most: _____

comments: _____

GROUP RESULTS

like the most: _____

dislike the most: _____

comments: _____

FIGURE 4.14 House image exercise.

215

A Site Alternatives session allowed participants to describe preferences for a variety of site planning characteristics. Through the use of drawings, different residential arrangements were depicted, showing variations in the amount and type of open space, the location of parking, and the density of the site. Although it is improbable that one particular site plan will satisfy all of the participants' requirements, responses suggested the types of site arrangements that met individual needs. Once participants became familiar with the drawings, the best solutions were chosen for outdoor children's play, privacy, neighborhood activities, and physical security. Individual selections were pooled within small groups for discussion and consensus.

An alternate approach for exploring site options with users is to present photographs that convey various densities by house type, such as high- and low-rise buildings. The choice of photographic images—new or old, single- or multifamily—also suggests the preferred character and location of residential areas, such as inner city or suburban (Figure 4.15).

House Model Game

A three-dimensional game developed by Jeff Bishop (1987), the House Model Game, provides each player with an opportunity to propose a housing layout based on personal preference. The eventual design is a result of a trade-off and the opportunity to evaluate a range of ideas from within the group. The game can be used to achieve a wide variety of objectives, some related to physical and social aspects of housing layout, others to the development of personal and group decision making. The House Model Game can be used to consider both urban and rural sites.

The size of the group can vary considerably. It has worked well with groups of 30 people, from ages nine and upward. No special equipment is necessary. House models can be constructed as shown in Figure 4.16 and made with any piece of folded paper. The site can be a blank sheet of legal-size paper. Each house comes with a private back garden, and 12 houses and gardens must be accommodated on the site. Basic site planning criteria are as follows:

- There should be a path to each house.
- There should be sunlight in every garden.
- Each house must have a place to park a car.
- There must be some public open space.

The objectives of the exercise are to find a layout that is attractive, easy to use, and as cheap as possible. Roads and parking can be drawn on the site as appropriate. Considerations for participants to think about are privacy, deliveries, safety, noise, views, landscaping, climate, wheelchairs, gardens, bicycles, energy conservation, and wayfinding (Figure 4.17). As individuals complete the exercise, they fasten their models to the site and evaluate each other's solution according to the

COMMUNITY

When planning environments for older adults it is necessary to consider the size of community in which social or residential facilities are located. What are the advantages and disadvantages of different-sized communities? Consider land cost, amenities, and services when making your comments.

	Advantages	Disadvantages
Urban	_____	_____
	_____	_____
	_____	_____
Suburban	_____	_____
	_____	_____
	_____	_____
Small Town	_____	_____
	_____	_____
	_____	_____
Rural	_____	_____
	_____	_____
	_____	_____

ACCESSIBILITY

When planning environments for older adults, how important are the services listed below? Please rate them according to their order of importance by placing a "1" next to the most important, and so on.

Park _____
Medical center _____
Public transportation _____
Retail stores _____
Entertainment _____
Schools _____

PLACE

Arrange the four housing sites in order of preference:

Best ___ ___ ___ ___ Worst

Livable Sites

FIGURE 4.15 Housing density score sheet.

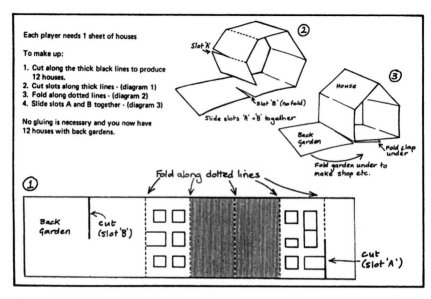

FIGURE 4.16 Construction of house model.

FIGURE 4.17 Large-scale housing layout. *(Photo: Jeff Bishop.)*

original criteria on a five-point scale ranging from *very attractive* to *very unattractive, very easy* to live in to *not easy* to live in, and *very cheap* to *very expensive*. A group discussion of the results can focus on the basic alternatives as well as the assumptions initially made by each player in responding to the question, For whom were you designing?

Trade-off games are a means of permitting citizens to participate more fully in the planning and decision-making processes that affect their lives and sense of well-being (Robinson, 1987).

Planning for Real

An active method of engaging people in the planning process is Planning for Real (Gibson, 1988), a kit complete with cutout buildings, neighborhood facilities, information cards, and case histories, devised and used mainly in Britain for neighborhood improvement. Its aim is to facilitate communication between professionals and the public. Local people initially construct a model of a community, large enough to allow everyone to participate and to focus on tangible issues. It is constructed in sections and moved to various locations in the community, such as churches, shopping centers, and schools. The kit contains 150 suggestions marked on cutouts that people then arrange on the model, gradually arriving at consensus. A model works, argues Gibson, its developer, because it begins to establish working relationships between professionals, citizens, and public officials (Figure 4.18).

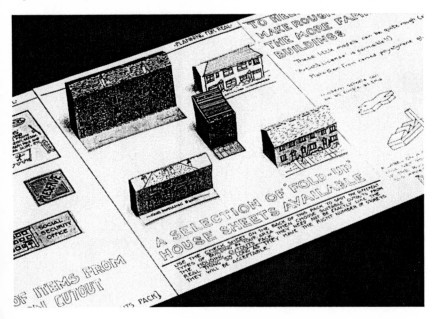

FIGURE 4.18 Planning for Real kit. *(Reprinted, by permission, from Reinhard Goethert , Action Planning for Cities, p. 89. Copyright 1997 by John Wiley & Sons, Inc.)*

The model enables people to see the problems and possibilities as a whole, making them more confident and adept at exploring ways to overcome problems and arrive at solutions. Finally, participants make concrete proposals, such as additions to buildings, gardens, and playgrounds, as well as neighborhood improvements. Participants in this process felt that the model allowed them to reach a "common ground quicker, because with words everybody's words are the same; but the imagination may be different" (Gibson, 1988, p. 204).

CHAPTER

5

Participation in Urban and Rural Environments

Traditional approaches to urban and neighborhood development were based on the master planning model, whereby policies and action strategies were linked to physical information, such as land use and building condition. More recently this approach has been replaced by a goal-based planning model, in which policies and actions are derived from social as well as physical information (e.g., client-user goals, census data, and demographic factors). The complexity of big cities, with their large numbers of people and institutions, usually results in a fragmentation of functions and a division of power, roles, and responsibilities so that there is a likelihood of many disconnections between the dimensions of a community. In a small town the dimensions of cultural norms, social structure, local economy, and decision making are much more interconnected than in a big city. Thus, the goal-based development plan used in the town of Bangalow, Australia, made connections between awareness, perception, decision making, and implementation.

The current interest in small towns is associated with a concern for what are believed to be the more manageable scales of human activity. Philosophically, smallness-seekers run the gamut from the anarchists who believe in minimal external control, to the critics of urbanization who find large cities unlivable and even unmanageable.

As a result, there have been apparent changes to small towns. Rather than being autonomous and distinctive places to live, they are no longer independent or even separable. Once characterized by limited growth and minimum resident control, small communities are experiencing renewed interest, with the people returning being significantly different from those who never left. There are also indications that small-town residents voice higher satisfaction with work, housing, and leisure time activity, and the rate of participation tends to be higher in small communities.

Despite the higher rating of subjective factors, such as quality of life, small towns are in need of help, particularly from the planners who produce master plans that look alike. The idiosyncrasies and characteristics of each small town are typically ignored. Every town has a personality, a unique combination of elements that create its identity. A town's character, or sense of place, is shaped by its architectural style, natural setting, cultural diversity, use of materials, and countless other local conditions that distinguish one place from another. The relationship of all these elements to each other is an important aspect of a town's identity (Sanoff, 1981).

There are four action modes generally used in small-town revitalization (Swanson, Cohen, and Swanson, 1979). In some of them proposed action is a one-shot effort, and in others activities are undertaken sequentially or simultaneously. In some, values are made explicit at the outset, whereas others project values that are implicit, not clarified or justified. In some, outside experts play a prominent role, and in others, local residents dominate the process.

The *categorical* approach tends to carry out one substantive project at a time. The presumption is that each problem may be solved in relative isolation, without regard to its interconnections with other problems. Recreation problems, housing problems, and infrastructure problems all receive separate treatments, while the cumulative direction for the community structure goes unattended. State and federal grants and programs, where support is available, nurture this piecemeal approach by focusing on specific problem areas. This approach encourages local people to think in categorical terms.

The *comprehensive planning* approach intends to overcome the piecemeal process through an overall assessment of community facilities and services. The major problems in a community are identified and recommendations are made, often without an analysis of the impact on the residents. This approach examines the problems, but never sets them in perspective as to how they relate to social structures, decision-making systems, and community values.

The *integrative* approach attempts to involve people in a process whereby they identify their own needs and preferred courses of action. These considerations are part of the process of organizing, choosing priorities, mobilizing support for a proposal, and engaging in the implementation of the project. Thus, a specific problem such as housing, sewage, or social services may be the beginning of a deeper exploration of the community's problem. The integrative approach seeks to connect problems to the social, political, and value contexts of the community. Consequently, the solutions to housing problems may be found in the social structure or political system, instead of in the narrowly defined rehabilitation or construction actions that commonly emerge from the categorical approach.

The *dialogical* approach emphasizes values clarification. It is concerned with having local residents articulate their values up front, understand how those values help or constrain achieving desired goals, and decide on the necessary changes that must be made. In many community improvement projects, the values being reinforced have tended to be those of the dominant persons or groups in town. To avoid this, those who advocate the dialogical format of community problem solving encourage community discussions of internal dynamics and values before engaging in specific projects. Basically, this is a process of community education whereby residents become aware of the forces acting on a community from within and without.

This balance of elements that creates a town's identity is under constant pressure for change. For this reason it is important that new development and change be guided by a conservation philosophy, a conscious policy of respect for the existing environment, and for the unique identity of towns. Thus, a renewed awareness is necessary to guide change within certain desired limits. Awareness is the beginning of a process leading to the understanding of problems, clarification of objectives, and the consequences of the strategies for change.

SWOT Analysis

The revitalization of a neighborhood or small town requires knowledge of its internal conditions as well as those external forces that may impinge on its development. An investigation to this end is referred to by Bernie Jones (1990) as an environmental scan, which includes the SWOT—strengths, weaknesses, opportunities, and threats—within a community. The information needed in a neighborhood or small-town planning process is categorized as physical, social, or economic. Jones identifies 13 areas of needed information:

- Natural environments
- Existing land uses
- Zoning
- Circulation
- Utilities
- Housing
- Community facilities and services
- Urban design features
- General physical condition
- History

- Demography
- Social analysis
- Economic base

A method of organizing this information is to employ the SWOT categories, using a map to annotate and identify positive as well as negative features. A useful technique for integrating the data is to compose a scenario describing what the community would be like at some point in the future if certain trends are continued or reversed. The KEEPS game (p. 278) is an exercise that can enable the public to be aware of the strategies effective in reversing undesirable trends.

Richmond Neighborhood Charrette

▶ Charrette Process   Participatory action research
 Community action planning Public forum
▶ Focus groups   Strategic planning
 Game simulation   Visioning
▶ Goal setting   ▶ Workshop
▶ Group interaction

Highland Park is a low-income neighborhood in Richmond, Virginia, where Highland Park Restoration and Preservation Program, Inc. (HP RAPP), a nonprofit community-based corporation, has a mission that includes creating and designing model neighborhood programs. Proposed as a model for future development throughout the community, a nine-block "Adopt-a-Block" incubator and the adjacent commercial strip were designated by the community for total revitalization.

The aim of the charrette process was to involve residents, especially skilled community leaders, and invited architects and planners to share their ideas regarding community development. A planned one-day event allowed neighborhood residents to select key issues and identify appropriate goals and strategies for their implementation. Community leaders and professionals participated in the charrette process as a resource to the residents to ensure that informed decisions would be made.

An initial meeting of local leaders, project coordinator Jeff Levine, and an invited design consultant, who constituted the Core Planning Team, resulted in identifying four major development areas for discussion at the charrette. These included business development, housing, image and safety, and education and culture. From this discussion, resource teams consisting of area specialists in each of the key issue areas generated appropriate goals and strategies for their implementation (Figure 5.1). Every effort was made to include goals and strategies for presentation

HOUSING

Rehabilitate housing in minor and/or major levels of deterioration

Identify the availability of low- and moderate-income housing

Establish policy to regulate rental property problems

Encourage low-income housing,

Encourage middle-income housing,

Promote increased home ownership

Increase the utilization of existing housing space by subdividing large homes into duplexes

Increase available rental housing using existing homes

Establish design guidelines for new and rehabilitated construction

Preserve the historical heritage of Highland Park

Increase the construction of small multifamily housing

Evaluate needs for the homeless

Remove blighted homes that are beyond rehabilitation

EDUCATION AND CULTURE

Provide education training for undereducated and unemployed

Provide job training

Provide continued education training for youth, adults, and disabled persons

Establish a local skill development/job market training center in the community

Establish a mentor program with local businesses, universities, and churches

Establish day-care centers

Establish after-school programs

Develop a self-awareness and esteem program

Sponsor art, culture, and special events to attract people to the area

Provide a racially, culturally, and ethnically integrated community

Reduce school dropout rate

Establish a community center

IMAGE AND SAFETY

Create a clean neighborhood

Create a Crime Watch Program unique to Highland Park community that will address economic concerns and policing

Eradicate violent crime

Establish work release and training program for drug offenders

Provide rehabilitation for substance abusers

Increase drug-free zone, remove illegal use and distribution of drugs

Install a home/building safety program

Improve landscape and lighting to decrease crime

Preserve the architectural character of the community

Boost community interest and civic pride

Improve pedestrian linkage and walkways

Promote the development of a center that is filled with lively, economically viable activities

Establish an environmental protection program

BUSINESS DEVELOPMENT

Improve businesses along Meadowbridge Road from 4th Avenue to Carolina Avenue

Develop programs that promote the growth of existing small businesses

Develop a marketing plan to encourage new businesses into the area

Complete a marketing analysis that determines the type of building in the business area

Provide for a concentration of a wide variety of goods, services, and activities in the area

Provide opportunities for more employment

Provide loans and grants for business development

Evaluate the need for parking to serve consumers

Provide for a mix of both public and private sector businesses

Establish special tax breaks and other incentives to promote the development of new businesses

FIGURE 5.1 Richmond's major development areas.

at the charrette that were realistic and achievable. This approach allowed area residents to examine a broad range of possible options from which to make choices.

Preparation for the charrette included the following:

- A promotion campaign, including graphic materials and banners to announce the forthcoming meeting
- Venue selection for the event, including the organization of space, equipment and food and media coordination
- Collection of data to inform participants about loan programs and the Community Reinvestment Act; gathering of information on historical development, housing conditions, crime, and area demographics
- A follow-up report and plan of action

The aim of the initial charrette event was to allow each participant to select three goals with the highest priority for each respective key issue, and to elect to participate in one of the key issue groups. The procedure for the selection activity was to provide each participant with 12 colored tabs (3 red, 3 yellow, 3 green, 3 blue), corresponding to the key issues. After hearing the presentation of key issues by the facilitator of each issue group, participants individually selected three goals they believed were important to the four key issues, then fastened the appropriate colored tab next to that goal statement (Figure 5.2).

FIGURE 5.2 Participants selecting key goals.

Individuals then selected a group in which they wished to participate. Group sizes ranged from 20 to 40 people, with a trained facilitator keeping the discussion focused. Each group received a list of strategies prepared by the resource team, along with the goals achieving the highest priorities. Group discussions focused on matching strategies to goals and developing an action plan for each strategy. Action plans answered the questions Who? How? and When?

Upon choosing the pertinent strategies for implementing a particular goal, a recorder completed a "strategy card," indicating the strategy, goal, key issue, and action plan. Action plans told how to implement each strategy, who would be involved with the implementation, and the time frame for implementation. Design implications for certain strategies required the presence of volunteer architects, who provided sketches to clarify the ideas (Figures 5.3a and 5.3b). Completed cards were reproduced for overhead presentation at the end of the charrette, and copies were distributed to all participants.

During the six years following the participatory event, the charrette resulted in a number of significant achievements. Business development goals were articulated as follows:

- To improve businesses in the main commercial area
- To nurture small businesses
- To provide opportunities for increased employment in the area
- To provide for a concentration of a wide variety of goods, services, and activities in the area

A student and faculty team from Hampton University developed a business plan and a model of the area showing how businesses could function. The plan was to create a catalyst for economic development along the main commercial strip. Recognizing the lack of sufficient business in the area as well as limited availability of funds, the community developed a proposal to seek support from the City of Richmond to establish an enterprise zone.

During the charrette, key goals were also established for the housing development area:

- To rehabilitate deteriorated housing
- To maintain the present density of the neighborhood
- To promote home ownership
- To create in-fill housing sympathetic to the Victorian character of the area

Through the support of local financing about 30 houses have been rehabilitated (Figure 5.4) by the architectural firm of Shelter Design, and designs for new in-fill housing have been prepared. A major historic property now houses the offices of HP RAPP.

AFTER

BEFCRE

(a)

(b)

OLD NEIGHBORHOOD - PRETTY HOUSES

FIGURE 5.3a & b Architect's sketches during the charrette.

FIGURE 5.4 Completed projects. *(Photo: Jeff Levine.)*

For the image and safety development area, key goals were established as follows:

- To create a distinct and continuous landscape street and open space character
- To improve maintenance and encourage small-scale improvements to existing buildings and sites
- To preserve and improve the distinctive visual and architectural character of the Adopt-a-Block area in Highland Park
- To preserve the history of Highland Park
- To preserve architecturally and historically important buildings
- To create a safe neighborhood

These goals were achieved by the residents' creation of a crime-watch program and a periodic neighborhood cleanup and landscape improvement program through the Adopt-a-Block model. The creation of an arboretum, also the outgrowth of the charrette, enhances a neighborhood park located on a vacant lot supporting a billboard. This was a pro bono project developed by landscape architect Charles Snead with the assistance of Shelter Design.

Key goals of the education and culture development area included the following:

- To sponsor art, cultural, and special events to attract people to the area
- To promote a racially, culturally, and ethnically integrated community

The achievement of these goals required the involvement of youth in the community development process. Operation Architecture, an environmental awareness program, involved middle-school students in a process of rediscovering the historical characteristics of their community. Partnerships between HP RAPP and local schools helped to establish periodic festivals for parents and children as well as a number of ecologically oriented projects conducted by students both in the classroom and in the community.

The citywide effect of the charrette was the Adopt-a-Block process, the block watch, and the community festivals, whereby a community coordinator has extended these activities to other communities. Many charrettes have occurred since the initial event. Exploring such topics as crime prevention through environmental design, residents and local police met at Virginia Commonwealth University to explore streetscape and neighborhood watch strategies. Building Better Communities, a series of inner-city neighborhood charrettes, brought participants from different communities to the Museum of Art to discuss various collaborative approaches.

Town of Bangalow, Australia*

▶ Charrette Process
Community action planning
▶ Focus groups
Game simulation
▶ Goal setting
▶ Group interaction

Participatory action research
Public forum
▶ Strategic planning
▶ Visioning
▶ Workshop

Bangalow is a small Australian town in New South Wales with a population of 780 people. The township and its immediate surrounding rural area consist of a population of 3,000. Bangalow lies in the valley of Byron Creek, 12 kilometers west of Byron Bay. With the coming of the railway in 1894 and the clearing of the "Big Scrub" rain forest, Bangalow thrived as a dairying district. Its comparative wealth in the early 1900s is evidenced by the fine commercial buildings in the town center. The town's historic character was noted in an assessment of environmental heritage (Shellshear, 1983), and efforts have been extended to reinforce the town's continuity with the historical past.

In 1990 a design resource team spent four days helping to preserve the town's past and to shape a new future. The team consisted of the present author and four architecture students from the University of Sydney, as well as several local architects and planners who served as consultants and information resources. This "charrette" process, a period of intensive planning, was decided upon as the most expedient and time-effective strategy to enable the town to reassess its future, inasmuch as the proposed bypass off the Pacific Highway would dramatically affect the potential of Bangalow as a rural tourist center and gateway to the hinterlands.

The visit of the design team began with a meeting of community leaders, followed by a bus and walking tour with interested citizens. The tour provided the design team with additional insights about the community from local professionals who had conducted feasibility studies of the implications of the bypass.

The second day consisted of interviews with interested townspeople, who presented conflicting opinions and attitudes about the town's future. The purpose of the interviews was to identify the range of issues that, from the resident's perspective, seemed to be crucial to the economic and social development of Bangalow.

*This project was sponsored by the Arts Council of New South Wales, the Bangalow By-Pass Ring Road Committee, and the Community Cultural Development Unit, Australia Council. The design team included Matt Devine, Ann McCallum, Roger Ackland, David Young, and David Huxtable. The project coordinator was Rory O'Moore with Helen O'Moore, Stacey Pollard, and Vicki Reynolds, all from the town of Bangalow.

The resource team's full schedule is shown below.

Resource Team Schedule

Evening before visit — Team arrival and informal social event

Day One

8:00–9:30 A.M. — Breakfast briefing with community leaders and resource people.

9:30–1:00 P.M. — Driving tour of Bangalow and surrounds with community leaders and local professionals; includes industrial and residential areas, educational institutions, and the bypass location

1:00–2:00 P.M. — Working lunch

2:00–4:00 P.M. — Walking tour of Bangalow

6:00–8:00 P.M. — Resource team discussion and preparation for Day Two interviews

Day Two

8:00–8:30 A.M. — Working breakfast

8:30–10:30 A.M. — Interviews with interested individuals and community leaders

10:30–12:30 P.M. — Model making and drawing workshop with schoolchildren

12:30–1:30 P.M. — Working lunch

1:30–5:30 P.M. — Interviews continue

6:00–12:00 midnight — Resource team preparation of workshop materials

Day Three

8:00–9:00 A.M. — Working breakfast

9:00–12:00 noon — Preparation for workshop

12:00–1:00 P.M. — Working lunch

1:00–6:00 P.M. — Preparation for workshop

6:30–9:00 P.M. — Community workshop

9:00–10:30 P.M. — Dinner with Director of Arts Council of NSW, community consultants, and community leaders

Day Four

8:00–9:00 A.M. — Working breakfast

9:00–12:00 noon — Measuring of key buildings and sites in the community

12:00–1:00 P.M. — Working lunch

1:00–6:00 P.M. — Continued gathering of information for future design and planning

6:00–8:30 P.M. — Dinner with community leaders for workshop summary and recommendations for future planning and management

Some residents displayed interest in converting Bangalow into a "heritage village with true charm," whereas opposing views expressed belief in "not looking back." Many seemed to agree, however, that recognition of the town's history was important. Gateways to Bangalow emerged as a popular issue, as well as signage and streetscape enhancement. Keen interest was shown for replacing the traditional verandahs (covered porches) and encouraging reluctant shopkeepers to invest in Main Street improvements.

Many residents also cited new and improved facilities for the visual and performing arts as a need, with an emphasis on places for the town's youth. Some people lamented the problem of resident apathy, yet others remarked about the "good community feeling." It was generally recognized that the community was heterogeneous, with many new families with young children moving to town. Consequently, the services in Bangalow were inadequate, forcing residents to shop in nearby towns.

Although most residents seemed optimistic about Bangalow's future, there was concern about their ability to satisfy all authorities that impose conflicting and arbitrary regulations on new development. Similarly, a popular view expressed was to limit residential development and ensure that green views from Main Street are preserved. The results of the interviews provided the necessary background to prepare for a community-wide workshop, which was held at the local bowling club on the third evening. This event was planned to provide an opportunity for the residents of Bangalow to meet face-to-face to consider the goals and strategies that would enable their ideas to be implemented. Public participation in Bangalow's future through a community workshop was a strategy for bringing together different generations of residents, an event that had not previously occurred in the town. The design team relied on the expertise of the community participants to shape their future in developing a list of goal statements prepared from previous interviews.

The objective for design intervention was to develop a process whereby citizens could identify important issues and outline specific alternatives and implementation procedures, so that they could change the plan as they believed necessary. Because conflicting values are inherent in any goal-oriented process, an approach was developed that encouraged community members to clarify their differences through a game simulation in which goals and implementation strategies were key factors that participants could manipulate.

Inasmuch as Bangalow's young people represent the future of the town, a special children's workshop was conducted with fifth- and sixth-grade students from the public school. The young people were involved in developing models of their future town, as well as wall murals depicting their likes and dislikes (Figure 5.5). The message from the 10- and 11-year-old children was clear: "More stuff for the kids." Features such as a pinball parlor, skating rink and park were specifically identified, but there was a general feeling that Bangalow lacked the necessary services and amenities associated with a self-sufficient community. The results of this two-hour activity were exhibited at the community workshop held at the Bangalow Bowling Club. Special activities were developed for the younger children

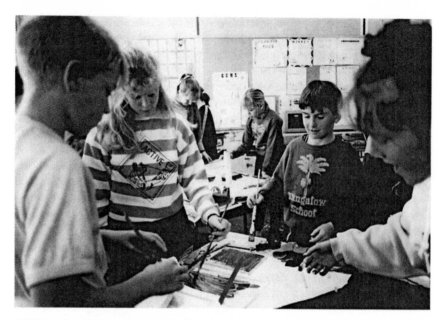

FIGURE 5.5 Children making models of their future town. *(Photo: Henry Sanoff.)*

attending the workshop while their parents were engaged in the goal-setting process. The children viewed a 20-minute video of their school workshop showing the making of their artwork.

To begin the community workshop, small groups of five persons each were formed. Participants were given the following list of goals:

- To recognize the area's natural and scenic resources as major assets
- To heighten public awareness to the town's unique historical character
- To provide youth-oriented activities
- To improve gateways to the town
- To enhance the community's natural resources
- To promote downtown revitalization
- To package and promote an image of innovation and tradition
- To encourage the arts to contribute to the development of the community
- To promote the town's historic resources
- To create avenues for public/private partnerships for community development

From the list provided, they selected four statements that seemed important in developing the town. The individual lists were then pooled, and through a process of collaboration four mutually agreed-upon statements were selected by consensus. Through a similar process, complementary strategies were selected that could effectively accomplish each of the goal choices. During both phases of the process group members were urged to support their individual choices and to persuade the total group to include their own particular selections (Figure 5.6).

The process provided the impetus for discussions with town members and the subsequent development of goals reflecting the wide range of possibilities for the town of Bangalow. The citizens of the town explored many ideas. These were summarized by a concern for the town's unique heritage, and for the provision of services and facilities for special populations and interest groups.

In addition to presenting the goal-setting exercise, the design team prepared sketches of proposed changes to features of the town that were identified by the residents during their interviews. This part of the workshop focused on six different aspects of the town, among which were the town entrance, building signage, infill and open space, and the adaptive reuse of vacant buildings. The intent was to allow participants to compare the existing situation with proposed changes in order to fully realize the potential impact of the changes (Figure 5.7).

The results of the workshop were analyzed by clustering similar goals and compatible strategies, along with comments made about changes in the town's appearance. On the fourth day a strategic plan was proposed to enable the residents of Bangalow to move toward their stated goals. The components of the strategic plan included a statement of purpose, drawing upon the goals developed at the community workshop, such as "To recognize the area's natural and scenic resources as major assets."

FIGURE 5.6   Twenty work groups participating in the planning session. *(Photo: Henry Sanoff.)*

Verandahs

Existing

What three features do you like best about the scene?

I. _____
II. _____
III. _____

What three features do you like least about this scene?

I. _____
II. _____
III. _____

Design Idea

What three features do you like best about the scene?

I. _____
II. _____
III. _____

What three features do you like least about this scene?

I. _____
II. _____
III. _____

FIGURE 5.7 Comparison of existing situation to proposed changes.

This statement defined what should be accomplished through the strategic plan, and it would be the responsibility of the participants in the process to shape this statement into a series of tangible outcomes. Because the goals are broad statements of intent, strategies are measurable tasks that support the accomplishment of goals. Action steps further advance the strategies by specifying activities that contribute to their achievement (Figure 5.8).

Implementation of the strategic plan required the formation of a new organization to provide the needed communication and coordination between civic, historic, government, and arts-related organizations. Although this would be an independent organization, it would bring together representatives from existing groups with the intention of integrating economic development and the cultural life of the town. Twenty-five people agreed to become part of a steering committee, with task forces created in Natural Resource Development, Urban Design, Cultural Facilities, Cultural Tourism, and Media Communication Education. The

GOAL:

To create a permanent home for performing and visual arts organizations in Bangalow.

STRATEGY:

Renovate the art gallery into the Bangalow Center for the Arts.
Establish steering committee to oversee facility planning and fund-raising.

Action Steps	Responsibility	Time-Line
Appoint committee	Spirit of Bangalow, Inc.	September 1990
Have support committee work with office staff	Spirit of Bangalow, Inc.	October 1990
Hold national design competition	Committee	March 1991
Hire capital campaign consultant and begin fund-raising	Committee	June 1991
Select architect	Committee	September 1991

FIGURE 5.8　An example of strategies and action steps.

identification of the task forces resulted from an analysis of the patterns of goal statements generated at the workshop.

Two months after the formation of a new organization called the Spirit of Bangalow, task forces reported significant progress toward fund-raising and implementation of numerous projects, including a community park, the restoration of an old movie theater into an arts center, and the restoration of verandahs. One year after the initial community workshop, substantial changes were made, such as the addition of several verandahs (Figure 5.9) and a children's park.

Participation in neighborhoods and with community organizations is widely recognized as a solution to many social problems. Over the last two decades, people in many neighborhoods and small towns have come together to create their own community-based organizations to tackle problems that government and the private sector have long neglected. They have formed countless block clubs, self-help groups, neighborhood associations, community organizing fund drives, and community development corporations. The public demand for participation, especially in planning, has grown to the point where governments have begun to incorporate into their legislation compulsory provisions for public participation, and public authorities have come to regard public involvement as a normal part of their practice (Shearer, 1984). In many situations it can be observed that the participation process is not considered a separate exercise from the design process.

Community participation is a complex concept. Planning for effective participation requires an analysis of the issues to be discussed, the individuals or groups that are to be affected, the resources that will be needed, and the goals for which the participation is being initiated. Although it is necessary to identify goals and objectives in planning for participation, it is also necessary to analyze the techniques

FIGURE 5.9　New verandahs added to the streetscape. *(Photo: Rory O'Moore.)*

available and the resources they require. Techniques such as the use of surveys, review boards, neighborhood meetings, conferences, task forces, workshops, and interviews represent a few of the options available to participatory designers. When people participate in the creation of their environment, they need the feeling of control; it is the only way their needs and values can be taken into consideration.

Town of Murfreesboro, North Carolina

▶ Charrette Process   Participatory action research
Community action planning   Public forum
▶ Focus groups   Strategic planning
▶ Game simulation   ▶ Visioning
▶ Goal setting   ▶ Workshop
Group interaction

Growth and development constitute a problem not only for large cities, but for small towns as well. Yet the methods used for citizen involvement in urban neighborhoods are equally suitable for use in small communities. This case study describes the delicate balance necessary between citizen learning and effective decision making.

Historically, the area surrounding the town of Murfreesboro, North Carolina, was inhabited by Native American villages. Incorporated in 1787, Murfreesboro was a trade center with a major shipping industry linked to the New England seaports, which accounts for the particular style of architecture found in the buildings of that period. The town was a center of commerce and education and was referred to as the "Athens of the South." Industry and commerce, however, fell off as a result of the Civil War and the subsequent depression until their rebirth following World War II.

In recent years the town of Murfreesboro, under the direction of the Murfreesboro Historic Association (MHA), rehabilitated and reused several of its old, historically significant buildings. As a result, the community benefited by the addition of space with potential to support a variety of activities, but also retained its important educational and cultural resources as reminders of the town's physical, social and economic development. In order for the MHA to make effective decisions and guide the future of the historic district, the Community Development Group devised a growth plan (Sanoff, 1978).

The concept of conservation through adaptive use has been applied in many communities throughout the country and is widely recognized as a viable approach in small communities as well as in urban areas. The increasing demand for residential and commercial development, coupled with the continuing deterioration of older structures within a community, raised questions concerning the importance of conserving old buildings. The dozens of reasons for preservation can be grouped under four main headings: cultural memory, successful proxemics, environmental diversity, and economic gain. These are described as follows:

- *Cultural memory.* Buildings are tangible reminders of the accomplishments and growth of a community throughout its history. Different architectural styles are a physical record of the environment in which the community's ancestors worked and lived.
- *Successful proxemics.* This refers to the relationship between people, the activities they engage in, and the places where they perform these activities. Before the development of the automobile as the primary means of transportation and the initiation of land use zoning, most neighborhoods displayed the characteristics of successful proxemics. Places of employment, schools, churches, and neighborhood stores were within walking distance of one's home. Today, the social interaction that once occurred as a result of walking to and from work or the neighborhood store has been lost. Consequently, the sense of town or neighborhood identity has diminished.
- *Environmental diversity.* People's everyday environment is becoming increasingly more homogeneous in appearance and in use. Zoning regulations, with restrictions on land use and density, building appearance, and location of a building on its site, were intended to produce an orderly environment, but the result is often homogeneity. Rapid, uncontrolled growth, too, created communities that are automobile dependent. These influences make the preservation of older buildings and neighborhoods, with their diversity of building types, a desirable alternative to many of the newer monotonous environments.
- *Economic gain.* Recycling old buildings to new uses makes it economical to save them, retaining much of the original building. Investments in rehabilitation not only add to the cultural resources of a community but also produce a higher market value for the improved property.

The town of Murfreesboro still contains neighborhoods that have successful proxemics. Recognizing that these neighborhoods, like others throughout the United States, have adapted because of the growing pressures for change, an alternative approach to development was deemed a necessity. Faced with limited resources and infrequent professional assistance, the MHA sought assistance to develop a process whereby citizens groups could identify important issues, explore alternative solutions, and select implementation procedures so that they could change the plan as they felt it should be changed. Because conflicting values are inherent in any goal-oriented process, an approach was developed that encouraged community members to clarify their differences through a design game in which goals and strategies were the key elements that participants could manipulate. The

Knowledge of Emerging Environmental Preservation Strategies (KEEPS) exercise (p. 279) provided groups interested in preserving the many qualities unique to older neighborhoods with an understanding of the strategies open to them. Organizing and planning for the preservation of the qualities the community had identified as important relied on consideration of the following factors:

- The environmental qualities the group chose to develop
- The community's goals
- The types of strategies the community could realistically use to accomplish their goals

This exercise prepared community residents to engage in the design development process. The KEEPS game provided the impetus for discussions with community members and the subsequent development of goals reflecting the wide range of possibilities for the town of Murfreesboro. Community members utilizing the nominal group technique (NGT), whereby individuals proposed, discussed, and compared statements and finally established their priorities, generated ten goal statements for the town, listed in order of importance as follows:

1. Preserve the history of Murfreesboro.
2. Preserve architecturally and historically important buildings.
3. Boost community interest and civic pride.
4. Control change in the historic district.
5. Use the river and ravines to full potential.
6. Restore many homes to period authenticity.
7. Influence restoration in other parts of town.
8. Involve more people in MHA's plans.
9. Improve business along Main Street,
10. Eliminate nonhistoric homes from the historic district.

The historic district and its adjacent environment was then subdivided into target areas, a particular geographic entity being defined by physical and/or social boundaries or certain characteristics that make it unique from others directly adjacent. In addition to the geographic areas, issues such as visual quality, historic district image, and regulation of development, were pertinent to each of the designated areas. For each geographic area or issue there were specific goals generated by community members, of determination of qualities unique to that particular area, and alternative plans and policies to achieve the stated goals. The alternative plans developed by the design team consisted of two parts—a general policy and suggestions for implementation.

The general policy consisted of a statement describing an ideal future for each particular area of the town. For example, for the Williams Street-South Side area (Figure 5.10) the general policy for the first alternative plan was as follows:

WILLIAMS STREET-SOUTH SIDE

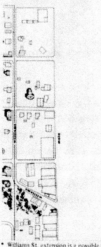

- Williams St. extension is a possible formal entrance to the area.
- Two dead ends means little vehicular traffic.
- The narrow setback of the buildings along Williams St. is conducive to public/commercial activity.

Rea Store—Williams St.

- Much pedestrian activity along street.
- Easy access to ravine from street.
- Daniel's Nursery increases the amount of plant life in the CBD.
- Commercial–residential transition gives diversity to street.

_____
_____
_____
_____
_____
_____
_____
_____
_____

goals related to area

ADD & DELETE AS THE GENERAL GOALS OF THE MHA CHANGE (see PROCEDURE FOR CHOOSING THE 'RIGHT' PLAN in the previous chapter)

- Boost the community interest and civic pride
- Control change in the historic district
- Use river and ravines to full potential
- Influence restoration in other parts of town
- Involve more people in the MHA's plans
- Improve business along Main St.
- Eliminate the non-historic homes from the historic district

_____
_____
_____
_____
_____
_____
_____
_____
_____
_____
_____

choosing the 'right' plan

EVERYTIME IMPLEMENTATION OF ANY GENERAL OR SPECIFIC SUGGESTION IS CONSIDERED UNDER ANY OF THE FOLLOWING ALTERNATIVE PLANS, GO THROUGH PROCEDURE FOR CHOOSING THE 'RIGHT' PLAN IN THE PREVIOUS CHAPTER

implementing the 'right' plan

IF THE MHA HAS DIFFERENT, BETTER, OR MORE EXACT SUGGESTIONS FOR IMPLEMENTING ANY OF THE FOLLOWING ALTERNATIVE PLANS, GO THROUGH THE DESIGN GUIDE LINES IN THE FOLLOWING CHAPTER TO DETERMINE IF THE SUGGESTIONS ARE ACCEPTABLE

alternative plan 1

SCRATCH OUT ALL SUGGESTIONS THAT ARE NO LONGER PERTINENT OR HAVE ALREADY BEEN IMPLEMENTED

policy
The historic district should be expanded to include the half-block to the south of Williams St. between Sycamore St. and Second St.

effect
Will promote unified development for both sides of Williams St.

general suggestions for implementation
- Ask the planning board to expand the existing historic district to include [1].
  - all residences on Fourth St. south of

qualities/importance of area

ADD & DELETE AS THE QUALITIES OF THE AREA CHANGE

- Commercial activities were originally located here.
- Location one block from Main St. offers access to goods and services.
- Southern boundary of local historic district—important visually.

Williams Street

- Residential use on south side of Williams St. important to ease transition from commercial area to residential.
- The street contains some of the oldest buildings in Murfreesboro.

Williams St.
- all properties north of the alley that connects Sycamore St. with the Williams St. extension.
- the lot south of Williams St. between Fifth St. and the Williams St. extension.
- all property between Williams St. and Main St., Fifth St. and Fourth St. except lot on the southeast corner of the block.
- Rea house and Hardee's Restaurant lots.
- all property between Williams St. and Main St., Third St. and Second St. except lot on the southwest corner of the block and the lot directly east of that one.

- Ask the planning board to prepare, or have the MHA prepare, a report on the quality of the area to be added. [1]
- Encourage owners in area to attend public hearing(s) concerning the proposal to zone the area historic district.

After historic district zoning has been secured:

- Encourage the planning board to adopt the practice of negotiating with developers, and other property owners, who request zoning changes on property outside the areas covered in this report. If the developer owns property within the Williams St.–South Side area, and will agree to grant to the MHA or to the town a preservation easement on this property—or will agree to relocate an obnoxious use to a site outside the area covered in this report—his zoning change application should be accepted. [1]

- Encourage the city to sell general obligation bonds to underwrite a rehabilitation loan and grant program for this area. If unsuccessful, encourage the city to recapture surplus revenues from increased property valuations in the central section of the historic district and reinvest in rehabilitation of residences on the south side of Williams St. [1]

FIGURE 5.10 Sample work sheet describing goals and qualities of the area.

alternative plan 1

⚑ SCRATCH OUT ALL SUGGESTIONS THAT ARE NO LONGER PERTINENT OR HAVE ALREADY BEEN IMPLEMENTED

policy
A Community Appearance Commission (CAC) should be established.

effect
Will enhance and improve the visual quality and aesthetic characteristics of Murfreesboro.

general suggestions for implementation

* Ask the City Council to appoint a Community Appearance Commission (CAC), in accordance with N.C. enabling legislation. [1]
EFFECT—will authorize the CAC to:
  –initiate, promote and assist in the implementation of programs of general community beautification.
  –seek to coordinate the activities of individuals, agencies and organizations, public and private, whose plans, activities and programs bear upon Murfreesboro's appearance.
  –provide leadership and guidance for individuals and public and private organizations in matters of area or community design and appearance.
  –make studies of the visual characteristics and problems of Murfreesboro, including surveys and inventories, and to recommend standards and policies of design for the entire area, any portion or neighborhood, or any project.
  –prepare both general and specific plans for the improved appearance of Murfreesboro or any part. The plans shall set forth desirable standards and goals for the aesthetic enhancement of Murfreesboro or any part.

* Encourage the City Council to include in the ordinance establishing the CAC the following powers [1]:
  –to request from any public organization its plans for public buildings, facilities, or projects to be located within Murfreesboro.
  –to review these plans and to make recommendations to the appropriate agency, the Murfreesboro planning board, or City Council regarding the aesthetic suitability of the plans.
  –to formulate and recommend to the City Council or planning board the adoption or amendment of ordinances that will serve to enhance the appearance of Murfreesboro and its surrounding areas.
  –to direct the attention of city officials to needed enforcement of any ordinance affecting the appearance of Murfreesboro.
  –to seek voluntary adherence to the standards and policies of its plans.
  –to enter in the performance of its official duties upon private lands.
  –to promote public interest in, and understanding of, its recommendations, studies, and plans, and to that end to prepare, publish and distribute to the public such studies and reports as will advance the cause of improved Murfreesboro appearance.
  –to conduct public hearings and meetings.

* Encourage the City Council to appropriate money for the CAC's use. [1]

* Encourage private agencies, foundations, organizations, individuals, the State or federal government, or any other source to contribute money to the CAC. [1]

* Encourage the City Council to form a joint city/county CAC. [1]

* Once the CAC is established:
  –Encourage the CAC to make a survey of the design resources within Murfreesboro. [1]
  –Encourage the CAC to recommend to the City Council that the existing historic district be expanded to the boundaries of the National Register Historic District. [2]
  –Encourage the City Council to add to the zoning ordinance:
    –an admendment stating that historic district zoning boundaries should be through the middle of a block, not along a street. [1]
    –an amendment stating that certain visually obnoxious land uses should not bound an historic district. This amendment must not affect the location of historic district boundary lines during historic district zoning implementation. nor should this prevent alternative solutions besides removal of conflicting land uses. [1]
    –an amendment establishing a sign ordinance, limiting size, location, and co of signs. [2]

specific suggestions for implementation

SUGGESTIONS PERTAINING TO SPECIFIC BUILDINGS—
* Restore the facades of the Peter Williams house, Murfree Law Office, Thompson house, Winborne Law Office, Dormer house, Lassiter house, and Howell house. [1–3]

* Offer to restore the exterior facade of the Vinson house if the owner agrees to keep it the house in its present location. [1]

SUGGESTIONS PERTAINING TO LANDSCAPING
* All properties owned by the MHA should be kept trimmed and neat. [1]

SUGGESTIONS THE MHA SHOULD MAKE TO OTHERS—
* Encourage the CAC to seek voluntary adherence to its standards and policies from:
  –Georgia-Pacific
  –the building materials supply establishment south of Williams St. between Williams St. extension and Fifth St.
  –East Main St. commercial owners [2]

alternative plan 2

⚑ SCRATCH OUT ALL SUGGESTIONS THAT ARE NO LONGER PERTINENT OR HAVE ALREADY BEEN IMPLEMENTED

policy
A general educational program on the design resources of Murfreesboro should be implemented.

effect
Will increase citizen environmental awareness.

general suggestions for implementation

* Conduct a survey, such as the following utilized in Doylestown, Pa., of the design stimuli (resources) in Murfreesboro. [1]

Doylestown, Pa., survey sheet

* Encourage an interested Chowan College class to do the design resources survey. [1]

* Encourage the city government and all Murfreesboro's residents to conserve these design resources. [1]

* Encourage the public schools in Murfreesboro to implement an environmental education program. The program should educate students about the built environment and its relationships to people and to the natural environment. [1]

* Conduct a series of programs, open to the public, on the design resources of Murfreesboro. Such programs might include [1]:
  –Slide programs about the design resources in Murfreesboro (and/or about specific parts of the design resources).
  –Participatory projects, to get the town's people involved in the actual conservation of the design resources. Projects might include: litter pick-up; identification of plants/trees by markers; development of a large map, located somewhere in the center of the town, locating the major design resources of Murfreesboro; etc.
  –Workshops on specific methods the general public can use to conserve design resources.

* Make a movie about the conservation of design resources in general to be circulated to communities around the state. [2]

* Develop a series of brochures concerning specific design resource elements to be circulated around the state. [2]

FIGURE 5.10 *(Continued)*

"The historic district should be expanded to include the half-block to the south of Williams Street between Sycamore Street and Second Street." The suggestions for implementation consisted of a group of statements describing the design recommendations for realizing the general policy. For example, for the Williams Street South Side area, an implementation suggestion was to "encourage rehabilitation of the commercial businesses on the Williams Street extension."

Typically, there were at least two options that could be pursued for each target area. The policies described an ideal future based on enhancing the target area qualities and satisfying the goals. The effects of each policy were predicted in order to indicate the results that would be expected if the policy were to be followed.

To further clarify the process, combining verbs and objects created the general and specific suggestions for policy implementation. For example, the verb "restore" was applied to the object, "the West Main Street group of significant buildings."

Within each alternative plan the suggestions for implementation were arranged according to their own priority system of three categories of importance. For each geographic target area, specific questions were asked by participants in order to determine which alternative plan to pursue. Key questions were prepared for the development process for the town, which was to be continued for at least 20 years. The questions were intended to alert community members to the inevitability of changing goals and area qualities that would require adding to the list of plan alternatives.

A community design workbook, prepared for the residents of the town, identified 15 geographic areas for Murfreesboro's continuing preservation efforts to emphasize the town's colonial past. The workbook, describing the community participation process as a component of the strategic plan, was given a First Award in the *Progressive Architecture* awards program. In the past two decades the workbook has been the primary resource in the development of Historic Murfreesboro. In addition to the restoration and reuse of many older buildings, vacant buildings in the rural area have been moved to the historic district (Figures 5.11 and 5.12), restored, and given new uses.

Today Murfreesboro reflects the commitment of its citizens in creating a major tourist attraction, with tour guides acquainting visitors with the town's natural and historic assets. Murfreesboro's continuing preservation efforts emphasize the town's colonial past but extend also to those things revered in living memory. The 1922 Murfreesboro High School, for example, has been recently acquired and restored by the Historical Association to provide auditorium space for cultural events as well as exhibition rooms for special collections.

FIGURE 5.11   Building being moved to the historic district. *(Photo: Henry Sanoff.)*

FIGURE 5.12   Vacant buildings relocated to the historic district.   *(Photo: Henry Sanoff.)*

Monroe Downtown Revitalization

Charrette Process	Participatory action research
▶ Community action planning	Public forum
Focus groups	▶ Strategic planning
▶ Game simulation	Visioning
▶ Goal setting	▶ Workshop
▶ Group interaction	

In the early part of the twentieth century the town of Monroe, North Carolina, was a major passenger and freight junction for the entire East Coast. By the 1960s previous decades of rapid growth had led many residents out of established neighborhoods into subdivisions and shifted business from the traditional downtown to the outskirts of town, leaving many vacant buildings in the downtown area.

After witnessing the dramatic physical change to the townscape produced by the destruction of much of Monroe's traditional architectural heritage, civic and business leaders initiated a visioning process to answer the question, "What kind of town do we want to be?" A series of workshops, organized by a design team led by Henry Sanoff, allowed community members to rediscover the town's assets and to create a vision of a downtown that would be a healthy, safe, and convenient place, providing a pleasant and attractive atmosphere for living, shopping, recreation and for civic, cultural, and service functions. The vision also stated that new development in forms and patterns would preserve and enhance the existing character of the downtown area (Figure 5.13). "The Union Observer," a county news section of the *Charlotte Observer,* and the Monroe weekly paper, the *Enquirer Journal,* reported on the visioning process, announced forthcoming workshops, and presented design recommendations in a series of illustrated articles.

From the initial vision statement, a follow-up workshop allowed 60 Monroe citizens, working in small groups, to identify the goals that would achieve their vision. Consensus to four general categories of goals was achieved:

- Preservation
- Participation
- Regeneration
- Visualization

To reach these goals, workshop participants proposed a number of steps to be taken. Preservation, declared the residents, enhances the value of places and objects of historical, cultural, or architectural value to the community, therefore:

- Preserve architecturally historic important buildings.
- Develop historic attractions in downtown.

Successful community development occurs when people who live and work in a community participate in the process of planning, development, and implementation, therefore:

- Heighten the public's awareness of the downtown's unique physical character.
- Increase public participation in the development of the downtown.

Downtown should thrive again as an activity center and a place to do business, therefore:

- Improve business activities in the downtown.
- Develop new activities and community facilities downtown.

New development should be compatible with the character of the original downtown architecture and provide an image of downtown as a place to enjoy and remember, therefore:

- Improve the visual character of the downtown.
- Develop guidelines to maintain a consistent downtown image.

A third workshop used ten maps corresponding to different sections of the downtown, each of which had a special character (Figure 5.14). Community

ISSUES

LACK OF LIFE

The lack of life in downtown is a consequence of the displacement of shops to the new mall, the lack of activities in downtown, the tight schedule and appearance of some shops, and the lack of character in downtown. These affect particularly the merchants and the downtown as a whole.

OPEN SPACE

There are several open spaces in downtown, usually without any particular treatment as open space.

The combination of different types of open space has an important influence on the downtown image. The sidewalks, streets, parking lots, and vacant lots are all equally important for the downtown visual quality.

VISUAL QUALITY

A very important consideration in the revitalization of the downtown area is its overall visual cohesiveness. Monroe downtown has buildings with different surface qualities (including color, texture, and shape) and buildings with different architectural relationships (including street facade sequences). There are also many viewpoints and landmarks (including forms that dominate or symbolize, such as the old Court House.

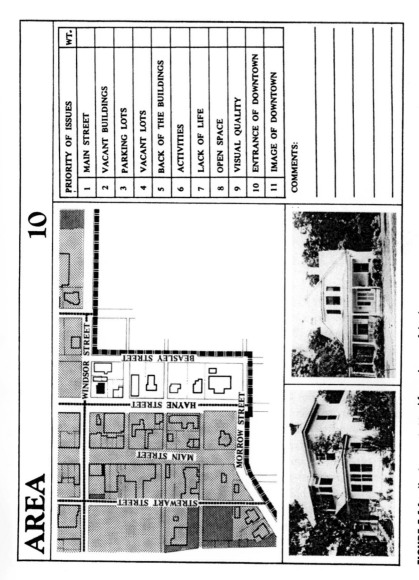

AREA 10

PRIORITY OF ISSUES	WT.
1 MAIN STREET	
2 VACANT BUILDINGS	
3 PARKING LOTS	
4 VACANT LOTS	
5 BACK OF THE BUILDINGS	
6 ACTIVITIES	
7 LACK OF LIFE	
8 OPEN SPACE	
9 VISUAL QUALITY	
10 ENTRANCE OF DOWNTOWN	
11 IMAGE OF DOWNTOWN	

COMMENTS:

FIGURE 5.14 Key issues prioritized for each area of the downtown.

members, working in small groups, identified and prioritized key issues in each section. The recommendation to which there was greatest agreement was to meet the need for a civic center by reusing a vacant historically significant building to provide for cultural activities in the downtown. Housing for the elderly, to be provided in an existing hotel, also received consensus from workshop participants. In addition, there was agreement to convert several of Monroe's older buildings to accommodate the increasing demand for downtown office space.

Implementation strategies consisted of the formulation of policies as well as design proposals. To allow community members to visualize the impact of the strategies, photographs of existing settings were used as a basis for proposing modifications to those settings. Figure 5.15 illustrates several implementation strategies and their proposed physical outcomes, which allowed community members to establish priorities for the most salient strategies to pursue.

Design proposals were developed for a community park, elderly housing, downtown commercial and office space, a pedestrian mall connecting a proposed civic center with retail shops in a vacant department store and adjacent warehouse, and a variety of landscape improvements.

Neighborhoods and Towns in Japan

If given the opportunity and having acquired the appropriate knowledge necessary to develop their own strategies, people can achieve the ability to determine the course of their own lives. The self-confidence they develop is in itself empowering. Empowerment can be viewed as a positive outcome of self-discovery and the ability to dialogue with different people. Confidence to engage in group processes is in itself a liberating force (White, Nair, and Ascroft, 1994). When individuals become self-reliant, their behavior will change—from dependence to independence and from alienation to involvement. A community of self-reliant people will be capable of diagnosing its own problems and developing innovative solutions. The recent community design movement in Japan reflects the self-determination and confidence of people who unite to define community needs. Public participation, however, is a relatively new idea in Japan inasmuch as planning decisions are usually made at the national level, leaving citizens on the periphery of the decision-making process. Yet, there is increasing interest in applying participation methods reported to have been successful in implementing plans to meet the needs of townspeople.

Recurring urban problems in Japanese cities led the Nippon Seinenkan Foundation, a community development organization, to request professional design assistance to conduct three projects incorporating citizen participation to find appropriate solutions. Employing the *Design Games* (Sanoff, 1979) approach to community participation, design teams were formed in the cities of Arakawa, Ohya, and Nanao, based on their requests for design assistance, and led intensive

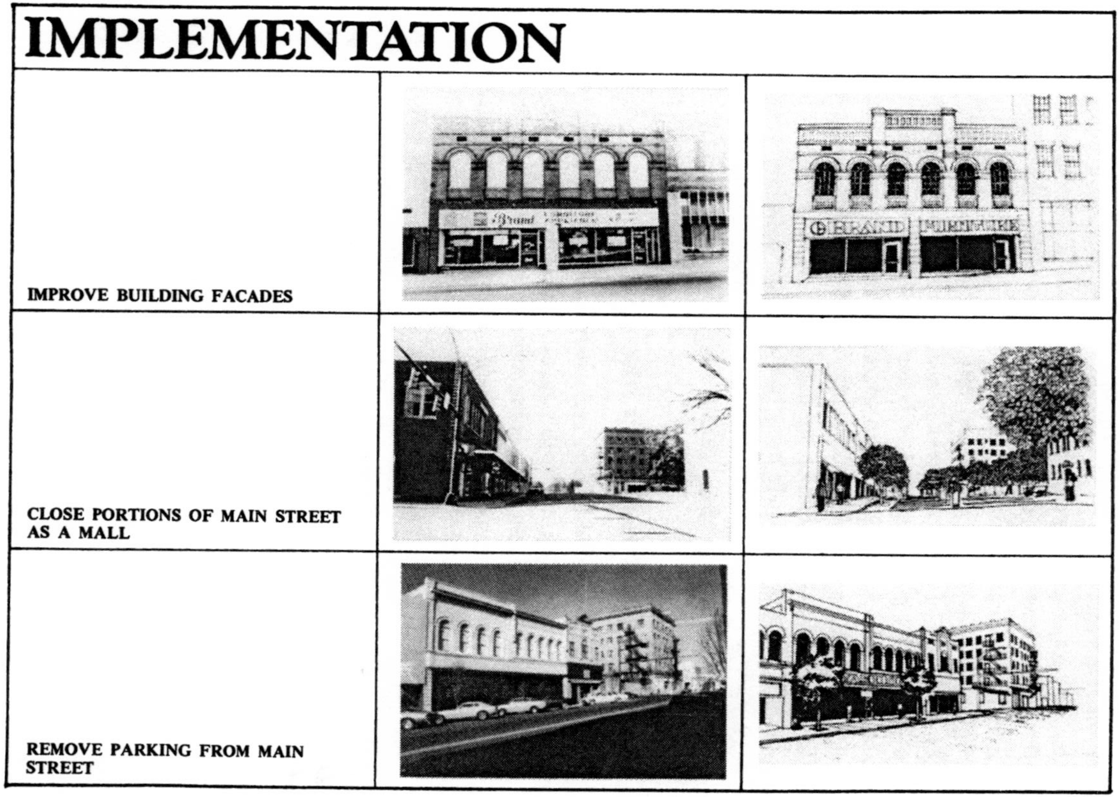

IMPLEMENTATION

IMPROVE BUILDING FACADES

CLOSE PORTIONS OF MAIN STREET
AS A MALL

REMOVE PARKING FROM MAIN
STREET

FIGURE 5.15 Proposed improvements.

three-day sessions that began with fact-finding and concluded with community participation workshops. The projects, which varied in size and scope, included the revitalization of a historic shopping lane in the city of Arakawa, the preservation and revitalization of the historic town of Ohya (famous for its stone used by Frank Lloyd Wright in the construction of the Imperial Hotel in Tokyo), and the identification of appropriate uses for a landfill area in the resort town of Nanao. These intensive processes involved community leaders and citizens of all ages in rediscovering their community problems and assets through walking tours, structured interviews, and focus group discussions.

Volunteer architects, planners, and interested citizens prepared graphic materials for a variety of workshops, which included a streetscape computer simulation whereby participants could identify key visual features, graphic symbols that depicted activities for participants to select and locate on a map, and design recommendations of targeted improvement areas. Workshops were conducted with schoolchildren, as well as with community members in a shopping mall, in a regional museum, and in a city hall. Participation in the workshops ranged from 40 to 80 people. The final step in the participation process consisted of developing action plans to implement the ideas generated in the workshops.

Introductory Workshop at Yamanakaka Lake

Forty architects, landscape architects, and community planners met with the design consultant for two days in May 1996, at a conference center at Yamanakaka Lake near Mount Fuji, to develop a planning strategy for each of three workshops to occur during the next several days. Representatives included design team members of each project area and volunteers from various parts of Japan interested in participating in the projects and learning about the design games participation process. The two-day program opened with introductions and project area descriptions. Participants then joined in several exercises, allowing them to experience the objectives of design games and how they differ from other participatory processes. The objectives included the following:

- To form small groups to encourage equal participation
- To employ consensus decision making to encourage participants to listen to each other
- To structure games that allow participants to learn about the design process
- To emphasize goal setting as a primary activator for solving environmental problems
- To use goal setting to activate the process of strategy selection

On the second day of the workshop participants formed working groups around the project areas and applied design games principles to their particular issues. Each of the groups was equally responsible for the organization of the three-day project that would occur in their towns (Figure 5.16). The results of this plan-

FIGURE 5.16 Planning team.

ning workshop prepared design team members for the events to occur in their communities.

Nakamachi Shopping Lane in Arakawa

▶ Charrette Process	Participatory action research
Community action planning	Public forum
Focus groups	Strategic planning
▶ Game simulation	Visioning
▶ Goal setting	▶ Workshop
▶ Group interaction	

Lying in the northeastern section of metropolitan Tokyo, Arakawa is one of 23 city wards and has a population of 180,000 people. Arakawa retains much of the townspeople's traditional life-styles, typified by many small shops and crafts people. The city is known for the Nakamachi shopping lane, one of the oldest districts of this type in Tokyo. The closing of an elementary school on the shopping lane, however, resulted in several vacant shops that formerly catered to young children. In addition, recent plans by the Tokyo Metropolitan Government called for a new supermarket to be built very close to this historic shopping lane. Recognizing these problems, the local merchant's association, the Nakamachi Merchants Federation, subsidized by local government, had been working to find ways of ameliorating the conditions facing the future of this shopping district.

Consequently, the marketing division of local government, a small group of individuals dedicated to preserving the character of Nakamachi, assumed responsibility for bringing a citizen participation process to Arakawa and requested assistance from the Nippon Seinenkan Foundation. One of the major areas of interest to the Foundation is community development, and this project represented the first community action effort initiated by the organization. The Foundation served as the conduit between the town and the community design consultant.

Several important factors were revealed when the design consultant and members of local government went on an initial walking tour of the area. Although there were signs of vitality in the Nakamachi area, most of the shoppers and shop owners were elderly people. Merchants typically lived above their shops, and shoppers either walked or arrived by bicycle. The shops mainly sold fresh vegetables, fruit, and seafood, and their owners took pride in their merchandise. The small privately owned shops had individual character and featured personal-touch shopping based on trust and face-to-face communication between shopper and customer (Figure 5.17).

FIGURE 5.17 Nakamachi shopping lane. *(Photo: Henry Sanoff.)*

An extremely narrow shopping lane accommodated cyclers and walkers. hoppers, presumably protected by a 3-foot painted green strip designated for pedestrians, were not easily contained within the designated area. Shop owners also encroached onto the green pedestrian area with the display of their merchandise. Although there seemed to be an awareness of the problems connected with the shopping lane, there appeared to be no clearly organized process within local government for resolving these difficulties, especially because major planning efforts were directed toward a new supermarket.

Fact-finding was the starting point of the three-day community design process in Arakawa. A previously publicized meeting attracted 27 interested citizens, who met in the Arakawa branch of the Tokyo Chamber of Commerce building. Participants at the meeting included shop owners, local citizens, and volunteer designers and planners. The goal of this initial meeting was to have local residents rediscover the shopping lane through a walking tour. On the tour citizens used disposable cameras to photograph the *liked* and *least liked* features of the shopping lane. Citizen-generated photos provided important reference points in the community workshop that followed, and the results were displayed on a large map of the district. To gain additional insights into the problems and future prospects of the shopping area, several design team members conducted interviews of 30 randomly selected shop owners. A three-person photographic team from Keio and Tokyo University, working in Tokyo's Urban Simulation Laboratory, videotaped the interview process and photographed segments of the shopping lane (Figure 5.18).

FIGURE 5.18 Interviews with shoppers and merchants. *(Photo: Henry Sanoff.)*

Team members and citizens accumulated a considerable amount of information necessary for developing the workshop materials. Information consisted of concerns expressed by shop owners and residents, as well as visual documentation of key features of the area. This material formed the basis of a two-part community workshop that began with goal setting. The intent of the workshop was to incorporate the citizens' ideas into a process whereby they could discuss and prioritize goals and identify the appropriate implementation strategies. Working in small groups of five people, all workshop attendees had an equal opportunity to participate. All made individual choices, defended their decisions, yet reached group consensus. Summarizing the results of each group provided the design team with a list of prioritized goals and implementation strategies. The key goals that received the highest level of agreement were as follows:

- Encouraging young shoppers to the district
- Improving the visual quality of the shopping lane
- Providing shoppers safety from bicycles
- Making the market friendly to elderly shoppers

Implementation strategies included converting the vacant school building into a community center, using vacant shops for parking bicycles and resting places, putting electric wires underground, and providing merchandise to encourage young shoppers. Associations made between goal setting and finding appropriate implementation strategies enhanced participants' awareness of the process of environmental change.

Clusters of individual buildings, sequentially photographed, were assembled into four streetscapes (Figure 5.19). Participants wrote comments on streetscape segment sheets included in their workshop packet. Their observations were then presented to the entire group through a video monitor. Visual simulation of the shopping lane allowed workshop participants to point out specific features to be changed and those to be preserved. With the aid of a miniature video camera, it was possible to move along the streetscape as the images were projected on a video monitor for all the workshop participants to observe.

Citizens' comments stressed the unsightliness of parked bicycles and vending machines, the visual disharmony of graphic materials including building advertising, and the lack of an identifiable entry to the shopping lane. Conclusions reached and observations of the design games workshop approach were communicated to the public through local and national newspaper reports.

As a result of combining the responses to the goal-setting process and the visual simulation, a clear agenda emerged toward a mutually acceptable direction. The agenda included the following actions:

- The visual simulation strategy would be continued to convey design proposals for the problem areas identified in the workshop.

FIGURE 5.19 Streetscape images being assembled. *(Photo: Henry Sanoff.)*

- All visual images would be displayed for public viewing and additional comments.
- The merchant's association in partnership with local government would develop and enforce improvement policies.

Merchants were excited to have straightforward comments from the residents and shoppers. Although they occasionally exchanged views, they rarely had an opportunity for discussions with their customers on an equal footing. Residents, too, were pleased to discuss their ideas about community development. Although local government does hold regular meetings with residents to get their input, responsible officials neither make comments on the opinions offered nor provide sufficient information about the topic under discussion. Normally, residents never participate in the meetings held by the Business Promotion Section of the ward, because they are organized for private business people. Therefore, the atmosphere of the workshop was unique and thus attracted the interest of ward officials and key business leaders in Arakawa. Consequently, plans are under way to reuse the vacant school building as a community center and to provide for bicycle storage in a vacant shop.

Ohya: The Rock District in Utsunomiya

▶ Charrette Process
Community action planning
Focus groups
▶ Game simulation
▶ Goal setting
▶ Group interaction

▶ Participatory action research
Public forum
Strategic planning
Visioning
▶ Workshop

Utsunomiya is a city whose historical roots can be traced back to the seventeenth century. Today it is one of the major inland industrial areas of Japan. Utsunomiya is also the home of the Ohya rock, a soft stone that resulted from volcanic eruptions and crust movement (famous for its use by Frank Lloyd Wright in the construction of the Imperial Hotel in Tokyo). Stone quarries and stone houses reflect the historic character of the area; however, many of the mines are abandoned and dangerous and other underground spaces are underutilized. Although the original stone is still quarried, a poor imitation of it is becoming increasingly popular. Today, Ohya is in a state of decline.

Because the city bureaucracy has not been able to implement any plans thus far considered, a local advocacy group composed of architects and planners from government and the private sector has formed. It is also believed that the citizens distrust bureaucrats—townspeople are on the periphery of the decision-making process and often lose interest in plans generated by local government. A local leader commented, "The district of Ohya has been wandering between lightness and darkness, reality and imagination. Though plans are proposed one after another, the reception from the townspeople is stone cold. There are many problems in the town; however, there are also many good sites and resources."

This special interest group has developed a project entitled "Only the residents can warm the heart of Ohya." Its members believe that it is in the interest of both the city and the residents to have a forthright discussion about what is needed and to move to implement plans that meet their needs. A community participation workshop was identified as an appropriate catalyst to initiate change in Ohya.

The three-day process in Ohya began with a meeting of the 35-person volunteer design team. Some of the team members came from other cities in Japan with an interest in learning about the design games approach. The Shiroyama community hall building, which also functions as an agency of Utsunomia City Hall, served as the home base for preparation of the workshop and community meetings. A bank of computers and drawing materials were made available in a large multipurpose meeting room, occupied by the design team for three days.

Because many team members were volunteers unfamiliar with the area, informing the team about the attributes and problems in the district was the first step in the process. Volunteer citizens from the Women's Group in Ohya led walking tours throughout the district to inform design team members about the problems and prospects of Ohya. Team members then conducted a map interview by dividing the district into five sampling areas, where a total of 100 residents were surveyed. Interviewees located on a map of Ohya their favorite and least favorite places in the district. Teams then went out to photograph the problem areas identified during the interviews (Figure 5.20).

Middle school students from two elementary schools also participated in the design process by conveying their ideas, through drawings, to the design team. Sixth-grade students drew and described features they would like to see in Ohya (Figure 5.21). More than 100 drawings were assembled and subsequently covered the walls of the workshop venue. Involvement of the students also engaged their teachers in this exploratory process. Parents, too, became involved in thinking about the future of Ohya as their children discussed the school drawing project. This awareness and information-gathering step concluded the first day of the community design process.

An analysis of the children's drawings, the interview results, and the photographic survey revealed nine types of problem areas. These included vacant buildings, danger zones for cars and pedestrians, lack of historic markers, lack of recreation areas for young children, and inaccessibility to the district's historic river.

Preparation of workshop materials occurred on the second day of the intensive community design process. With the assistance of graduate architecture students from Utsunomiya University, design proposals were generated in response to the problem areas. Photographs of targeted areas served as a basis for developing the design alternatives. Design proposals that entailed the removal of debris and other

FIGURE 5.20   Historic building constructed of local stone.

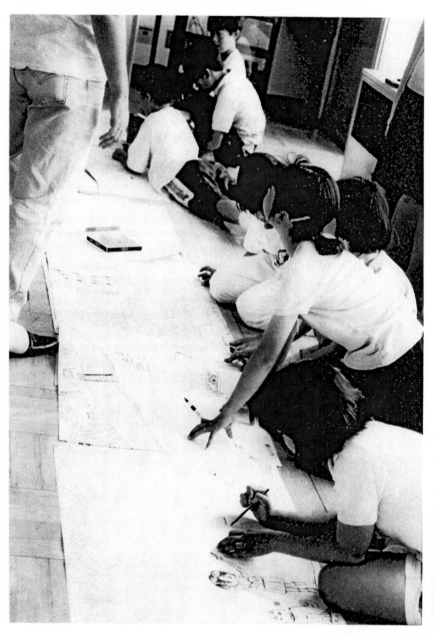

FIGURE 5.21 Students drawing ideas for their community.

minor modifications were developed through computer graphics methods. At the same time, other team members brainstormed possible goals and implementation strategies that might be selected in conjunction with the design proposals.

The aim of the community design workshop was to encourage participants to select and prioritize goals and to find appropriate implementation strategies associated with specific design proposals. Each participant received a workshop packet that included goal statements and illustrations of design proposals. These allowed participants to record their decisions for later use by design team members.

As customary in Japan, interested citizens registered in advance for the community workshop. The City Hall meeting room was organized with 16 tables, each accommodating five people. This arrangement allowed all participants to voice their opinions while making and discussing their individual choices. Eighty people, of all ages, from Ohya and Utsunomiya joined the design team in the one-day workshop. Many children who participated in the drawing exercise were present, along with their parents and teachers. Elderly citizens, who had never experienced such a community meeting, felt comfortable in sharing their knowledge and experience with younger participants.

To familiarize citizens with the events leading up to the workshop, a five-minute video opened the meeting. It consisted of a series of 60 still images of the walking tour, the interviews, the children's exercise, and the preparation of workshop materials, recorded with a digital camera during the entire process.

Goal setting, the opening workshop activity, engaged participants in a lively discussion as they revealed their concerns about the future of Ohya. Work groups devoted two hours to discussing community goals and how they may benefit its citizens. The following are the goals that topped each group's list of priorities:

- Places for children to play
- Tourist development
- Preservation of Ohya's streetscape
- Preservation of the town's natural resources
- Revitalization of the characteristics of Ohya

Appropriate signage to historic areas and historic markers were described as effective physical methods for promoting tourism. Street and monument lighting was noted as an important element in making the town visible and active at night. Revitalization of the river for fishing and recreation was seen to be equally appropriate for tourists and residents. Participants also agreed that abandoned mines should be filled and that underground spaces could be developed for theatrical and musical performances.

A traditional lunch prepared by a women's group and served by residents of the city allowed workshop participants to continue their discussions and to learn more about each other's interests. Work groups continued into the afternoon as they reviewed nine design proposals developed from the initial resident survey of undesirable community features (Figure 5.22). Participants made individual decisions, then collaborated to reach agreement as they prioritized those physical features that

FIGURE 5.22 Design proposals for problem areas in the community.

現況　提案

○この提案には、どの手法が合ってますか？

○この提案の、どこが好きですか？

○この提案の、どこが嫌いですか？

現況　提案

○この提案には、どの手法が合ってますか？

○この提案の、どこが好きですか？

○この提案の、どこが嫌いですか？

現況　提案

○この提案には、どの手法が合ってますか？

○この提案の、どこが好きですか？

○この提案の、どこが嫌いですか？

would have the greatest impact on Ohya. Each working group presented its recommendations to the larger group to allow the design team to identify issues for discussion at subsequent workshops.

It was encouraging and impressive to see elderly people, especially women, who rarely have an opportunity to express their opinions, actively participating in the discussions. In local areas, meetings tend to be male dominated, allowing for few occasions for discussion between men and women. Moreover, the participants were comfortable in being able to openly express their agreement as well as their opposition to the design proposals. Workshop participants also enjoyed seeing the students' drawings on the wall, and the elementary school students were equally proud of their contribution.

A follow-up community workshop consisted of specific design solutions for promoting tourist activities, the highest-priority action issue. Projects were identified that could be accomplished by citizens, as well as those that would require local government support. To build on the momentum of the community workshops, several citizen participation projects were identified where work could begin immediately. For example, stone markers could be placed at designated locations around Ohya to inform tourists of the key community attractions (Figure 5.23). A street lighting design proposal was also developed and presented to local government officials for implementation. The local design team has effectively aroused the community, motivating it to participate in a major revitalization process, in which citizens have taken a leadership role in effecting change.

FIGURE 5.23 Stone markers: A citizens project.

FIGURE 5.23 *(Continued)*

Nanao

▶ Charrette Process   Participatory action research
Community action planning   ▶ Public forum
Focus groups   ▶ Strategic planning
▶ Game simulation   Visioning
▶ Goal setting   ▶ Workshop
▶ Group interaction

The port city of Nanao has historical significance in its cultural assets and traditional performing arts. Fishing villages scattered along the coast of the Sea of Japan in the Nanao vicinity lend visual interest to this area of the Ishikawa Prefecture. Nanao is also the sister city to Monterey, California, and features a fisherman's wharf not unlike those found in California.

The city has recently reclaimed an 8-acre area next to the fisherman's wharf that is scheduled to be filled by 1998. Originally, the reclamation was part of "Nanao: Marine City Project," proposed by the Junior Chamber of Commerce in 1989 as a symbolic "greenland." Subsequent research by the Transport Ministry concluded in the authorization of the prefecture to proceed with the reclamation plan, which later became part of the port project. The basic plan was prepared without consultation with the citizens; consequently, a citizens group organized and submitted its own request to the mayor of Nanao. With the goal of motivating people to think about their city, the Nanao Secretariat invited people of all ages to participate in planning new uses for this reclaimed area.

A small group of architects and planners in Nanao formed a volunteer design team and initiated a community planning process. The three-day design process in Nanao began when a chartered boat tour took the design team, 60 middle school and high school students, their teachers, and several parents around the future perimeter of the land to visualize the scale of the future site. Adolescents and teenagers were selected to participate in this tour because they had been excluded from previous discussions about the future of this reclaimed area. On board, they freely discussed their ideas for the site as they realized the scale of this area and the type of activities that could be accommodated.

The community participation program in Nanao included a search through earlier newspapers for articles describing the intent of the landfill, a review of previous proposals, and a public opinion survey conducted during the Noto International Tent Village festival. Such a review provided insight into possible uses for the new site, which included cultural, recreational, and athletic activities. Although the 8-acre site could enhance the breadth of activities currently available in Nanao, citizens would be required to make trade-offs in selecting the most suitable for the community.

Recognizing that the workshop would include children, teenagers, and adults, an appropriate strategy was needed to engage all participants at their own levels of competence. Consequently, a mapping design game using graphic symbols to correspond to land uses formed the basis of the community workshop. Design team members prepared more than 50 symbols for different activity areas. The symbols were identical in size, but each corresponded to a specific unit of area. Activity data sheets included the population capacity, the area requirement, and the number of symbol units that would have to be fastened to a large map of the landfill.

The community workshop was held in a central area at the fisherman's wharf shopping mall on a Sunday morning (Figure 5.24). This public venue gave the workshop high visibility to members of the community. Children and teenagers worked together in small groups of three to five. In addition to using the symbols to locate appropriate activities on a map, students used the map as a base to construct a three-dimensional model of their proposals. Each team was provided with a package of model making materials, including straws, foam pieces, colored paper, a variety of plastic shapes, and glue. Team members collaborated in each step of the process.

Adults began by identifying community goals and linking them to appropriate activities. Key goals addressed the need for a landscape that included the use of water and places for recreation, and the need for a place to hold regular events such as concerts or even a flea market. Activities to satisfy these goals included the development of flower gardens, a landscaped plaza, a children's play area, a park with a water feature, a restaurant, and a concert hall. All groups produced design solutions, at the same scale, for the landfill area (Figures 5.25a and 5.25b). Representatives from each group concluded the workshop with a brief presentation of

FIGURE 5.24 Workshop consisting of 12 work groups. *(Photo: Henry Sanoff.)*

their ideas. It was assumed that each group would opt for activities suited to its own age and interests, but participants were surprised when students selected features that would allow for their parents' recreational activities as well as their own.

Representatives of each planning team presented their landfill proposals to the larger community of about 250 residents at the local art museum. An open question-and-answer session revealed a supportive response to many of the ideas proposed and unanimous agreement about the viability of the community design process (Figure 5.26).

Following the community presentation design teams developed charts and models, based on the workshop results, for presentation at the local high school to hear comments by students, as well as by resident groups. Responding to the students' and residents' reactions to the proposals, design models were subsequently exhibited at the Montrey Plaza, the site of the original workshop. A review of the comments allowed the design team to develop one design proposal. This proposal reflected the community's interests, which contrasted with that of the local government that did not involve the community in its decisions. A comparison of the two proposals, conducted by the residents, indicated that the prefecture's proposal did not effectively use the view, did not reflect a unified concept, and did not use the open stage area effectively. The two proposals, that developed by the prefecture and that developed by the community design process, were presented to the residents of Nanao to allow the broader community to select an appropriate solution.

FIGURE 5.25a   Work groups developing ideas for the landfill.   *(Photo: Henry Sanoff.)*

FIGURE 5.25b   Children's work groups.

FIGURE 5.26 Presentation of proposals to the larger community. *(Photo: Henry Sanoff.)*

Through this broad community process the results of the design team were favored, and a citizens council was organized by the prefecture government to ensure that the results of the workshop would be considered in the final scheme. To facilitate this process, people who organized the workshop became participants in the citizens council.

A formal evaluation of the charrette process revealed it to be very successful, and part of this success is attributable to the attention to detail and organization typical of many Japanese events. The spirit of collective decision making, an integral aspect of Japanese culture, was evident at every stage of preplanning and during the charrette process itself. People typically registered in advance of the workshop, which allowed key logistics problems to be solved prior to the arrival of the design team. Participants represented all levels of decision making and community interests. In all cases the press documented the process and the major results, informing the public of the events and of the decisions that had been made.

In Japan, design games workshops are viewed as an important approach for achieving public involvement in decision-making processes. A growing number of Japanese professionals and citizens believe it is necessary for the public to share in decisions that determine the quality and direction of their lives. In the past six years many benefits have resulted from the design games approach for communities, users, and designers. There are biannual national conferences devoted to gaming workshops in which participants are required to present community projects that employed gaming strategies for citizens' participation. Two national conferences have been held since 1993, with more than 400 attendees in each and about

100 completed projects to date, all of which were initiated by local citizens groups. The first national conference was held in Kochi in 1993, and the second, two years later in the northern part of Kyushu.

Diamachi Fureai Park

Charrette Process	Participatory action research
▶ Community action planning	Public forum
▶ Focus groups	Strategic planning
▶ Game simulation	Visioning
▶ Goal setting	▶ Workshop
▶ Group interaction	

Nagoya, a city in Japan of 2 million people is divided into 16 wards. In Showa, a ward of 100,000 people located in the center of Nagoya, children usually play in their homes, in the streets, or in parking lots because it is the only neighborhood in the city with few parks. Yoshie Ohno, a concerned mother of three children, approached the officials at Nagoya City Hall to request a safe outdoor place for children to play and meet other children. Although the public officials were sympathetic to her request, they did not generate any action. Later she learned that a neighborhood nursery school was planning to build a park for its children, so she met with the school head to propose a collaborative project between parents and staff of the nursery school and neighborhood residents. An initial meeting of neighborhood parents and children resulted in an agreement to four wishes:

1. Children cannot safely play outside; therefore, they wished for a place to play ball, to jump rope, and to swing and slide.
2. Parents wished for a place to meet easily with their neighbors.
3. Community members wished for a park to serve children, their parents, elderly persons, and people with disabilities.
4. Parents and nursery school staff wished they could work together and agreed to "make a park."

Local park officials and community members developed a process for securing City Hall approval for the park by initiating a signature-collecting campaign. A petition signed by more than 18,000 people requesting the park was presented to the mayor of Nagoya. The petition indicated that Showa ward, in comparison with other wards in the city, had no park and that their neighborhood, Gokiso, was a suitable location. They particularly stressed the fact that children have the right to be able to play safely out-of-doors.

The Nagoya City Council approved the request for the park and instructed the community leaders to search for an appropriate location. Organized visits to other community parks allowed neighborhood residents to become acquainted with a variety of options. A questionnaire circulated throughout the community identified the possible locations, the park theme, and the activities for the park. Neighborhood residents conducted the questionnaire, held meetings with City Hall officials, photographed key features of other parks, developed a business plan, and identified professional needs. The neighborhood organization sought advice from consultants about how children play, how to construct a park, and how to develop a design game to allow community members to participate in the design process. A designer from Nagoya City Hall also volunteered to provide the professional guidance necessary to construct the park. The points agreed to by all community members were that the park would be neighborhood based and that neighbors would be the primary users and therefore responsible for its upkeep. Five basic themes evolved from the neighborhood survey:

- Children want a place to play ball.
- Parents and young children needed a place of their own.
- Shade trees and flower gardens were needed.
- Water should be integrated into the park.
- The park should be accessible and welcoming to people with disabilities.

A design game workshop involving residents of the neighborhood answered several important questions:

- How can our park help in achieving a strong sense of community?
- How can we make a good park?
- What are the conditions for a good park?

The workshop included approximately 60 people, as well as elderly and disabled people from the neighborhood, working together for one day to design their park. A design kit, prepared in advance, included a catalog of play equipment, a game board, a variety of colored markers, scissors, and other materials. Young children made drawings of the features they would like to see in the park, and older children and adults worked in groups of six to construct three-dimensional scale models of their park. Each team presented its ideas for appropriate activities for children of all ages, and they evaluated their schemes' ability to satisfy the following criteria:

- Adequate space for young children to play
- Adequate space to play ball
- Space for children of all age levels to play
- Quiet space for resting
- Safety zone around each piece of equipment

- Accessibility to people with disabilities
- Safe and secure environment
- Ability of a car to enter the park

Design proposals included a slide and swings for the younger children, ball playing for the older children, and a garden and sitting area for parents to observe their children and for neighbors to meet. Plans and a construction schedule were prepared when agreement on the types of park activities was reached. Construction of the park was primarily a volunteer effort that included children and adults from the community. Children and their parents designed and did the mosaic work on the concrete bench and walls that were constructed by 95 volunteers from the community (Figure 5.27). The park was completed in three months.

The operation of the park, too, is a volunteer effort. Play leaders help to organize children's activities in the park (Figure 5.28), and other volunteers participate in planting, watering, and various types of routine maintenance.

User Responses to the Completed Park

A young mother, who recently moved to the neighborhood, is a daily visitor to the park because her children meet with other children to form play groups. Young children are happy to run barefoot and play with mud and water. Older adults

FIGURE 5.27 Community members constructing mosaic wall. *(Photo: Yoshie Ohno.)*

FIGURE 5.28 Community-constructed fountain in the park. *(Photo: Yoshie Ohno.)*

report that the park is a source of information about activities and events in the city. The park is also the location of many festivals, attended by as many as 600 people. Typical festivals include a variety of games, locally prepared food, and a bazaar. During the Star Festival bamboo is decorated with colored paper, and at the Full Moon Festival bowls are made from mud and painted. Boy Scouts hold periodic festivals, and students from the nearby college frequently help visitors to the park.

Therapeutic Gardens

A community garden called "Flower Land" was created in the Setagaya district of Tokyo at a time when concepts of "universal design" were not part of the vocabulary. Consequently, the garden was not designed to be accessible to people with disabilities. A landscape architect and community designer, Naho Mochizuki, who was also teaching courses on horticultural therapy, proposed a community workshop to renovate the existing garden to make it more accessible to all community residents. The purpose of the workshop was

- To generate community participation in redesigning the community garden
- To provide a learning experience for people on the value of working together and learning from each other
- To educate people on the concept of universal design and horticultural therapy through a green project

Factors considered in achieving a successful project included the identification of areas that could be improved for the greatest impact, the creation of a garden that would serve as an educational experience, and a process that would result in planting in the spring.

A series of six workshops were held over a period of several months. Participants included neighborhood residents in wheelchairs and with visual impairments, district officials, and community designers. The opening session began with a discussion of the principles of universal design, followed by a firsthand evaluation of the accessibility of Flower Land by the workshop participants. The evaluation was conducted with the use of blindfolds and wheelchairs to allow neighborhood residents to identify problems areas where changes were needed.

A second workshop session was held to identify the areas where improvements could be made and to develop a planning process for the community garden. Specific tasks were established for small work groups, which included braille guides of Flower Land for blind persons, guided tours for disabled people, and planning work areas for disabled people. The third session focused on creating models and design solutions based on the ideas developed by each of the work groups. A fourth session focused on implementing the design ideas. With the assistance of a carpenter, many residents participated in constructing a multipurpose worktable for people in wheelchairs, a raised flower bed with workbenches for the blind, and various wind chimes and hanging wooden pots.

With the coming of spring, the fifth session was held to develop a planting plan and to train volunteer guides to assist people with disabilities. The intent was to create a garden that was safe and exciting to all the senses (Figure 5.29). The completed garden was named "Kizuki Garden" (*Kizuki* means "taking the root of a tree" and "gained awareness"). Not only was the workshop process a valuable experience for the participants, it was instrumental in the formation of a community development volunteer group, "Group Shepherd's Purse," supported by local government.

Today Kizuki Garden is managed and maintained by horticulture students of the original course at Flower Land, and programs for people with and without disabilities are planned and implemented by the members of Group Shepherd's Purse.

FIGURE 5.29 Community garden. *(Photo: Naho Mochizuki.)*

Urban Participatory Games

Urban Infill

At the core of urban design is the streetscape. What we describe as infill is also referred to as redevelopment, which is a renewal or recycling process. Infill, which refers to building on vacant urban properties, requires less energy to build and maintain, and denser development conserves energy and building materials. Infill is also good for communities because it reduces the fuel consumption, pollution, and travel time associated with commuting.

Today, because of neglect and rapid decay, many streetscapes are in need of repair or replacement. Moreover, an empty site is often a blighted site. In many cases, however, when action is proposed in communities without the support of historic-district or similar regulations, its visual impact does not lend itself readily to analysis, and there is a lack of recognized guidelines to evaluate its significance and weigh its beneficial or detrimental consequences. Such problems have led to charges of insensitivity and even litigation against those responsible for urban development projects.

To make certain that there is some continuity in the process of restoring older streetscapes, it is necessary to evaluate new building proposals very carefully. This is best achieved by comparing each new proposal with design guidelines to ensure the preservation of those unique qualities that make older buildings visually distinctive. Compatibility in a streetscape can be attained if certain features are maintained through the collective development of design guidelines. Such features include the following:

- Setbacks
- Character
- Scale
- Building use
- Roof silhouette
- Surface variation
- Use of ornamentation
- Proportion of window and door openings
- Relative height

The Best-Fit Slide Rule

The Best-Fit Slide Rule (Figure 5.30) is a discussion tool developed to examine streetscape infill solutions and their consequences (Sanoff, 1990). It is a visual guide for determining compatibility by identifying those factors to be considered in contemplating new construction. As a strategy for discussion, it can bring together professionals, public officials, landowners, and citizens groups to explore the consequences of various infill alternatives prior to construction (Figure 5.30). Developing an awareness of the complex issues related to streetscape infill, through a hypothetical exercise, can enable community members to focus on the social, economic, and visual implications of changing the fabric of an existing streetscape. Because participants respond to a design situation with varying values and beliefs, the exercise offers an opportunity for them to share those differences and learn from each other. Participants use the game props to clarify and reconcile differences.

The Slide Rule is most effectively used in small-group settings in which participants make individual choices, defend their decisions, and reach consensus about the most appropriate fit. The process requires each group member to select one of thirteen options for the infill of the residential streetscape (Figures 5.31a and 5.31b). Participants then try to maintain their positions and debate them, but the final goal of the exercise is a solution that is acceptable to the group.

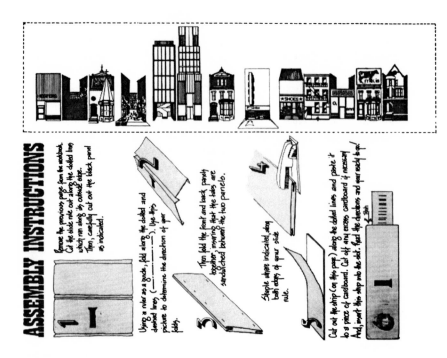

DIRECTIONS:

This typical block face can be found in most communities where residential areas have remained unaltered for many decades. Today, neglect and rapid decay have placed many blocks of this type in need of replacement or repair. In order to insure that there is some continuity in the process of restoring older residential areas, it is often necessary to evaluate new building proposals very carefully. This is done by comparing each new proposal with specific criteria developed to insure the preservation of those unique qualities that make older buildings visually distinctive.

On your slide rule you will find a drawing of Front Street, a typical residential block in downtown SERCORP. One of the buildings has been condemned by SERCORP's building department because it is unsafe for occupancy. There are twelve proposals for reusing the site of the condemned building.

As an interested citizen it is your job to insure the selection of a proposal which will preserve Front Streets unique character. Using the criteria checklist provided, review each of the twelve design proposals and decide which proposal fits best within the available space. Only that proposal which satisfies all eight criteria can be considered acceptable.

CRITERIA CHECKLIST

Each proposal must be evaluated using the criteria below and must be similiar to the adjacent buildings regarding the following:

- alignment of window and door openings
- relative height
- roof silhouette
- proportion of window and door openings
- use of ornamentation
- building use
- surface variation
- relative width

FIGURE 5.30 Best Fit Slide Rule.

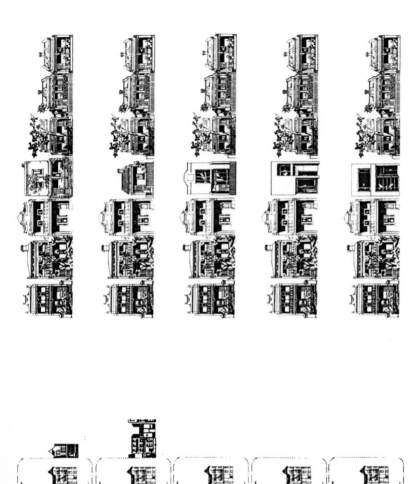

FIGURE 5.31a Slide Rule options. *(Drawing: Greg Centeno and Henry Sanoff.)*

FIGURE 5.31b Slide Rule options. *(Drawing: Henry Sanoff.)*

The thirteen options for the infill site, located in the center of a hypothetical urban residential street, include alternative building uses as well as visual appearance. Typically, the issues participants discuss are related to the impact of the changing uses created by business or commercial additions and their corresponding parking requirements and increased traffic. Similarly, concerns about residential stability are as integral to the discussions as is architectural style.

Developing an awareness of the complex issues pertaining to infill, through an abstract exercise, can enable community members to focus on the social, economic, and visual implications of changing the fabric of an existing residential streetscape. The technique of using a hypothetical street as a stimulus for generating a discussion of important issues permits all participants to learn from each other without being encumbered with and confounded by the personal, political, economic, and site constraints of a real situation. To follow up on the discussion generated by the participants in the Best-Fit Slide Rule exercise, the actual streetscape under consideration can be presented in a similar way, along with alternative infill proposals. At this point, participants may already be aware of such issues as building use, ornamentation, roof silhouette, relative height, proportion of door and window openings, and surface variation, so the discussion can include other issues related to the streetscape. The visual impact of a building's image is significant in conveying the consequences associated with the selection of building alternatives.

Knowledge of Emerging Environmental Strategies (KEEPS)

The KEEPS game is designed to provide groups interested in preserving the many environmental qualities unique to older neighborhoods, districts, and towns with an understanding of the strategies open to them (Figure 5.32). Organizing and planning for the preservation of the qualities identified relies on the consideration of (Sanoff, 1978):

- The environmental qualities the group seeks to develop
- Individual goals
- The strategies the group can realistically use to accomplish their goals

To begin, each player identifies and records those neighborhood or town qualities that have been lost or that should be retained. Group members record and discuss the qualities each has identified. Next, from the goal list provided, each player selects no more than four goals that seem to be important in developing the environmental qualities the group has decided upon. When all members of the group have made their individual choices, the individual lists are pooled. Through discussion, the group chooses a total of four goals, with the additional constraint that the four statements must be incorporated into a unified conservation program. Players are urged to forcefully support their individual choices, even if other members of the group differ. Discussion should continue until group members persuade or are persuaded to include four goals that reflect the group's priorities. This may require considerable discussion.

keeps
Knowledge of Emerging ■ *Environmental Preservation Strategies*

KEEPS is a game designed to provide groups interested in preserving the many environmental qualities unique to older neighborhoods, districts and towns with an understanding of the strategies open to them. Organizing and planning for the preservation of the qualities your group has identified as important, relies upon the consideration of:
—The environmental qualities your group seeks to develop.
—Your goals.
—The type of strategies your group can realistically use to accomplish your goals.
To begin, each player selects from the goal list provided, no more than four goals that seem to be important in developing the environmental qualities your group has decided upon. When making your initial selections, brief notes should be made justifying each choice. When all the members of your group have made their goal choices, the individual lists are pooled.
Through negotiation the group must choose a total of four goals, with the additional constraint that the four statements must be incorporated into a unified conservation program. Players are urged to forcefully support their individual choices, even if other members of the group differ.

Discussion should continue until group members persuade or are persuaded to include four goals that reflect the groups priorities. This may require considerable discussion
When consensus is reached the group should enter its choices on the record sheet
Next, using the strategies list, each player should individually select no more than four implementation strategies that can be used to effectively accomplish each of the goal choices. Work through each goal completely before starting a new one. And, keep in mind that some strategies may relate to more than one of your goal choices. After all members of your group have made their strategy selections, pool your lists and negotiate on your final group selections. As before, players are urged to persuade the total group to include their own particular selections. Your complete record sheet now contains the framework of a collaboratively generated conservation program. Combine the results of all the working groups and use these as a framework for future discussions and actions. Remember, the future is up to you . . . and KEEPS is what we are playing for

GOALS
—Preserve historically significant sites, landmarks, objects, and buildings.
—More public and private involvement in decisions which could alter the character of the area.
—Heightened public awareness to the area's unique physical character.
—Optimal use, or re-use of sites in the area.
—Preservation of the neighborhood's visual characteristics.
—Influence public and private investment for the good of the area.
—Neighborhood development which is compatible with the long range objectives for town development.
—Public awareness to the area's historic resources.
—Preservation of neighborhood social cohesiveness.
—Maintenance and upgrading of properties.
—Increased public participation in the development of the area
—Influence neighborhood improvement programs in other parts of town.
—Control of growth and development in the area.

STRATEGIES
—Encourage property owners to increase property maintenance.
—Encourage civic organizations to clean up, or maintain sites.
—Offer preliminary architectural services to businesses and individuals interested in developing sites.
—Encourage private planting programs.
—Move some historically significant building to infill a key unoccupied site
—Encourage pedestrian activities in key areas by petitioning for walkway improvement programs.
—Contact other organizations that have initiated similar projects for advise
—Have an area wide 'planting day.'
—Develop detailed design guidelines to maintain a consistent area image.
—Organize for bulk purchase of materials
—Acquire public agency support
—Encourage the demolition of buildings that are hopelessly beyond repair.
—Use local media sources to obtain issue visibility.
—Look into the possibility of federal and state grants.
—Lobby for zoning changes which can insure the implementation of your goals.
—Purchase and restore key buildings and sites to 'period authenticity'.
—Sponsor continuing area wide 'clean up day' programs.
—Identify and evaluate historically significant buildings and sites.
—Purchase, rehabilitate, and adaptively reuse significant buildings and sites.
—Develop property easement programs
—Put utilities underground.
—Purchase, rehabilitate and sell.
—Purchase, rehabilitate and rent
—Control of outdoor advertising
—Develop a revolving fund.
—Tree planting and maintenance of publically owned property

The drawings above characterize a sequence of changes that have occured in a town not unlike your own. For the purpose of this exercise you can assume that your present town is at stage two in the process of change, rapidly moving towards stage three if no action is taken. As a community planning group you are interested in preserving certain qualities that were lost as well as maintaining or improving characteristics that would make your town more humane.

To begin, each individual in your workgroup (from three to five players) should briefly list important environmental qualities. Then, as a group, discuss each persons views about the town until agreement is achieved. Next, proceed to the goal selection phase.

environmental qualities
_____
_____
_____
_____
_____

RECORD SHEET

1 _____
2 _____
3 _____
4 _____

FIGURE 5.32 KEEPS game.

When consensus is reached, the group enters its choices on a record sheet. Next, using the strategies list, each player selects no more than four implementation strategies that can be used to effectively accomplish each of the goal choices. Each goal should be worked through completely before starting a new one. Some strategies, however, may relate to more than one goal. After all members of the group have made their strategy selections, the lists are pooled to arrive at the final group choices.

The completed record sheet now contains the framework of a collaboratively generated action program. If several groups are engaged in the exercise simultaneously, the results should be combined and used as a framework for future discussions.

Bibliography

Abt, C. 1970. *Serious Games*. New York: Viking Press.

Argyris, C., and D. Schon. 1991. "Participatory Action Research and Action Science Compared: A Commentary." In *Participatory Action Research*, edited by W. Whyte. Newbury Park, CA: Sage Publications.

Alexander, C. 1985. *The Production of Houses*. New York: Oxford University Press.

Alinsky, S. 1972. *Rules for Radicals*. New York: Vantage Books.

Altman, I., and A. Wandersman. 1987. Neighborhood and Community Environments. New York: Plenum Press.

Arnstein, S. 1969. "A Ladder of Citizen Participation." *AIP Journal* 35:215–224.

Avery, M. 1981. *Building United Judgment: A Handbook for Consensus Decision Making*. Madison, WI: The Center for Conflict Resolution.

Axelrod, R. 1984. *The Evolution of Cooperation*. New York: Basic Books.

Baird, G., J. Gray, N. Isaacs, D. Kernohan, and G. McIndoe. 1996. *Building Evaluation Techniques*. New York: McGraw Hill.

Batchelor, P., and D. Lewis. 1985. *Urban Design in Action: The History, Theory and Development of the AIA's Regional/Urban Design Assistance Teams Program (RUDAT)*. School of Design, North Carolina State University–Raleigh and American Institute of Architects. Vol. 29. Washington, DC.

Baum, A., and S. Valins. 1977. *Architecture and Social Behavior: Psychological Studies of Social Density*. Hillsdale, NJ: Lawrence Erlbaum Associates.

Becker, F. 1977. *Housing Messages.* Stroudsburg, PA: Dowden Hutchinson & Ross.

———. 1988. "Form Follows Process at Dynamic Lloyds of London." *Facilities Design and Management* (Feb.):54–58.

Becker, F., and F. Steele. 1995. *Workplace by Design.* San Francisco: Jossey-Bass.

Bishop, J. 1987. *Building Design for Non-Designers: An Innovative Distance Learning Pack.* Bristol, England: School for Advanced Urban Studies.

Bordenave, J. D. 1994. "Participative Communication as a Part of Building the Participative Society." In *Participatory Communication: Working for Change and Development,* edited by S. A. White, K. S. Nair, and J. Ascroft. Thousand Oaks, CA: Sage Publications.

Boyte, H. C. 1991. "Beyond Community Service: Turning On Youth to Politics." *The Nation* 252, 18:626–628.

Bratt, R. G. 1987. "The Role of Citizen-Initiated Programs in the Formulation of National Housing Policies." In *Citizen Participation in Public Decision Making,* edited by J. DeSario and S. Langton. New York: Greenwood Press.

Bremer, M. 1993. *SimCity 2000 User Manual.* Walnut Creek, CA: Maxis.

Brill, M., with S. Margulis and E. Konar. 1984. *Using Office Design to Increase Productivity.* Vol. 1. Buffalo, NY: Workplace Design & Productivity.

Brody, R. 1982. *Problem Solving: Concepts and Methods for Community Organizations.* New York: Human Sciences Press.

Broido, M. 1971. *Communal Housing.* A Report by a CHIMERA Working Group. London: University College.

Brown, D. L. 1983. *Managing Conflict at Organizational Interfaces.* Reading, MA: Addison-Wesley.

Bruner, J. S. 1967. *Towards a Theory of Instruction.* Cambridge, MA: Harvard University Press.

Bryson, J. M. 1988. *Strategic Planning for Public and Nonprofit Organizations.* San Francisco: Jossey-Bass.

Bullard, R. 1990. *Dumping in Dixie.* Boulder: Westview.

Burns, J. 1979. *Connections: Ways to Discover and Realize Community Potentials.* New York: McGraw Hill.

Carnegie Foundation for the Advancement of Teaching. 1988. *An Imperiled Generation: Saving Urban Schools.* Princeton, NJ: Carnegie Foundation for the Advancement of Teaching.

Cashden, L., B. Fahle, M. Francis, S. Schwartz, and S. Stein. 1978. A Critical Framework for Participatory Approaches to Environmental Change. In *Participatory Planning and Neighborhood Control,* edited by M. Francis. New York: Center for Human Environments, City University of New York.

Castells, M. 1983. *The City and the Grassroots.* Berkeley: University of California Press.

Checkoway, B. 1986. "Building Citizen Support for Planning at the Community Level." *Interdisciplinary Planning: A Perspective for the Future.* New Brunswick, NJ: Center for Urban Policy Research.

———. 1994. "Paul Davidoff and Advocacy Planning in Retrospect." *APA Journal* 60, 2:139–142.

City of Rock Hill. 1987. *Theme Group Handbook*. Rock Hill, NC: Rock Hill.

Comerio, M. 1984. "Community Design: Idealism and Entrepreneurship." *Journal of Architecture and Planning Research* 1:227–243.

Comstock, D. E., and R. Fox. 1993. "Participatory Research as Critical Theory: The North Bonneville, USA, Experience." In *Voices of Change: Participatory Research in the United States and Canada*, edited by P. Park, M. Brydon-Miller, B. Hall, and T. Jackson. Westport, CT: Bergin & Garvey.

Connolly, W. E. 1969. *The Bias of Pluralism*. New York: Atherton Press.

Connor, D. M., and S. G. Orenstein. 1995. "Combining Conflict Resolution and Public Participation for Challenging Cases: The Bridges of Winnipeg Case." *Consensus*. (Oct.) p. 2.

Creighton, J. L. 1994. *Involving Citizens in Community Decision Making: A Guidebook*. Washington, DC: Program for Community Problem Solving.

———. 1995. "Trends in the Field of Public Participation in the United States." *Interact: The Journal of Public Participation* 1, 1:7–24.

Curry, R. 1998. *History of the Association for Community Design*. New York: Pratt Institute Center for Community and Environmental Development.

David, T. 1982. "Functional Dimensions of Classroom Environments." In *Mind Child Architecture*, edited by J. C. Baird and A. D. Lutkus. Hanover, NH: University Press of New England.

Davidoff, P. 1965. "Advocacy and Pluralism in Planning." *Journal of the American Institute of Planners* 31:331–338.

de Bono, E. 1985. *Conflicts: A Better Way to Resolve Them*. London: Harrap.

Delbecq, A. L., A. H. Van de Ven, and D. H. Gustafson. 1975. *Group Techniques for Program Planning: A Guide to Nominal Group and Delphi Processes*. Glen View, IL: Scott Foresman.

Deshler, D., and D. Sock. 1985. "Community Development Participation: A Concept Review of the International Literature." Paper presented at the International League for Social Commitment in Adult Education, Ljungskile, Sweden.

Dickey, M. 1996. "Practice: Chicago Hope." *Landscape Architecture* 86, 4:50–55.

Dorman, G. 1981. *Middle Grades Assessment Program: Users Manual*. Chapel Hill, NC: Center for Early Adolescence.

Duke, R. D. 1974. *Gaming the Futures Language*. New York: John Wiley & Sons.

Duncan, J. 1985. "The House as a Symbol of Social Structure: Notes on the Language of Objects Among Collective Groups." In *Home Environments*, edited by I. Altman and C. Werner. New York: Plenum Press.

Easterbrook, G. 1995. *A Moment on the Earth: The Coming of Age of Environmental Optimism*. New York: Viking Press.

Eldin, M., and M. Levin. 1991. "Cogenerative Learning: Bringing Participation into Action Research." In *Participatory Action Research*, edited by W. Whyte. Newbury Park, CA: Sage Publications.

Faraday, A. 1970. "Feeling Is Believing." *New Society* 405, 7:5.

Forester, J. 1988. *Planning in the Face of Power*. Berkeley: University of California Press.

Francis, M. 1998. "Proactive Practice: Visionary Thought and Participatory Action in Environmental Change." *Places* 12, (spring)1:60–62.

Francis, M., L. Cashden, and L. Paxson. 1984. *Community Open Spaces: Greening Neighborhoods Through Community Action and Land Conservation.* Covela, CA: Island Press.

Friere, P. 1990. *Pedagogy of the Oppressed.* New York: Continuum Publications.

Friedmann, A., C. Zimring, and E. Zube. 1978. *Environmental Design Evaluation.* New York: Plenum Press.

Friedmann, J. 1987. *Planning in the Public Domain.* Princeton, NJ: Princeton University Press.

———. 1992. *Empowerment: The Politics of Alternative Development.* Cambridge, MA: Blackwell.

Fromm, D. 1991. *Collaborative Communities.* New York: Van Nostrand Reinhold.

Frost, J. L., and B. L. Klein. 1983. *Children's Play and Playgrounds.* Austin, TX: Playscapes International.

Gaventa, J. 1993. "The Powerful, the Powerless, and the Experts: Knowledge Struggles in an Information Age." In *Voices of Change: Participatory Research in the United States and Canada,* edited by P. Park, M. Brydon-Miller, B. Hall, and T. Jackson. Westport, CT: Bergin & Garvey.

Gibson, T. 1988. *Planning for Real: Users' Guide.* Telford, UK: Neighborhood Initiatives Foundation.

Godschalk, D. R., D. W. Parham, W. R. Potapchuk, and S. W. Schukraft. 1994. *Pulling Together: A Planning Development Consensus Manual.* Washington, DC: Urban Land Institute.

Gold, S. J. 1992. *Refugee Communities: A Comparable Field Study.* London: Sage Publications.

Goldberg, B., and C. Bee. 1991. "Redesigning Schools: Architecture and Restructuring." *Radius* 3, 1:1–7.

Goodman, R. 1971. *After the Planners.* New York: Simon & Schuster.

Goodey, B. 1974. *Urban Walks and Town Trails.* University of Birmingham, UK: Centre for Urban and Regional Studies.

Gove, P. B. and Merriam-Webster. 1986. *Webster's New International Dictionary.* Springfield, MA: Merriam-Webster.

Greenblat, C. S., R. D. Duke, 1981. *Principles and Practices of Gaming Simulation.* Beverly Hills, CA: Sage.

Greene, S. 1992. "Cityshape: Communicating and Evaluating Community Design." *Journal of the American Planning Association* 58, 2:177–189.

Grubb, H. A. 1997. "Cultural Outreach Center" Master's thesis, North Carolina State University.

Gustavsen, B. 1985. "Workplace Reform and Democratic Dialogue." *Economic and Industrial Democracy* 6:461–479.

Habermas, J. 1990. *Moral Consciousness and Communicative Action.* Cambridge, MA: MIT Press.

Habitat (1987). *Global Report on Human Settlements*. New York: Oxford Press.

Habraken, N. J. 1986. "Towards a New Professional Role." *Design Studies* 7, 3:102–108.

Haines, D. 1996. "Patterns in Refugee Resettlement and Adaptation." In *Refugees in America in the 1990s*, edited by D. Haines. Westport, CT: Greenwood Press.

Halprin, L., and J. Burns. 1974. *Taking Part: A Workshop Approach to Collective Creativity*. Cambridge: MIT Press.

Hamdi, N. 1991. *Housing Without Houses: Participation, Flexibility, Enablement*. New York: Van Nostrand Reinhold.

Hamdi, N., and R. Goethert. 1997. *Action Planning for Cities*. New York: John Wiley & Sons.

Handy, C. 1997. *The Hungry Spirit*. London: Hutchinson.

Hardie, G. 1988. "Community Participation Based on Three-Dimensional Models." *Design Studies* 9, 1:56–61.

Hart, R. 1979. *Children's Experience of Place*. New York: Irvington Publishers.

Hatch, R. 1984. *The Scope of Social Architecture*. New York: Van Nostrand Reinhold.

Heath, D. H. 1991. *Fulfilling Lives: Paths to Maturity and Success*. San Francisco: Jossey-Bass.

Hester, R. T., Jr. 1987a. "Making the Grassroots Whole." *Built Environment* 13, 1:45–60.

———. 1987b. "Landstyles and Lifescapes: 12 steps to Community Development." *Landscape Architecture* 75, 1:78–85.

———. 1990. *Community Design Primer*. Mendocino, CA: Ridge Times Press.

———. 1996. "Wanted: Local Participation with a View." In *Public and Private Places*, edited by J. Nasar and N. Brown. Salt Lake City: Environmental Design Research Association.

Hurwitz, J. G. 1975. "Participatory Planning in an Urban Neighborhood. Soulard, St. Louis, Missouri: A Case Study." *DMG Journal* 9, 4:348–357.

Jones, B. 1990. *Neighborhood Planning: A Guide for Citizens and Planners*. Chicago, IL: American Planning Association.

Kaplan, R. 1987. "Simulation Models and Participation." *Designers & Clients. Proceedings of the 18th Environmental Design Research Association Conference*, edited by J. R. Harvey and D. Henning. Ottawa, Canada.

Kellett, R. 1998. *Net Energy Communities*. Eugene, OR: Center for Housing Innovation, University of Oregon.

Kingsley, G. T., J. B. McNeely, and J. O. Gibson. 1997. *Community Building Coming of Age*. Washington, DC: The Development Training Institute. The Urban Institute.

Kretzman, J. P., and J. L. McKnight. 1993. *Building Communities from the Inside Out: A Path Towards Finding and Mobilizing Community Assets*. Evanston, IL: Center for Urban Affairs and Policy Research, Northwestern University.

Kritchevsky, S., E. Prescott, and L. Walling. 1974. "Planning Environments for Young Children: Physical Space." In *Alternative Learning Environments*, edited by G. Coates. Stroudsburg, PA: Hutchinson & Ross.

Kurth-Schai, R. 1988. "The Roles of Youth in Society: A Reconceptualization." *The Education Forum* 52, 2:113–132.

Lach, D., and P. Hixson. 1996. "Developing Indicators to Measure Values and Costs of Public Involvement Activities." *Interact: The Journal of Public Participation* 2, 1:51–63.

Lake, R. W. 1993. "Rethinking NIMBY." *Journal of the American Association of Planning* 59, 1:87–92.

Lancourt, J. E. 1979. *Confront or Concede.* Lexington, MA: Lexington Books.

Landscape Architecture. 1987. "Runyon County Master Plan and Design Guidelines." 77, 6:60–63.

Langton, S. 1978. *Citizen Participation in America.* Lexington, MA: Lexington Books.

Lawrence, R. 1989. Translating Anthropological Concepts into Architectural Practice. In *Housing, Culture and Design: A Comparative Perspective,* edited by S. Low and E. Chambers. Philadelphia: University of Pennsylvania Press.

Lewin, K. 1946. "Action Research and Minority Problems." *Journal of Social Issues* 2:34–36.

Lineberry, R. L. 1986. *Government in America: People, Politics and Policy.* Boston: Little, Brown.

Lozare, B. V. 1994. "Power and Conflict." In *Participatory Communication: Working for Change and Development,* edited by S. A. White, K. S. Nair, and J. Ashcroft. Thousand Oaks, CA: Sage Publications.

Lumsdaine, E., and M. Lumsdaine. 1993. *Creative Problem Solving: Thinking Skills for a Changing World.* New York: McGraw Hill.

Markus, T. 1993. *Buildings and Power.* New York: Routledge.

Mason, R. O., and I. Mitroff. 1981. *Challenging Strategic Planning Assumptions: Theory, Cases, and Techniques.* New York: John Wiley & Sons.

Mazmanian, D., and J. Nienaber. 1994. "Fishbowl Planning: Environmental Planning, Economic Development, and Democratic Technique." In *Critical Studies in Organization and Bureaucracy,* edited by F. Fischer and C. Sirianni. Philadelphia: Temple University Press.

McCamant, K., and C. Durrett. 1989. *Cohousing: A Contemporary Approach to Housing Ourselves.* Berkeley: Ten Speed Press.

McCoy, M., P. Emigh, M. Leighninger, and M. Barrett. 1996. *Planning Communitywide Study Circle Programs: A Step-by-Step Guide.* Pomfret, CT: Civic Practices Network. Topsfield Foundation.

McDonald, A. 1986. *The Weller Way: The Story of the Weller Streets Housing Co-operative.* Boston: Faber and Faber.

Medoff, P., and H. Sklar. 1994. *Street of Hope: The Fall and Rise of an Urban Neighborhood.* Boston: South End Press.

Midgley, J. 1986. *Community Participation, Social Development and the State.* New York: Methuen.

Moore, C. W. 1986. *The Mediation Process: Practical Strategies for Resolving Conflicts.* San Francisco: Jossey-Bass.

Moore, G. T., and J. A. Lackney. 1993. *Educational Facilities for the Twenty-First Century: Research Analysis and Design Patterns.* Milwaukee: University of Wisconsin, CAUPR.

Moore, R. C., and H. H. Wong. 1998. *Natural Learning: Creating Environments for Rediscovering Nature's Way of Teaching.* Berkeley, CA: MIG Communications.

More, E. 1998. *Managing Changes: Exploring State of the Art.* Greenwich, CT: JAI Press.

Naparstek, A. J., D. Dooley, and R. Smith. 1997. *Community Building in Public Housing.* Washington, DC: U.S. Department of Housing and Urban Development.

North Carolina Department of Labor. 1998. *Introduction to Migrant Housing Inspections in North Carolina.* Raleigh, NC: Division of Occupational Health and Safety.

Nutt, P. C., and R. W. Backoff. 1987. "A Strategic Management Process for Public and Third-Sector Organizations." *Journal of the American Planning Association* 53:44–57.

Okubo, D. 1997. *The Community Visioning and Strategic Planning Handbook.* Denver, CO: National Civic League Press.

Pais, W. 1995. "The Challenge of Creating Multicultural Communities." *CoHousing* 8, 1:6–8.

Park, P., M. Brydon-Miller, B. Hall, and T. Jackson. 1993. *Voices of Change: Participatory Research in the United States and Canada.* Westport, CT: Bergin & Garvey.

Peattie, L. 1968. "Reflection on Advocacy Planning." *Journal of the American Institute of Planning* 34:80–88.

Pettigrew, A., and R. Whipp. 1993. *Managing Change for Competitive Success.* London: Blackwell Business.

Pittman, K. J. 1996. "Community, Youth, Development: Three Goals in Search of Connection." *New Designs for Youth Development* 12, 1:4–8.

Poister, T. H., and G. Streib. 1989. "Management Tools in Municipal Government: Trends over the Past Decade." *Public Administration Review* 49:244.

Preiser, W. F. E., H. Z. Rabinowitz, and E. T. White. 1988. *Post-Occupancy Evaluation.* New York: Van Nostrand Reinhold.

Rabe, B. 1994. "Beyond NIMBY: Participatory Approaches to Hazardous Waste Management in Canada and the United States." In *Critical Studies in Organization and Bureacracy,* edited by F. Fischer and C. Sirianni. Philadelphia: Temple University Press.

Ramasubramanian, L. 1994. "Integrating Theory, Method, and Knowledge: Strategies for Improving Research Utilization." Unpublished paper. Milwaukee: University of Wisconsin–Milwaukee.

Rapoport, A. 1982. *The Meaning of the Built Environment.* Beverly Hills: Sage Publications.

Red Rockers. 1973. *Shelter.* Bolinas, CA: Shelter Publications.

Regnier, V. 1994. *Assisted Living Housing for the Elderly: Design Innovations from the United States and Europe.* New York: Van Nostrand Reinhold.

Regnier, V., and J. Pynoos. 1987. *Housing the Aged: Design Directives and Policy Considerations.* New York: Elsevier.

Rescher, N. 1993. *Pluralism: Against the Demand for Consensus.* Oxford: Clarendon Press.

Ring, P., and A. Van de Van. 1994. "Developmental Processes of Cooperative Interorganizational Relationships." *Academy of Management Review* 19, 1:90–118.

Robinson, I. M. 1987. "Trade-off Games as a Research Tool for Environmental Design." In *Methods in Environmental and Behavioral Research,* edited by R. B. Bechtel, R. W. Marans, and W. Michelson. Stroudsburg, PA: Hutchinson & Ross.

Rosner, J. 1978. "Matching Method to Purpose: The Challenges of Planning Citizen Participation Activities." In *Citizen Participation in America,* edited by S. Langton. New York: Lexington Books.

Sachner, P. 1983. "Still Planning with the Poor: Community Design Centers Keep Up the Good Work." *Architectural Record* 17:126–131.

Sanoff, H. 1978. *Designing with Community Participation.* New York: McGraw Hill.

———. 1979. *Design Games.* Los Altos, CA: William Kaufmann.

———. 1981. "Human Exchange Techniques for Citizen Participation in Town Revitalization." *Design Studies* 2, 3:157–164.

———. 1983. *Arts Center Workbook.* Raleigh: North Carolina State University and North Carolina Arts Council.

———. 1988. "Participatory Design in Focus." *Architecture and Behavior* 4, 1:27–42.

———. 1989. "Facility Programming." In *Advances in Environment, Behavior and Design,* Vol. 2, edited by E. H. Zube and G. T. Moore. New York: Plenum.

———. 1990. *Participatory Design: Theory and Techniques.* Raleigh: School of Design, North Carolina State University.

———. 1991. *Visual Research Methods in Design.* New York: Van Nostrand Reinhold.

———. 1994. *School Design.* New York: Van Nostrand Reinhold.

Sanoff, H., and J. Sanoff. 1988. *Learning Environments for Children.* Atlanta: Humanics.

Sargent, H. 1972. "Fishbowl Planning Immerses Pacific Northwest Citizens in Corps Project." *Civil Engineering* 42:54–57.

Schine, J. 1990. "A Rationale for Youth Community Service." *Social Policy* 20, 4:5–11.

Schon, D. 1971. *Beyond the Stable State.* London: Temple Smith.

Seidel, A. 1982. "Usable E.B.R.: What Can We Learn from Other Fields." In *Knowledge for Design,* edited by P. Bart et al. Washington, DC: Environmental Design Research Association.

Sharon, A. 1976. *Kibbutz and Bauhaus.* Tel-Aviv, Israel: Massada Printing Ltd.

Shearer, D. 1984. "Citizen Participation in Local Government: The Case of Santa Monica, California." *International Journal of Urban and Regional Research* 8:573–586.

Shellshear, T. 1983. *Byronshire Environmental Study: Working Paper No. 6—Heritage.* Sydney, Australia: Planning Workshop Pty. Ltd.

Smith, F., and R. T. Hester. 1982. *Community Goal Setting.* Stroudsburg, PA: Dowden Hutchinson & Ross.

Sommer, R. 1979. "Participating Design." *Ideas* (Herman Miller, Ann Arbor, MI): 3, 4.

Steelcase/Harris. 1987. *Office Environment Index.* Grand Rapids, MI: Steelcase Corporation.

Swanson, B. E., R. A. Cohen, and E. P. Swanson. 1979. *Small Towns and Small Towners.* Beverly Hills, CA: Sage Publications.

Thomas, R. L., M. C. Means, and M. A. Grieve. 1988. *Taking Charge: How Communities Are Planning Their Futures.* Washington, DC: International City Management Association.

Threllfall, M. 1986. "Insideoutside: The School Environment." *Children's Environment Quarterly* 3, 3:30–39.

Tjosvold, D. 1993. *Learning to Manage Conflict: Getting People to Work Together Productively.* New York: Lexington Books.

Turner, J. F. C. 1977. *Housing by People.* New York: Pantheon.

U.S. Department of Agriculture. 1980. *National Farmworker Housing Survey.* Rosslyn, VA: InterAmerica Research Associates.

Verba, S. 1961. *Small Groups and Political Behavior: A Study of Leadership.* Princeton: Princeton University Press.

Verba, S., and N. H. Nie. 1972. *Participation in America.* New York: Harper & Row.

Wates, N. 1978. "Support Christiania." *The Architects Journal* (January 25):142–145.

———. 1996. *Action Planning.* Prince of Wales Institute of Architecture, 14 Gloucester Gate, London NW1 4HG.

Wates, N., and C. Knevitt. 1987. *Community Architecture: How People are Creating Their Own Environment.* London: Penguin.

Weinstein, C. S., and T. David. 1987. *Spaces for Children: The Built Environment and Child Development.* New York: Plenum Press.

Wener, R. 1989. "Advances in Evaluation of the Built Environment." In *Advances in Environment, Behavior and Design,* edited by E. H. Zube and G. T. Moore. New York: Plenum Press.

White, S. A., and P. K. Patel. 1994. "Participatory Message Making with Video: Revelations from Studies in India and the USA." In *Participatory Communication: Working for Change and Development,* edited by S. A. White, K. S. Nair, and J. Ascroft. Thousand Oaks, CA: Sage Publications.

White, S. A., K. S. Nair, and J. Ascroft. 1994. *Participatory Communication: Working for Change and Development.* Thousand Oaks, CA: Sage Publications.

Whyte, W. F. 1991. *Participatory Action Research.* Newbury Park, CA: Sage Publications.

Williams, B. A., and A. A. Matheny. 1994. *Democracy, Dialogue, and Social Regulation.* New Haven: Yale University Press.

Winders, R., and L. S. Gray. 1973. *The Urban Trail.* Sheffield, UK: Pavic Productions.

Wisner, B., D. Stea, and S. Kruks. 1996. "Participatory and Action Research Methods." In *Advances in Environment, Behavior, and Design,* Vol. 3, edited by E. Zube and G. T. Moore. New York: Plenum.

Worsley, P. 1967. *The Third World.* Chicago: University of Chicago Press.

Wulz, F. 1986. "The Concept of Participation." *Design Studies* 7, 3:153–162.

Zucker, C. 1995. "The Importance of Interdisciplinary Teamwork." *Urban Design Symposium.* Washington, DC: Library of Congress.

Additional Readings

Albrecht, J. 1988. "Towards a Theory of Participation in Architecture: An Examination of Humanistic Planning Theories." *Journal of Architectural Education* 42, 1:24–31.

Aleshire, R. A. 1970. "Planning and Citizen Participation: Costs, Benefits and Approaches." *Urban Affairs Quarterly* 5, 6:369–393.

Alexander, C. 1975. *The Oregon Experiment.* New York: Oxford University Press.

———. 1979. *The Timeless Way of Building.* New York: Oxford University Press.

———. 1981. *The Linz Cafe.* New York: Oxford University Press.

Altschuler, A. A. 1970. *Community Control.* Indianapolis: Bobbs-Merrill.

"Architecture and Community." 1985. *The Architectural Review* CLXXVII:1058.

Bacon, V., and M. Jenck. 1986. Briefing—A Means to Match User Interests and Design. In *What Is the Point of Community Architecture?* edited by J. Scott, and M. Jencks. Oxford, UK: Oxford Polytechnic, Department of Town Planning. Working Paper No. 95, November, pp. 29–38.

Baer, M. A., and D. Jaros. 1974. "Participation as Instrument and Expression: Some Evidence from the U.S." *American Journal of Political Science* 18, 5:365–384.

Barnett, J. 1966. "A Planning Process with Built-in Political Support." *Architectural Record* 139:141–146.

Becker, F. 1990. *The Total Workplace.* New York: Van Nostrand Reinhold.

Behesti, M. R. 1985. "Design Coalition Team." *Proceedings of the International Design Participation Conference,* Vols. 1, 2, and 3. Eindoven, The Netherlands: Department of Architecture, Building and Planning.

Biagi, R. 1978. *Working Together: A Manual for Helping Groups Work Effectively*. University of Massachusetts Citizen Involvement Training Project.

Bion, W. R. 1975. "Experience in Groups." In *Group Relations Reader*, edited by A. D. Colman and W. H. Bexton. Sausalito, CA: Grex.

Blumberg, P. 1969. *Industrial Democracy: The Sociology of Participation*. New York: Schocken Books.

Bonta, J. P. 1979. "Simulation Games in Architectural Education." *Journal of Architectural Education* 33, 1:12–18.

Borton, T. E., and K. P. Warner. 1971. "Involving Citizens in Water Resources Planning: The Communication Participation Experiment in the Susquehanna River Basin." *Environment and Behavior* 3, 9:284–306.

Brieland, D. 1971. "Community Advisory Boards and Maximum Feasible Participation." *American Journal of Public Health* 61, 2:292–296.

Burke, E. M. 1968. "Citizens Participation Strategies." *Journal of the American Institute of Planners* 34, 5:287–294.

———. 1969. "Citizen Participation Is Necessity: How Can We Make It Work." *Journal of Housing* 26, 12:599–602.

———. 1981. *A Participatory Approach to Urban Planning*. New York: Human Sciences Press.

Burns, J. 1979. "Citizens Take Part in the Process of Urban Design." *Nation's Citizen's Weekly* 2:43.

Butcher, H., P. Collins, A. Glen, and P. Sills. 1980. *Community Groups in Action: Case Studies and Analysis*. London: Routledge & Kegan Paul.

Cahn, E. S., and B. A. Passett. 1971. *Citizen Participation: Effecting Community Change*. New York: Praeger.

Carp, J. C. 1986. "Design Participation: New Roles, New Tools." *Design Studies* 7, 3:125–132.

Chesterman, D., and C. Stone. 1987. "New Approaches to Public Housing." *Architecture Australia* 76, 4:37–43.

Churchman, A. 1987. "Can Resident Participation in Neighborhood Rehabilitation Programs Succeed?" In *Neighborhood and Community Environments*, edited by I. Altman and A. Wandersman. New York: Plenum.

Clavel, P. 1994. "The Evolution of Advocacy Planning." *APA Journal* 60, 2:146–149.

Cohen, R. 1973. *Psych City: A Simulated Community*. New York: Pergamon.

Comerio, M. C. 1987. "Design and Empowerment: Twenty Years of Community Architecture." *Built Environment* 13, 1:15–28.

Community Architecture Information Services and Royal Institute of British Architects. 1986. *Building Communities: Proceedings of the 1st International Conference in Community Architecture, Planning and Design*. London: Royal Institute of British Architects.

Conan, M. 1987. "Dweller's Involvement in Housing Design: A Development Perspective." *Journal of Architecture and Planning Research* 4, 4:301–309.

Connor, D. M. 1988. "A New Ladder of Citizen Participation." *National Civic Review* 77, 3:249–257.

Crosbie, M. 1984. "Television as a Tool of Urban Design." *Architecture* 73, 11:54–61.

Cross, N. 1982. "Participation." *Architects Journal* (January):76–78.

Cunningham, B. 1976. "Action Research: Toward a Procedural Model." *Human Relations* 29:215–238.

Dale, D. 1978. *How to Make Citizen Involvement Work.* Amherst: University of Massachusetts. Citizen Involvement Training Project.

Damer, S., and C. Hague. 1971. "Public Participation in Planning." *Town Planning Review* 42, 3, 217–232.

Davis, S. 1995. *The Architecture of Affordable Housing.* Berkeley, CA: University of California Press.

Devereux, E. C., Jr. 1960. "Community Participation and Leadership." *Journal of Social Issues* 16:29–45.

Dew, J. R. 1997. *Quality Centered Strategic Planning.* New York: Quality Resources.

Downs, A. 1975. "HCDA: Getting People into the Act." *Planning* 41, 1:12–14.

Draper, T. A. 1971. *Citizen Participation.* Toronto: New Press.

Duke, R. D., and C. S. Greenblat. 1979. *Game Generating Games: A Trilogy of Games for Community and Classroom.* Beverly Hills: Sage Publications.

Erskine, R. 1976. "Designing with User Participation." *RIBA Journal* 84:273.

Evans, B. 1985. "Community Kroll: Participant of Vision." *The Architectural Review* CLXXVII:1058.

Fagence, M. 1977. *Citizen Participation in Planning.* Oxford: Pergamon.

Fanning, O. 1975. *Man and His Environment: Citizen Action.* New York: Harper & Row.

Farrelly, E. M. 1987. "Community Architecture, Contradiction in Terms?" *Architecture Review* 1081:27–31.

Fordyce, J. E., and R. Weil. 1971. *Managing with People.* Reading, MA: Addison-Wesley.

Francis, M. 1983. "Community Design." *Journal of Architectural Education* 36, 5:14–19.

———. 1988. "Negotiating Between Children and Adult Design Values." *Design Studies* 9, 2:67–75.

Franck, K. A., and S. Ahrentzen. 1991. *New Housing New Households.* New York: Van Nostrand Reinhold.

Friedmann, J. 1973. "The Public Interest and Community Interest." *Journal of American Institute of Planners* 39, 1:2–7.

Gibson, T. 1986. "Decision Making in Neighborhood Design and Development." *Design Studies* 7:3.

———. 1986. *Us Plus Them: How to Use the Experts to Get What People Really Want.* London: Town and Country Planning Association.

Gittel, M. 1980. *Limits to Citizen Participation.* Beverly Hills: Sage Publications.

Godschalk, D. 1972. *Participation, Planning and Exchange in Old and New Communities: A Collaborative Paradigm.* Chapel Hill: University of North Carolina Press.

Gran, G. 1983. *Development by People: Citizen Construction of a Just World.* New York: Praeger.

Greenblat, C. S. 1980. Group Dynamics and Game Design. *Simulation and Games* 11, 1:35–58.

Habraken, N. J. 1972. *Supports: An Alternative to Mass Housing.* New York: Praeger Publishers.

Halprin, L. 1969. *The RSVP Cycles: Processes in the Human Environment.* New York: Braziller.

Hamdi, N., and B. Greenstreet. 1981. *Participation in Housing.* Working Papers Nos. 57 and 58. Oxford, UK: Oxford Polytechnic, Department of Town Planning.

Hasell, J., and J. L. Taylor. 1981. "Gaming/simulation: An Approach to the Study of Environmental Change and Development." In *Design and Research Interactions: Proceedings of the 12th International Conference of the Environmental Design Research Association,* edited by A. E. Osterberg, C. P. Tienan, and R. A. Findley. Ames: Iowa State University.

Hester, R. T., Jr. 1983. "Process Can Be Style: Participation and Conservation in Landscape Architecture." *Landscape Architecture* 73:49–51.

———. 1984. *Planning Neighborhood Space with People.* New York: Van Nostrand Reinhold.

———. 1987. "Participatory Design and Environmental Justice: Pas de Deux or Time to Change Partners?*"Journal of Architecture and Planning Research* 4, 4:289–299.

Hinrichs, C. L. 1985. "Designing the Design Coalition Team: Owner/User Participation in Architecture." *Design Coalition Team. Proceedings of the International Design Participation Conference,* Eindoven, Holland, 236–251.

Holod, R., and D. Rastorfer. 1983. *Architecture and Community: Building in the Islamic World Today.* New York: Aperture.

Illich, I. 1977. *Disabling Professions.* London: Calder & Boyars.

Jackson, J. S., III, and W. L. Shade. 1973. Citizen Participation, Democratic Representation and Survey Research. *Urban Affairs Quarterly* 9:57–89.

Johnson, C., and P. Rose. 1986. "User Involvement in Government School Design." In *People and the Man Made Environment,* edited by R. Thorne and S. Arden. Sydney: University of Sydney.

Johnson, J. 1979. "A Plain Man's Guide to Participation." *Design Studies* 1, 1:27–30.

Keyes, L. C., and E. Teitcher. 1970. "A View from the Establishment: Limitations of Advocacy Planning." *Journal of the American Institute of Planners* 36, 4:225.

Knevitt, C. 1977. "Down Your Way: Current Projects by Rod Hackney." *Architects Journal* 65, 5:630–636.

Kordesh, R. L. 1991. "Community for Children." *National Civic Review* 80, 4:362–373.

Kroll, L. 1986. *The Architecture of Complexity.* London: Batsford.

Kukkonen, H. 1984. *A Design Language for a Self Planning System.* Helsinki: ACTA Polytechnica Scandinavica. Aelsinki Civil Engineering and Building Construction Series No. 82.

Lang, J. 1987. *Creating Architectural Theory: The Role of the Behavioral Sciences in Environmental Design.* New York: Van Nostrand Reinhold.

Lawrence, R. 1981. "Participatory Architectural Design: A Review Essay." *Simulation and Games* 12, 4:499–509.

———. 1987. "Basic Principles for Public Participation in House Planning." *Design Studies* 8, 2:139–143.

Law-Yone, H. 1982. "Games for Citizen Participation." *Simulation and Games* 13, 1:51–63.

Lennard, S. H. C., and H. L. Lennard. 1988. *Livable Cities II.* Carmel, CA: Center for Urban Well Being.

Levin, A. 1960. "Citizen Participation." *Journal of the American Institute of Planners* 26, 8:195–200.

Lewis, D., and R. Gindroz. 1974. "Toward a Design Process That Re-enfranchises Citizens and Consumers." *AIA Journal* 62, 5:28–31.

Lind, A. 1975. "The Future of Citizen Participation." *The Futurist* 9, 316–328.

Linn, K. 1968. "Neighborhood Commons." *Architectural Design* 38, 8:379–382.

Lisk, F. 1985. *Popular Participation in Planning for Basic Needs.* Cambridge, UK: Cambridge University Press.

Litwak, E., and H. J. Meyer. 1966. "A Balance Theory of Coordination Between Bureaucratic Organizations and Community Primary Groups." *Administrative Science Quarterly* 7:31–58.

MacDonald, D. 1997. *Democratic Architecture.* New York: Whitney.

Maidment, R., and R. Bronstein. 1973. *Simulation Games: Designs and Implications.* Columbus: Merrill.

Malpass, R. 1979. "A Reappraisal of Byker, Part 2: Magic, Myth and the Architect." *The Architects Journal* 169:1012–1018.

Marans, R., and K. F. Spreckelmeyer. 1981. *Evaluating Built Environments: A Behavioral Approach.* Ann Arbor: University of Michigan, Institute of Social Research.

Marcus, C. C., and W. Sarkissian. 1986. *Housing as If People Mattered: Site Guidelines for Medium Density Family Housing.* Berkeley: University of California Press.

Marris, P., and M. Jackson. 1991. *Strategy and Context: Reflections on the Community Planning and Action Programs.* New York: The Rockefeller Foundation.

Maziotti, D. F. 1969. "The Underlying Assumptions of Advocacy Planning: Pluralism and Reform." *Journal of the American Institute of Planners* 35, 7:225–232.

Moore, C. 1984. "Working Together to Make Something." *Architectural Record* 172:94–103.

Moore, R. C. 1986. *Childhood's Domain: Play and Place in Child Development.* London: Croom-Helm.

Mosely, M. 1995. "The Youth Service Movement: America's Trump Card in Revitalizing Democracy." *National Civic Review* 84, 3:267–271.

Nicholson, S., and B. K. Schreiner. 1975. *Community Participation in City Decision Making.* Milton Keynes, UK: The Open University Press.

Null, R. L., and K. F. Cherry. 1996. *Universal Design: Creative Solutions for ADA Compliance.* Belmont, CA: Professional Publications.

Null, R. L., and J. Wysocki. 1978. "Simulation Games—Give Them a Try." *Housing and Society* 5, 2:52–55.

Oberdorfer, J. 1986. "The Felton Town Plan: A Participatory Village Masterplan." In *The Costs of Not Knowing: Proceedings of the 17th Annual Conference of the Environmental Design Research Association,* edited by J. Wineman, R. Barnes, and C. Zimring. Atlanta, GA.

———. 1988. "Community Participation in the Design of the Boulder Creek Branch Library." *Design Studies* 9, 1:4–13.

O'Brien, D. 1975. *Neighborhood Organization and Interest Group Process.* Princeton, NJ: Princeton University Press.

Olsen, M. E. 1982. *Participatory Pluralism: Political Participation and Influence in the United States and Sweden.* Chicago: Nelson Hall.

Ouye, J., and J. P. Protzen. 1975. "Choices of Participatory Planning." *DMG-DRS Journal* 9:304–312.

Owens, R. 1986. "Participation Panacea." *Architects Journal* (June):24–25.

Pateman, C. 1970. *Participation and Democratic Theory.* Cambridge: Cambridge University Press.

Phillips, B. E., and R. T. LeGates. 1981. *City Lights: An Introduction to Urban Studies.* New York: Oxford Press.

Polyzoides, S. 1975. "Participatory Architecture: Action Plus Form." *DMG Journal* 9, 4:321–324.

Porteous, T. D. 1971. "Design with People: The Quality of the Urban Environment." *Environment and Behavior* 3, 2:155–178.

Porterfield, G. A., and K. B. Hall Jr. 1995. *A Concise Guide to Community Planning.* New York: McGraw Hill.

Potapchuk, W. R. 1991. "New Approaches to Citizen Participation: Building Consent." *National Civic Review* 80, 2:158–168.

Propst, R., J. Adams, and C. Propst. 1976. *Facility Influence in Productivity.* Ann Arbor: Herman Miller Research Corporation.

Ravetz, A. 1976. "Appraisal: Byker." *The Architects Journal* 163, 15:731–742.

———. 1980. "PSSHAK 19 Months On." *The Architects Journal* 171:425.

———. 1980. *Remaking Cities: Contradictions of Recent Urban Development.* London: Croom Helm.

Sanoff, H. 1985. "The Application of Participatory Methods in Design and Evaluation." Special Issue. *Design Studies* 6, 4:1–3.

———. 1988. "Integrating Research and Design Participation." Special Issue. *Design Studies* 9, 1:4–61.

———. 1998. "Participation in Design and Planning." In *Encyclopedia of Housing,* edited by W. van Vliet. Thousand Oaks, CA: Sage Publications.

Schon, D. 1983. *The Reflective Practitioner.* New York: Basic Books.

Schumacher, E. F. 1973. *Small Is Beautiful: A Study of Economics as If People Mattered.* London: Blond & Briggs.

Schuman, T. 1987. "Participation, Empowerment and Urbanism: Design and Politics in the Revitalization of French Social Housing." *Journal of Architectural Planning and Research* 4, 4:349–359.

Sewell, W. R. D., and J. T. Coppock. *Public Participation in Planning*. London: John Wiley & Sons.

Shindler/Raiman, E., and R. Lippitt. 1972. *Team Concepts for Community Change: Concepts, Goals, Strategies and Skills*. Riverside: University of California Press.

Smith, R. W. 1973. "A Theoretical Basis for Participatory Planning." *Policy Sciences* 4, 9:275–296.

Snowden, O., and M. Snowden. 1963. "Citizen Participation." *Journal of Housing* 9:435–439.

Susskind, L., and M. Elliot. 1983. *Paternalism, Conflict, and Coproduction: Learning from Citizen Action and Citizen Participation in Western Europe*. New York: Plenum.

Taylor, J., and R. Walford. 1978. *Learning and the Simulation Game*. Beverly Hills: Sage Publications.

Thomson, K., J. Bissetta, and T. Webb. 1994. *Participation Works*. Medford, MA: The Lincoln Filene Center at Tufts University.

Tobey, G. B. 1973. *A History of Landscape Architecture: The Relationship of People to the Environment*. New York: Elsevier.

Turner, B. 1988. *Building Community*. London: Habitat International Coalition.

Ury, W. L., J. M. Brett, and S. B. Goldberg. 1988. *Getting Disputes Resolved: Designing Systems to Cut the Costs of Conflict*. San Francisco: Jossey-Bass.

Verderber, K. S., and R. F. Verdeber. 1977. *Inter-Act: Using Interpersonal Communication Skills*. Belmont, CA: Wadsworth Publishing Co.

Walker, J. M. 1975. "Organizational Change, Citizen Participation, and Voluntary Action." *Journal of Voluntary Action Research* 4:4–22.

Wandersman, A. 1979. "User Participation: A Study of Types of Participation, Effects, Mediators, and Individual Differences." *Environment and Behavior* 11, 2:186–208.

———. 1981. "A Framework of Participation in Community Organizations." *Journal of Applied Behavioral Science* 17, 1:27–58.

Wandersman, A., and P. Florin. 1990. "Citizen Participation, Voluntary Organizations and Community Development: Insights for Empowerment Through Research." *American Journal of Community Psychology* 18, 1:41–54.

Ward, A., and J. Hunt 1987. "The Alternatives Aotea Center Project, Auckland, New Zealand." *Journal of Architectural Education* 41, 1:34–45.

Ward. C. 1978. *The Child in the City*. New York: Pantheon.

———. 1983. *Housing: An Anarchist Approach*. London: Freedom Press.

Wates, N., and C. Wolmar. 1980. *Squatting: The Real Story*. London: Bay Leaf.

Weiss, Z. 1971. "Community Design Centers: Mechanism for Citizen Participation in the Planning Process." *Planning*. Selected papers from the ASPO National Planning Conference, New Orleans. Chicago: American Society of Planning Officials.

Wheeland, C. M. 1991. "Empowering the Vision: Citywide Strategic Planning." *National Civic Review* (fall):393–405.

Williams, S. 1976. "City Participation in City and Regional Planning: An Effective Methodology." *Town Planning Review* 47:349–358.

Wolfe, M. 1985. *Community Group Homes*. New York: Van Nostrand Reinhold.

Woolley, T. 1988. "Ten Topics for Participators." *Open House International* 13, 3:49–53.

Wrona, S. 1981. *Participation in Architectural Design and Urban Planning.* Warsaw: Poland: Warsankry Politechniki.

Zeisel, J. 1972. "Fundamental Values in Planning with The Non-paying Client." In *Architecture and Human Behavior,* edited by C. Burnette. Philadelphia: American Institute of Architects.

———. 1981. *Inquiry by Design: Tools for Environment-Behavior Research.* Monterey, CA: Brooks-Cole.

Index

CPSIA information can be obtained at www.ICGtesting.com
Printed in the USA
BVOW04*2105140114

341759BV00005B/32/P